FIRMICUS MATERNUS:
THE ERROR OF
THE PAGAN RELIGIONS

ANCIENT CHRISTIAN WRITERS

THE WORKS OF THE FATHERS IN TRANSLATION

EDITED BY

JOHANNES QUASTEN   WALTER J. BURGHARDT

THOMAS COMERFORD LAWLER

No. 37

FIRMICUS MATERNUS:
THE ERROR OF
THE PAGAN RELIGIONS

TRANSLATED AND ANNOTATED

BY

CLARENCE A. FORBES, Ph.D.
Professor of Classical Languages
Ohio State University

NEWMAN PRESS

New York, N.Y./Ramsey, N.J.

De Licentia Superioris S.J.
  Nihil Obstat
        J. Quasten
            Cens. Dep.

Imprimatur
            Patricius A. O'Boyle, D.D.
                Archiep. Washingtonen.
                    die 2 Martii 1968

Library of Congress
Catalog Card Number: 70-118037

ISBN: 0-8091-0039-8

PUBLISHED BY PAULIST PRESS
Editorial Office: 1865 Broadway, New York, N.Y. 10023
Business Office: 545 Island Road, Ramsey, N.J. 07446

PRINTED AND BOUND IN THE UNITED STATES OF AMERICA

CONTENTS

FIRMICUS MATERNUS:
THE ERROR OF
THE PAGAN RELIGIONS

INTRODUCTION

LIFE OF FIRMICUS

The explicit of the sole surviving manuscript of the *De errore profanarum religionum* gives the full name of the author: Iulius Firmicus Maternus V(ir) C(larissimus). Even more fully the explicit of the *Matheseos libri* gives Iulius Firmicus Maternus Iunior V. C. or Iulius Firmicus Maternus Siculus V.C. The identity of authorship of these two books, one pagan and the other Christian, was long disputed and generally denied by nineteenth-century scholarship. Nevertheless, identity of authorship was proved to the hilt in 1897 by a solid doctoral dissertation directed by Eduard Wölfflin and written by Clifford Herschel Moore.[1] Moore, guided by the sure touch of Wölfflin, found in the two books a convincing number of the same pet words, pet phrases, and syntactical and stylistic usages. Soon after Moore's dissertation appeared, Kroll and Skutsch (later aided by Ziegler) issued a new Teubner edition of the *Mathesis* with even more extensive stylistic proofs that there was only one Firmicus Maternus. Dispute on this matter came to an end.

We have no knowledge of Firmicus' life beyond what may be extracted from his writings, particularly from the prooemia to several books of his eight-book work on astrology. The dates of his birth and death are unknown, but his *floruit* was in the reigns of Constantine the Great and his sons Constantius and Constans. Firmicus states clearly (*Math.* 1 pr. #4) that he was a Sicilian by birth and residence: "totius Siciliae situm, quam incolo et unde oriundo sum" (*oriundo* meaning "by birth" or " by origin").[2] He pinpoints his home as Syracuse, proudly calling Archimedes his fellow townsman.[3] In the *De errore* (7) he devotes a purple passage of description to the Sicilian vale of Enna and its flowers, and the *communis opinio* credits him with founding his description on autopsy.[4]

Firmicus belonged to the senatorial class, for such is the meaning of the V(ir) C(larissimus) attached to his name in the manuscript tradition.[5] As an aristocrat he received a fine education for a public career—much the sort of education that had been explained and recommended by Quintilian. Besides getting a thorough training in rhetoric, which made a lasting impression on his written style, he formed an intelligent acquaintance with natural philosophy and literature. His writings show that he was "a man of considerable intelligence, studious tastes, and great moral earnestness."[6]

It is surprising that anyone should have denied, as did Fabricius in the eighteenth century, that Firmicus was *doctus utriusque linguae*. On a priori grounds one would suppose that even as late as the fourth century a person of senatorial rank would receive a school education in Greek —still more so in Sicily, where the Greek culture had ebbed but not disappeared under Roman domination.[7] Firmicus knew and quoted Homer, Plato, Aristotle, Porphyry, and technical Greek works on astrology.[8] He employed an unusually large number of loanwords from the Greek.[9] His etymologies from the Greek, fantastic as they are, nevertheless betray knowledge of the language.[10]

As to whether his aristocratic education was acquired wholly in Syracuse, as could easily have been the case, or partly in Rome, we cannot determine even by indirect evidence. Moore (48) argued that the conspicuous frequency of the *genetivus identitatis* (or *inhaerentiae*) in Firmicus is a feature of African Latin, and that Firmicus is more likely to have been influenced by *Africitas* in Syracuse, close to African shores, than in Rome; but Kroll, in his review of Moore's dissertation, brushed aside this flimsy argument—"as if he couldn't ever have learned anything of the *genetivus identitatis* in Rome!"[11]

Firmicus had three successive careers: first as an advocate, next as a pagan astrologer, and finally as a Christian polemicist. In the beginning his rhetorical and aristocratic training found a natural outlet in active practice at the bar, where he firmly resisted dishonesty, greed, and browbeating of the downtrodden.[12] But discovering that for his pains he reaped nothing except animosity, in disgust he abandoned the bar, drew away from the earthly converse of scoundrelly human beings, and turned to high converse with the celestial lore of astrology.[13]

Among the cultured and able friends of Firmicus was a high official of the imperial government, Q. Flavius Maesius (or Messius) Egnatius Lollianus Mavortius, governor of Campania, and later consul, proconsul of Africa, and praetorian prefect.[14] The year of his consulship is known to have been 355. Firmicus, however, says in the *Mathesis* (prooem. 8) that in the year when he finished the work Mavortius was simultaneously proconsul of Africa and designate consul ordinarius; our assumption would be that he was consul designate in 354, since he attained the consulship in 355. We shall presently rehearse the evidence sifted by Mommsen and almost universally accepted, which shows that Firmicus wrote the *Mathesis* approximately in the years 334–37; how could he in this work speak of Mavortius as consul designate when we know that the consulship was not forthcoming until two decades later? Mommsen's solution was that Constantine made Mavortius proconsul of Africa in 337 and let it be understood that he was consul ordinarius *in petto* for the following year; but when Constantine's death ensued on May 22, 337, his sons and successors did not consider themselves bound by their father's known intentions, and preferred to award the consulship to someone else.[15] By this combination of evidence we gather that Mavortius was proconsul of Africa in 337 and received in that year the dedication of the freshly completed work on astrology by his friend Firmicus Maternus.[16]

From internal evidence we can know during what years Firmicus wrote the *Mathesis*. Astronomical computations show that a solar eclipse took place on July 17, 334.[17] Now Firmicus in Book 1, using the phrase "ut de recentioribus loquar," mentions a solar eclipse in the consulship of Optatus and Paulinus, i.e., 334; it therefore appears that he began to write in or about that year. Later in Book 1 he alludes to the rulers as Constantine and the two Caesars, his sons; this would necessarily antedate the death of Constantine on May 22, 337.[18]

A further clue to the dating comes from the horoscope[19] of a man whose father was twice consul ordinarius, and who himself was governor of Campania, proconsul of Achaia, proconsul of Asia, and city prefect of Rome. Mommsen observed that from the end of the third century repeated consulships were a privilege reserved to the emperors and members of the imperial family; the only exception, under special circumstances, was C. Ceionius Rufius Volusianus, consul in 311 and 314.[20] His son

Ceionius Rufius Albinus was city prefect of Rome from December 30, 335 until March 10, 337, and is the anonymous person whose horoscope Firmicus described in Book 2 of the *Mathesis*.[21] This date coincides with the others mentioned above. Grateful for Mommsen's acute observations, scholars have agreed that the *Mathesis* was written in the years from 334 to 337.

We have Firmicus' own account of how he was led to write his long and ambitious work on astrology. Tired to the bone from traveling, probably from Sicily, he came in the dead of winter to Campania to visit his friend the governor Mavortius. He was heartily welcomed and given every opportunity for rest and refreshment. When he had thoroughly recuperated, Mavortius engaged him in a long and friendly conversation about Sicily and its natural phenomena. The scientific flavor of the conversation led to mention of the famous sphere of the Syracusan Archimedes, and then Mavortius launched into a brilliant discourse on the signs of the zodiac, the sun, moon, and planets, the Milky Way, the geocentric view of the universe, etc. Stimulated in imagination and filled with enthusiasm, Firmicus volunteered to write a book which would rehearse in Latin the astrological lore accumulated by Egypt and Babylon. Though the task proved to be long and arduous and was sometimes abandoned in moments of despair, Mavortius gave steady encouragement and kept insisting that the opus should be pushed forward to its conclusion. Finally, after years of effort, Firmicus finished writing *Matheseos libri VIII*,[22] which is for us the largest surviving Latin treatise on astrology. Inevitably he dedicated the treatise to Mavortius, apostrophizing him as "Mavorti decus nostrum" in the opening words and reiterating the honorific phrase many and many a time.[23] The book was not only the largest but also the last theoretical treatise on astrology to appear in Western Europe before the arrival of the Arabs; "not persecution or prosecution, but the lack of proper manuals caused the disappearance of 'scientific' astrology in the West for four or five centuries after Firmicus composed his astrologers' handbook."[24]

Firmicus believed that he was filling a gap which needed to be filled, for he claimed that every other branch of knowledge had been made available by books in the Latin language, but astrology alone was missing. Here are his exact words in the last sentence of the preface to Book 5: "Pura mente et ab omni terrena conversatione seposita et cunctorum flagitiorum labe purgata hos Romanis tuis libros scripsimus, ne omni disciplinarum arte translata solum hoc opus extitisse videatur ad quod Romanum non adfectasset ingenium."

The astrological interests of Firmicus were not confined to his one major effort, the *Mathesis*. Thrice he proclaimed to Mavortius his intention of Latinizing the *Myriogenesis* of Aesculapius, and once he promised at a future time to write an interpretation of the astrology of Nechepso; but these promises remained unfulfilled.[25] But he did write and dedicate to a friend named Murinus a one-book treatise *De domino geniturae et chronocratore;* and he says that he wrote another one-book treatise *De fine vitae.*[26] These writings do not survive.

In the early decades of his life the pagan Firmicus would have had opportunity to become initiated in one or more of the mystery religions. Observing the general correctness of his factual statements about these cults, scholars have been led to look closely for evidence that he was an initiate. Friedrich found such evidence. He pointed to the fact that Firmicus was a *vir clarissimus*, and most of the pagan aristocrats were initiates in at least one of the mystery cults.[27] He held that Firmicus was an initiate at least of Mithraism, and that such was the meaning of a phrase in the *De errore* (5.2): "sicut propheta eius tradidit nobis." Particularly if *nobis* is interpreted as the "editorial we," Friedrich's view is attractive, and it won assent from Clemen and Coman and quasi approval from Heuten.[28] It is, however, not necessary to interpret *nobis* in a personal and autobiographical sense; and Boll invited our attention to Firmicus' pages of highly moral counsel and admonition to astrologers, where we read the unconditional precept: "Numquam nocturnis sacrificiis intersis, sive illa publica sive privata dicantur."[29] This precept would lay the mystery religions under an interdict for astrologers. But Heuten recalled that even if Firmicus was not an initiate, he lived among aristocrats who were, and from them he could have learned the exact facts and formulae which he provides for his readers.

The general and natural view has prevailed that Firmicus was converted to Christianity at some time in the years, approximately a decade, intervening between the composition of the *Mathesis* and that of the *De errore*. Apparently he alluded to his conversion when he wrote: "At ego nunc, sacrarum lectionum institutione formatus, perditos homines religioso sermone convenio."[30] Skutsch in 1910, however, came forward with the surprising argument that Firmicus was already a Christian or at least intimately acquainted with Christianity when he wrote the astrological work; the argument stemmed from two noble doxologies in the prooemia of Books 5 and 7, doxologies which bear marked resemblances to the Christian prayers of the so-called *Constitutiones apostolorum*.[31] Skutsch observed correctly that in spite of St. Augustine's polemic, there were a few cases in ancient and modern times where believing Christians were devotees of astrology, though of course they denied the divinity of the celestial bodies. But Skutsch's main thesis, stemming from the doxologies, came under immediate fire from Wendland, who called Firmicus' prayers Stoic rather than Christian in tone and origin; and soon Norden entered the fray, saying that the common denominator of the prayers was Orientalized Neoplatonism, which to be sure had absorbed something from Stoicism.[32] Skutsch had laid some weight on a sentence with a Christian ring which he found in exactly the same wording in Firmicus' astrological book (5 praef. 3) and his apologetic treatise (26.3): "Voluntas dei perfecti operis substantia est." But this emphatic statement of the power of the divine will is in full accord with Neoplatonism,[33] and Norden was able to point to the same sentence ("Voluntas dei ipsa est summa perfectio") in a Latin translation from the *Hermetica*.[34] This Neoplatonic formulation appealed to the high-minded pagan Firmicus, and after his conversion was still entirely acceptable and therefore reusable. Worth repeating are Norden's closing words on the subject: "It was neither Christianity nor Greek philosophy but Orientalized Neoplatonism on which, as on a golden bridge, the astrologer and in general hundreds of cultured men of all professions walked across the river which flowed between the old way and the new."

Although we lack documentation, we may easily suppose that the conversion of Firmicus caused joy on earth as well as in heaven. "On peut imaginer la joie des chrétiens lors de la conversion d'un des hommes en vue du paganisme romain, de rang sénatorial, auteur de plusieurs traités d'astrologie, écrivain ciceronianisant distingué et très érudit en lettres classiques, Firmicus Maternus."[35]

But all that we know of the life of the distinguished convert after he walked across the golden bridge to Christianity is that he wrote the treatise *De errore profanarum religionum*.[36] As Cumont observed with a mild soupçon of humor, "Firmicus Maternus, après avoir écrit un mauvais traité d'astrologie, finit par combattre l'Erreur des religions profanes.' "[37] Fortunately it is easy to date the composition of this treatise within reasonably narrow limits. Firmicus addresses repeatedly the brother-emperors Constantius and Constans, the latter of whom was killed in the year 350;[38] thus a *terminus ante quem* is established. The *terminus post quem* comes from a clear reference to Constans' expedition against the Britons in 343.[39] Firmicus' statement (29.3) that during the reign of Constantius and Constans "Persica vota conlapsa sunt" must allude either to the conquest of Nisibis in 346 or to the victory over King Sapor in 348. Behind a generalized allusion to earthquakes (3.5) Boll saw a reminiscence of the particular quakes of 344 and 345; but how can we be sure of this when earthquakes are such commonplace occurrences in Mediterranean lands?[40] If Firmicus did succeed in arousing the emperors to enact measures of repression against the pagans, then perhaps he wrote in or just before 346, when a new imperial decree threatened death and confiscation of property for anyone who sacrificed to pagan gods.[41] Finally, Firmicus spoke with satisfaction (12.2) of "today's" severe Roman legislation against pederasty—very likely a complimentary allusion to a new and drastic statute on the subject which emanated from Constantius and Constans in December of 342.[42]

THE BACKGROUND AND THE BOOK

After the entente established in 313 by Licinius and Constantine between the Roman Empire and the Christian Church,[43] and still more after the conversion of Constantine and the general triumph of Christianity, one might have expected Christian apologetics to fall silent as being no longer needed. But actually some of the most vehement apologists, Firmicus among them, wrote after the Council of Nicaea in 325. Constantine granted full tolerance to pagans as well as to Christians; the temples remained unmolested, and the devotees of Isis, Mithra, Liber, and the Great Mother continued to maintain the Oriental cults which were the most vital and popularly appealing aspects of paganism in the fourth century. Particularly in the city of Rome the senatorial aristocracy formed a hard core of support for paganism and of resistance to Christianity.[44] The pagans did not become a minority until the fifth century, while in the early lifetime of Firmicus, before the conversion of Constantine, it has been estimated that two thirds of the Empire's population was still pagan.[45]

Constantine, while awarding many special favors to Christianity, believed it would be highly impolitic to undertake a sudden abolition of paganism and all its works. He knew that in the hearts of the Roman people, of whom Plutarch said that they were more religious than the gods themselves, Mithraism and other Oriental cults were too firmly rooted to be instantaneously removed by fiat. His wisdom called for a period of slow transition to the new situation in religion. Constantius and Constans, his sons and successors, were in harmonious accord with this general policy, as is shown by their acts and enactments. A law issued by Constantius in 341 ordered that "superstition shall cease; the madness of sacrifices shall be abolished."[46] In the following year the two emperors jointly commanded the urban prefect not to harm the temples outside the city walls of Rome, but nevertheless to stamp out all superstition.[47] Does this mean that paganism must perish or go underground just as Firmicus is on the point of writing *De errore* (*ca.* 346–50)? *Pace* Geffcken, nothing of the kind took place.[48] Enforcement of the antipagan laws was in the hands of the pagan ruling class, the members of which certainly did not propose to persecute themselves unless under the stimulus of a *force majeure*. The urban prefect of 342, charged by the emperors with the task of stamping out superstition, was the aristocrat Catullinus, probably a pagan; and his immediate predecessor, in the earlier part of 342, was none other than Firmicus' unregenerate pagan friend Lollianus Mavortius. We may plausibly suppose that Catullinus acted with majestic deliberateness and in fact contrived to do little or nothing by way of executing the imperial decree. Well aware that Constans was Pontifex Maximus, and that Constantius enjoyed among the pagans the repute of not being an extremist,[49] Catullinus and his successors reasoned that the word "superstition" was aimed at magic and private divination, and was not meant to include the old established state religion, sanctioned as it was by the *mos maiorum*. Firmicus claims that the law led to the destruction of some temples, and we may take this to be true.[50] But the official cult of the Roman State continued unmolested; the vestal virgins kept the holy fire alight, and Jupiter and the Sun were the favored deities of Rome.[51] As the easy restoration of paganism by Julian a few years later demonstrated, no irreparable rent had been made in "the ancient fabric of Roman superstition, which was supported by the opinions and habits of eleven hundred years."[52]

After the death of Constans in 350, the complacency of Constantius toward the old Roman religion delighted the hearts of those inveterate traditionalists, the Roman senators. Symmachus described the conduct of Constantius when he visited Rome in 357: "He made no diminution in the privileges of the vestal virgins; he filled up the priesthoods with aristocrats; he did not refuse financial support for the Roman ceremonies; and following the delighted Senate through all the streets of the Eternal City, he gazed calmly at the temples, read the names of the gods inscribed on their façades, inquired about the dates of the buildings, and expressed admiration for their builders."[53] In the very same year he unabashedly took this sightseeing tour of the Roman temples, Constantius issued an edict from Milan: "If any persons should be proved to devote their attention to sacrifices or to worship images, We command that they shall be subjected to capital punishment."[54] Thus the edicts breathed fire and brimstone, but their enforcement, not being backed by preponderant public opinion, was lax and ineffective;[55] and paganism, though somewhat curbed and annoyed, made shift to survive in considerable strength. Martroye, observing that in the fourth century the *fiscus* continued to pay the expenses of maintaining the ancestral Roman cult, argued that the animus of the imperial antipagan legislation of that century was to extirpate magic and private divination, not to do away with the forms, liturgy, priests, and buildings of the long-established state religion.[56] This interpretation would fit the behavior though not the words of Constantius in the decade when Firmicus was writing and thereafter.

To zealous Christians the spectacle of the slow and reluctant retreat of paganism was galling. Listening impatiently to the steady ebb tide with its "melancholy, long, withdrawing roar, retreating," they clamored for swift, decisive, drastic action.[57] Renan has claimed that no one at that time understood the true spirit of freedom and tolerance as we know it now; and when Christianity gained the upper hand, after undergoing centuries of persecution, it was no more inclined toward tolerance than the pagan rulers had been.[58] What Constantine had aimed to establish was not complete freedom of religious worship, but rather a *modus vivendi* between the long-hostile Church and state.[59] For some at least, this was not enough. "Intoxicated by their success, some Christians were not going to be satisfied until their first advantage should be followed by a complete victory and until the secular arm should drive away from the last pagan altar its last worshiper."[60]

Precisely such was the mood of the distinguished and literate convert Firmicus Maternus. It is true that, as a recent convert, he had never been a victim of persecution and thus was not animated by any personal thirst for revenge on the forces of paganism. But holding the view that the pagan deities, as far as they were not figments of the imagination, were demons guided by Satan and dedicated to the spread of moral depravity, Firmicus was in no mood for gradualness or compromise.[61] His book, addressed to the two reigning emperors,[62] has been called by Boissier "a handbook of intolerance."[63] Rand lumped Arnobius and Firmicus together and dismissed them with the rebuke that they were "learned, misinformed, virulent, and to us tolerant moderns somewhat repulsive."[64] It has been conjectured that Firmicus' violence was in part psychologically motivated, because he felt embarrassed at being a member of a minority group which, though ostensibly in the saddle, was still scorned by the pagan majority.[65]

Firmicus, profiting as a polemicist from the early years when he had been a lawyer,[66] laid down a barrage of anti-pagan arguments, vehement denunciations, and impassioned appeals. Himself a former devotee of Porphyry and Neoplatonism, he now wished to abjure the man and the doctrine. "Porphyrius, defensor sacrorum, hostis dei, veritatis inimicus, sceleratarum artium minister"—such are the epithets of detestation which he heaps upon the outspoken opponent of Christianity whom he had once cherished as "noster Porphyrius."[67] Now Porphyry held that there are multitudinous demons, some good and some bad.[68] Firmicus also believed in demons, but said they were all bad, the creatures and agents of the devil.[69] If Neoplatonists honored some demons, under the mistaken impression that they are beneficent, they were in Firmicus' eyes guilty of a satanic cult which was obnoxious to the laws of the Roman Empire. Thus he sought to demolish the most intellectual form of contemporary paganism.[70]

In addressing the emperors directly, Firmicus appealed to their covetousness, their patriotism, and their sense of duty as Christian rulers. He held before them a glittering temptation: they could enrich the *fiscus* if they would confiscate the accumulated wealth of the temples. He exhorted them to ruthlessness with the ferocity of a latter-day Cato: "Amputanda sunt haec penitus atque delenda et severissimis edictorum vestrorum legibus corrigenda." He held up as a shining example to any Roman rulers or high magistrates the drastic severity with which the consul Postumius suppressed the Bacchanalia in 186 B.C.: "Nec tam diu vindices gladii consulis conquierunt quam diu hoc malum fuisset radicitus amputatum. O digna Romani nominis animadversio!" He meant the reigning emperors to feel tacitly rebuked because they had acted less energetically and drastically than Postumius had done.[71] He reminded them of the stern words of the Old Testament, "Sacrificans diis eradicabitur," and assured them it was their duty under the law of God to kill those who served the gods of the pagans.[72] But this was to invoke Jewish law rather than Christian doctrine—a shocking procedure, and clear proof that Firmicus had not read or certainly had not understood the Pauline Epistles.[73] "There is something a little painful," says de Labriolle, "in the spectacle of this intolerance on the part of those who had formerly been persecuted and, scarcely delivered from their own nightmare, were hastening to become persecutors in their turn."[74]

Firmicus' impassioned demand for the extirpation of paganism by ferocious means wielded by the state strikes a new note in Christian literature. The express conviction of such humane thinkers as Tertullian and Lactantius had been that enforced conversion is unreal and ineffective for salvation.[75] The Christian emperors mostly did not state their views unless by implication, but Theodoric spoke up in the early sixth century and stoutly affirmed that religion cannot be forced.[76] Familiar in modern times is the couplet of Samuel Butler:

He that complies against his will
Is of the same opinion still.[77]

But Firmicus, no reader of Tertullian and Lactantius, drew a medical analogy. Men who are victims of disease, said he, do not know what is good for them; they are likely to crave what they should not have and perversely reject strong remedies of real value.[78] In such cases physicians wisely use force to apply the right remedies to unwilling patients, all in the best interest of the patients' own welfare. Likewise the emperors had a grim obligation to "amputate" (Firmicus' own word). "Nolunt quidam et repugnant, et exitium suum prona cupiditate desiderant. Sed subvenite miseris, liberate pereuntes. Ad hoc vobis deus summus commisit imperium, ut per vos vulneris istius plaga curetur. . . . Melius est ut liberetis invitos quam ut volentibus concedatis exitium."[79] By *exitium* Firmicus meant "damnation," and from this fate he was demanding that the emperors should rescue their subjects even against their will. This was the first appearance of the doctrine that enforced conversion is desirable, justifiable, and indeed imperative.

We note, too, that it was to the state, represented by the brother-emperors, that Firmicus looked for the enforcement of conversion and the extirpation of paganism. Firmicus was no advocate of the separation of Church and state; quite the contrary. As an adult convert, eager to demonstrate his zeal for his new-found faith, he was prone to excess. Doubtless remembering how the state had persecuted the Church, though he abstained from alluding to this unhappy page of history, he now vehemently insisted that the state should become *defensor fidei*, persecute paganism with unsparing rigor, and destroy it root and

branch. He even used in his medical analogy the dreaded
words *ignis et ferrum*—"cautery and scalpel" in the medical sense, but there are chilling overtones of a nonmedical
nature for those who survey the subsequent history of the
Church in Europe.

Surely Firmicus knew the recent imperial decree of 341:
"Superstition shall cease; the madness of sacrifices shall be
abolished"; and the watered-down affirmation of the same
in 342. But he also knew that these decrees were being
honored more in the breach than in the observance, and
he was clamorous for stronger decrees with definite penalties attached and aggressive enforcement. Turning to the
Theodosian Code (16.10.4), we encounter an imperial
decree whose date is clearly given as 346 (though scholars
have disputed the correctness of the date): the temples
are to be closed everywhere "so as to deny to all abandoned
men the opportunity to commit sin"; anyone guilty of the
crime of sacrificing must be struck down with the avenging
sword; and provincial governors who fail to enforce the
edict are subject to execution. This sterner decree has been
thought by Alfons Müller[80] to have been evoked partly
by the appeal of Firmicus to the Caesars, and indeed it is
not only in accord with Firmicus' wishes but also, unlike
any other antipagan decree in the Theodosian Code, employs a favorite appellative of Firmicus for the pagans:
perditi, "abandoned men."[81] Although this new decree
likewise was feebly enforced, and in particular did not
lead to any executions, it may be that the issuance of the
decree was a response to Firmicus or to the mood which
he represented.

Now since Firmicus overtly endeavored, perhaps with
a modicum of success, to mold imperial policy affecting

the Church, we may reasonably call his book in part a political pamphlet. Here speaks the Roman man of action, unlike the theoretical Greek apologists for Christianity.[82] The book voices for the first time ideas which took hold with wide-ranging consequences in the Middle Ages. There should be, in effect, a union of Church and state. The state should operate as the secular arm of the Church, should legislate against and be intolerant of non-Christian religious activity, and should have the kindness to save souls by forcible conversion. The ruler, be he king or emperor or sovereign of whatever kind, has the duty under God's law to exercise the ruling power, even by stringent measures, in behalf of the eternal salvation of all his subjects. Religious persecution is the right and may be the duty of the state as the secular arm. "This philosophy first found full expression in the work of Firmicus Maternus and it has formed a large part of the political and theological basis for religious persecution from that time to this."[83]

Besides being a political pamphlet, Firmicus' book is, of course, an essay in Christian apologetics, with the apparent mottoes that the best defense is an attack and the best approach to truth is through a study of error. Firmicus assails the pagan religions in the same aggressive and trenchant way as Arnobius before him. Since he deals not with the truths of Christianity but with the errors of paganism, he naturally says little of the former and concentrates on the latter. Other Christian writers of his generation have provided us with far less informative material on paganism; "Firmicus is a singular source of precious information on the pagan religions of his time, especially on the mystery religions."[84] Like Eusebius, he attacks not

only the outmoded Olympian gods but also and more particularly the currently flourishing cults of Mithra, Cybele,
and the other Oriental divinities. Other apologists, con-
trariwise, had thought it more needful to attack the official
Roman worship rather than the merely tolerated Oriental
religions. In the arguments wheeled up by Firmicus, as
contrasted with his valuable data, one finds little novelty
except in details. One new feature is in his diligent effort
to counterpose specific biblical revelation against specific
pagan ceremonies and formulas.[85] The total result is a book
which contrives in a small compass to give a fairly complete
refutation of paganism.

Emperor worship, however, is never assailed by either
Arnobius or Firmicus, though it had been earlier attacked
by the apologists Theophilus and Tertullian.[86] Firmicus
thought it impolitic to castigate emperor worship in a
treatise respectfully addressed to the brother-emperors. In
fact, by forever mouthing the phrase *sacratissimi impera-
tores*[87] or its equivalent, he seems to lean perilously close to
Caesarolatry.

Nor should the reader look for a refutation of astrology.
In condemning the errors of paganism, Firmicus carefully
preserves silence about his former hobby of astrology, of
which he had written the most complete exegesis in Latin.
What did other post-Nicene writers have to say about this
popular subject, which proclaimed fatalism and denied
free will?[88] We turn to Cumont for an answer: "At the
end of the fourth century a polemic against paganism was
almost inseparable from a refutation of astrology. The
latter held an important place in the doctrine and cult of
certain mysteries, like those of Mithra, and the educated
classes as well as the mob let themselves be governed by

the chimeras of this pseudo science."[89] St. Augustine himself was in the vanguard of those who thundered against astrology; and Ambrosiaster, the only writer who was discernibly somewhat influenced by Firmicus' *De errore*, condemned the starry art in the roundest terms: "Nihil tam contrarium Christiano quam si arti matheseos adhibeat curam. . . . Igitur fugiendum omnibus modis ab hac arte monemus. Curiosi enim eius et inimici dei sunt et sine sollicitudine numquam sunt."[90]

Far from turning against astrology, as logic required, the ex-astrologer retained a secret admiration for the art.[91] In a chapter bristling with deplorable etymologies, he dwells at particular length on the sun (*sol* from *solus*) and inserts an unacknowledged verbatim quotation of twenty consecutive words on the planets and the fixed stars from a declamation called *The Astrologer*, by Pseudo-Quintilian.[92] "Encore dans son ouvrage chrétien, il s'est inspiré de la déclamation *mathematicus*, toute imprégnée de croyance aux dogmes de l'astrologie" (Weyman).

Since Firmicus' main objective was destructive criticism, he has little to offer in a positive way. It cost the ex-lawyer no effort to become a vigorous polemicist, denouncing what he had renounced. It was moderately easy for him to show that paganism is riddled with contradictions, absurdities, and errors, and having done this he makes no effort to defend Christianity in terms which could make immediate sense to potential converts. All he does is affirm his faith and quote Scripture—usually the Old Testament. If his arguments were unlikely to win converts, so was his manner. "Son ironie méprisante devait blesser les païens et les endurcir plutôt que de leur faire avouer leur erreur."[93] "The treatise of Firmicus is neither an ornament to early Christian literature nor an asset to Christian polemics."[94] Perhaps Firmicus, like Miniver Cheevy, was born too late; in the fourth century his feeble light was outshone by the dazzling luminaries of the golden age of Christian Latin literature.

A few sentences will give a hasty synopsis of the book. The beginning is lost, because of the disappearance of the first two folios of the unique manuscript, P. Four chapters (2–5) describe and denounce the worship of the divinized elements, water, earth, air, and fire. Euhemeristic criticism is then wheeled up to disparage sundry Greco-Roman and Oriental cults which were at that time alive or even flourishing: Liber, Ceres, Adonis, Cyprian Aphrodite, Jupiter Sabazius, the Corybantes, and the Macedonian Cabirus (6–11). The *chronique scandaleuse* of the gods of Greek mythology is given a quick survey in a single chapter (12). Serapis is demoted from divine to human rank by the legerdemain of etymology (13). The Penates turn out to be nothing but divinized food, Vesta the hearth fire, and the Palladium a worthless image constructed out of the bones of Pelops (14–15). There were five Minervas, none admirable (16). Etymology is now invoked again to contribute to the *Götterdämmerung*, and this effort wreaks utter havoc, philological and theological (17). Several informative chapters discuss the mysteries and six of their sacred formulas (*symbola*), with equations between these formulas and Christian liturgy, doctrine, symbolism, etc. (18–27). The conclusion urges the emperors to annihilate paganism and asks divine blessings for them and the Empire (28–29).

Sources

In discussing paganism and its errors Firmicus could draw upon a fund of firsthand knowledge. The historian of religion G. van der Leeuw states that few writers before or after Firmicus could match his expertise regarding the mystery religions.[95] The possibility that Firmicus was an initiate at least in Mithraism has been weighed in our account of his life;[96] van der Leeuw goes farther, saying: "Still more probable is that he was a member of diverse religious communities, cumulating them in the manner then popular." At any rate, it is widely agreed that on the mysteries Firmicus has the value of an independent source. We would not, however, be justified in supposing that Firmicus has given us exclusively the report of a firsthand observer of paganism in the fourth century. "Legentibus nobis tradit antiquitas," he said in one passage (16.1); and there is superabundant evidence that Firmicus the Christian depended upon books just as much as Firmicus the astrologer had done. Similarly the apologist Arnobius (5.5) declared that he drew information "ex reconditis antiquitatum libris et ex intimis mysteriis."[97]

In a work on the misguided pagan religions, it was natural that pagan sources of information should be laid under contribution. Since Firmicus was stylistically a Ciceronian and a devotee of Ciceronian rhetorical methods, we may look first at his borrowings from Cicero.[98] One would readily surmise that the De natura deorum might contain information pertinent to Firmicus' theme, and we need only turn to the second book, chapters 66–69, to find our surmise corroborated.

Firmicus, discussing the divinization of Air, has the following (4.1): "aerem nomine Iunonis . . . consecrarunt. Iunonem . . . Iovis volunt ex sorore factam. Effeminarunt sane hoc elementum. . . . Aer interiectus est inter mare et caelum." Now look at Cicero (*Nat. deor.* 2.66): "Aer autem, ut Stoici disputant, interiectus inter mare et caelum Iunonis nomine consecratur, quae est soror et coniunx Iovis. . . . Effeminarunt autem eum. . . ." The same statements, in the same sequence (except for "interiectus inter mare et caelum"), in the same phraseology, with the contracted perfect form "effeminarunt" beginning a sentence in each author. A clearer case of the transmission of ideas could not be asked: this is Stoicism channeled via Cicero and in Ciceronian diction to Firmicus.

Another example: Firmicus (14.2) has a lexical item about the Penates: "Omne quod vescuntur homines penus vocatur: hinc et cella penaria, hinc et dii penates." And the Ciceronian parallel (*Nat. deor.* 2.68): "di Penates, sive a penu ducto nomine (est enim omne quo vescuntur homines penus). . . ." For such philological lore regarding Latin, Cicero was habitually dependent on Varro; this time, therefore, the transmission is Varro via Cicero to Firmicus. Parenthetically, Firmicus had made word-for-word borrowings from Cicero's *De natura deorum* also in the *Mathesis*.[99] As for Cicero's explanation of Apollo-*sol* (from *solus*) and Diana-*luna*-Lucina (*Nat. deor.* 2.68), I quote Pease's note *ad locum:* "Our passage is imitated and paraphrased by Firm. *De Errore,* 17. 1–2." Elsewhere Firmicus gives verbal evidence of chance recollections from the *Catilinarians* and the *De divinatione.*[100] And the description of the Sicilian Enna (12) is indebted to the eyewitness account of Cicero, as well as to Ovid.[101]

The theory that Firmicus' knowledge of the pagan religions was heavily indebted to Cornelius Labeo, the lost and undatable Neoplatonist writer on Etrusco-Roman religion, was a pet idea of Heuten.[102] Since we have only a few fragments of Labeo, Heuten was obliged to lean heavily on *Kombinationsforschung*. He argued that Labeo was a common source for several of the Latin apologists, and indeed there had been much talk of Labeo's influence on Arnobius. But only a few years after Heuten wrote, the Arnobian scholar and translator McCracken spoke disparagingly of "the Labeo myth," said that "the Labeo myth has, in my opinion, been thoroughly exploded," and discredited Labeo as a significant source for Arnobius.[103] Ziegler, in his second edition of Firmicus in 1953, gave a condensed and sensible discussion of the sources without mentioning Labeo. Pastorino, giving no generalized account of Firmicus' sources, nevertheless vigorously attacked Heuten's theory at sundry places in the notes.[104]

Other researchers before Heuten, not led astray by the Labeo myth, found an indisputable source in the *Declamationes maiores* of Pseudo-Quintilian, a work seemingly composed in the second century and naturally attractive to the rhetorically-schooled Firmicus.[105] The person who first sniffed the trail was Carl Weyman in 1898.[106] This was before Ziegler brought out his excellent Teubner edition of Firmicus, and Weyman was dependent on the highly unsatisfactory text of Halm (CSEL). At the beginning of Chapter 17, where the parchment MS. of Firmicus is worn and dimly legible, a long sentence about the sun, the fixed stars, and the planets was read in a very doubtful fashion by Halm. Now the fourth *Declamatio* of Pseudo-Quintilian is entitled *Mathematicus*, "The Astrologer"—a subject of obvious interest to the ex-astrologer Firmicus. Looking through this declamation, Weyman saw the following definition of fixed stars and planets: "quaedam velut infixa ac cohaerentia perpetua semelque capta sede conlucent, alia toto sparsa caelo vagos cursus certis emetiuntur erroribus."[107] He surmised that a re-examination of the MS. of Firmicus would show that he had copied this definition verbatim, and indeed Boll, then working in the Vatican Library, was able promptly to confirm this. Ziegler's edition and all those subsequent to it give Firmicus' words exactly as above, with no omissions or alterations of the word order—an acknowledgment that only through the help of Pseudo-Quintilian was it possible to read correctly the MS. of Firmicus.

At about the time when Weyman scored his little triumph of *Quellenforschung*, Albert Becker chanced to be working diligently on Pseudo-Quintilian. Encouraged by Weyman's discovery, Becker looked further for parallels and found seven more.[108] Still others in large numbers were unearthed by G. Stegen in an unpublished 1932 doctoral dissertation of the University of Liége (see Heuten 23 n. 1).

Casual reminiscences of words and phrases from Vergil, rarely from other authors, testify not so much to Firmicus' sources as to his general culture. Let a small table of these reminiscences suffice in the absence of the Latin text; the verbal comparisons, if not indicated here, are fully shown in the apparatus criticus of Ziegler's Teubner edition.

Larger drafts were made on Ovid for the description of Enna, as noted above, and on Livy for information about the Bacchanalia at Rome.[109]

With Greek writers Firmicus betrays less acquaintance.

AUTHOR AND PASSAGE			DE ERRORE
Sallust, *Cat.*	13.3	"muliebria pati"	4.2, 12, 4
Vergil, *Ecl.*	3.63		7.2
Geo.	2.513		3.4
Aen.	1.27		3.1
	1.204	"per varios casus"	27.8
	2.587		16.2
	3.673		28.6
	4.215		6.7
	5.331		28.13
	6.276	"turpis egestas"	18.6
	7.302		3.4
	7.329		5.1
	10.897f.	"et illa effera"	15.1
Horace, *Od.*	1.6.18		7.2 (dub.)
Maecenas, ap.			
Sen. *Ep.*	114.5		4.2
Germanicus,			
Aratea	1		12.4

He quotes in Greek two and a half hexameters of Homer (6.8:*Il.* 6.135–37). In the *Mathesis*, though not in the *De errore*, he names and quotes Plato and Aristotle, but gives no sign of knowing them well. Neoplatonism was more familiar to him, and in the pagan portion of his life he adhered, by and large, to the doctrines of that school. Hence in the *Mathesis* he spoke with high regard of Plotinus and Porphyry, calling the latter "noster Porphyrius."[110] The astrological sympathies of Porphyry[111] made him particularly congenial to Firmicus pagan, but his powerful anti-Christian writings made him anathema to Firmicus convert. Translating into Latin a few words of Porphyry's Περὶ τῆς ἐκ λογίων φιλοσοφίας ("On the Philosophy from Oracles"), the zealous convert identi-

fied the author as "Porphyrius defensor sacrorum, hostis
dei, veritatis inimicus, sceleratarum artium magister"
(13.4). Another passage of Firmicus may be aimed at
Porphyry. Porphyry had taken Plato's tripartite division of the soul (θυμός, νοῦς, ἐπιθυμία) and sought to explain that the so-called "parts" are only activities, and
therefore the soul can be understood to be indissoluble
and immortal. Firmicus kept the focus on the trichotomy
and, repeating old and trite arguments, declared that trichotomy implies mortality. Ziegler argued that Firmicus
was assailing his own former theology of Neoplatonism,
and particularly a view of Porphyry. Neoplatonic is
Firmicus' interpretation (5.3–4) of the triform goddess
of the Mithraic mysteries as parallel to Plato's tripartite
soul. Where Porphyry gave factual information discredit-
able to paganism, Firmicus was glad to borrow: so in regard to human sacrifice for Jupiter Latiaris.[112]

In attacking the pagan deities, Christian apologists found
a wondrously handy weapon in euhemerism, the doctrine
that the gods were merely distinguished human beings who
had been divinized. It seems that the central doctrine of
Euhemerus was widely known but his book was not.
Zucker in 1905 decried the tendency of nineteenth-century scholarship to find euhemerism everywhere in the
patristic writers and to suppose that they were using
Euhemerus as a direct source.[113] Euhemerism in Christian
polemic, said Zucker, might stem from the Latinization of
Euhemerus by Ennius, but at any rate no patristic writer
read Euhemerus in Greek. Lactantius, the principal source
of our surviving fragments of the Ennian version of Euhemerus, obviously read the Latin translation; but few others
did even that. Though Lactantius and Minucius Felix

(21.1) refer to Euhemerus by name, Firmicus and most of the other apologists do not. Lactantius and Firmicus are exceptional in that they narrate complete myths and give a full display of the euhemeristic interpretation.[114] Firmicus employs the euhemeristic method in Chapters 6, 7, and 10, where he gives accounts of Zagreus, the Theban Dionysus, the rape of Proserpina, and the Cyprian Aphrodite; but only in the opening sentence of Chapter 10, on temple-prostitution in honor of Cyprian Aphrodite, does he parallel a surviving statement of Euhemerus, known from Lactantius.[115] Even here verbal resemblances are lacking; again it appears that Firmicus was making only indirect use of Euhemerus.[116] As we see how several apologists repeat an identical bit of euhemeristic interpretation, we are impelled to believe that they used a common but lost euhemeristic source. Ennius may have been the vehicle of transmission in some cases, but obviously not where an item is found not only in the Latin apologists but also in Clement of Alexandria or Athenagoras.

We turn now to the biblical and Christian sources of Firmicus. It is, in the first place, a matter for mild surprise that Firmicus should quote the Bible at all; the comparative researches of Laurin have discovered that whereas the Greek apologists quote the Bible liberally, the Latin apologists never do—Firmicus being the conspicuous exception.[117] But even Firmicus was far from being an adept in biblical scholarship, as the present paragraph will show. Long ago Bernhard Dombart ascertained that of fifty-nine verbatim scriptural citations in the De errore, forty-seven are borrowed with little or no variation from two treatises of Cyprian, largely in the same sequence in which Cyprian gave them.[118] Five more citations appear in both Firmicus and Cyprian, but with such distinctive variations in the Latin text that borrowing is out of the question.[119] Finally, we have in Firmicus seven citations, all from the Old Testament, which do not appear at all in Cyprian. Add to these eleven biblical allusions without quotation, and you arrive at the total of seventy biblical allusions or quotations which are listed by Ziegler in his index of sources.[120]

Certain arguments of Christian apologetics had become clichés, repeated ad infinitum; for these commonplaces it is futile to go source-hunting.[121] Indeed Firmicus did not read widely and diligently in the relevant works of his forerunners; the natural expectation that his late arrival in the series of the apologists would insure his dependence on Tertullian, Minucius Felix, and Arnobius proves to be largely illusory. There is not the smallest indication that Firmicus had read either the *Apologeticus* or the *Ad nationes* of Tertullian. Moore (30) pointed to three passages in Firmicus that have parallels in Minucius, but only one of the three shows resemblance of diction and details, and even in this case Kroll convincingly argued that Firmicus' passage with fuller data does not depend on Minucius' passage with more meagre data.[122] A common polemical source, lost and unknown to us, would most reasonably account for Firmicus' resemblances to several other apologists, Greek and Latin; and for such a source Heuten steadfastly argued.

There is considerable evidence that Firmicus read and imitated the *Protrepticus* of Clement of Alexandria, a book whose size is not formidable and which, like the *De errore*, gives a drastic portrayal of the folly and immorality of pagan cults and mysteries. The parallels are all found in the lengthy second chapter of Clement, except for a

striking phrase coined by Clement in his fourth chapter
(σκηνὴν πεποιήκατε τὸν οὐρανόν) and borrowed by no
other author except Firmicus ("Scaenam de caelo
fecistis").[123] In his enumeration of the five Minervas
(16.1), Firmicus, though adding rhetorical amplification,
generally follows Clement, even in the matter of naming
Titanis as the mother of the fifth Minerva—a detail unknown in the parallel passages of Cicero and Arnobius.[124]
The Greek wording of a certain religious slogan quoted by
Firmicus (26.1) is elsewhere found only in Clement.[125]
Other parallels with Clement concern the Cyprian Cinyras,
Sebazius, five examples of divine pederasty, five human
objects of the roving love of Poseidon, and the little-known
story of Dionysus and his promise of reward to Prosym-
nus.[126]

The one Latin apologist whom Firmicus is most likely
to have read, judging by impressive but perhaps not con-
clusive resemblances, is Arnobius. Ziegler in his Teubner
text, while not stating any conclusion, took the trouble
to make running citations of numerous parallels. Defending in his critical apparatus the MS.-reading "summitatem"
(4.3), Ziegler used as his sole argument the fact that this
rare word appears twice in Arnobius.[127] Finding the phrase
"necesse est esse mortale" in Firmicus (5.4), Ziegler noted
that Arnobius has the same phrase in the same word
order three times (7.3, 7.5, 7.28). Cornelius Brakman,
writing in 1917,[128] adduced more parallels which had escaped the eye of Ziegler, and said that undoubtedly
Firmicus, coming late in life to Christianity, had found it
wise to read attentively the book of the rhetor of Sicca—
a book which, like the one Firmicus proposed to write,
delivered a strong attack on paganism. Brakman also at-

tributed to Arnobius' influence the affinity which Firmicus displayed for the explanatory genitive or *genetivus inhaerentiae*,[129] but this notion of Brakman deserves rebuke, for the explanatory genitive is extremely common in the *Mathesis*, where it certainly did not come from reading Arnobius.[130] McCracken in his translation of Arnobius stated a hesitant view: "Many of the parallels are of dictions which might have been and probably were commonly current in the period, and the similarities of content may be presumed to come from frequent identity of topics. It is possible that the author of the *De errore profanarum religionum* had read Arnobius but it is not proven."[131] There are, however, approximately thirty parallels in the twenty-nine chapters of Firmicus, and the frequent identity of topics may be no accident, since Firmicus shows no such parallelism of subject matter with the other apologists. It is my view that Arnobius was a source for Firmicus.

In Christology and doctrinal matters, which do not loom large in Firmicus' onslaught on paganism, we see strong influences from St. Paul and touches from Irenaeus. Aside from catch phrases like "man of God" and "spiritual rock," Paul is quoted verbatim only once (24.4; 1 Cor. 15, 55), but Paulinism is rampant in the doctrinal Chapters 24 and 25. In drawing parallels or contrasts between the Tree of the Fall and the Cross, and between Adam and Christ (Ch. 25), Firmicus followed Irenaeus. Recalling that in Irenaeus "Old Testament Scripture is constantly quoted simply as the Voice of God, or of the Divine Logos, and as of plenary authority,"[132] Vecchi sees a clear proof of Firmicus' discipleship to Irenaeus in his invariable attribution of the authorship of the Old Testament to the

Holy Spirit "speaking through the mouths of the sacred writers."[133]

To the above discussion of sources we may append the observation that Firmicus was never mentioned, except as an astrologer, by any contemporary or subsequent patristic or non-Christian or medieval writer; and only in certain passages of Ambrosiaster, *Quaestiones Veteris et Novi Testamenti*, a work dated about 375 A.D., have traces been found of the unacknowledged influence of the *De errore*.[134]

RELIABILITY OF FIRMICUS AS A SOURCE

On this subject it may be pardonable to borrow heavily from Heuten's pages (16–18) on the subject, especially since Heuten had the signal good fortune to glean the views of Franz Cumont in personal conferences with that renowned scholar of ancient religions. Heuten summarizes Cumont's estimate: "Firmicus est un pédant borné, qui accumule sans distinction des faits qu'il ne comprend pas, et il n'en est pas moins un des peintres les mieux informés, les plus précis et les plus sûrs de la religion de l'empire."

Those who seek to know the status and views of late paganism in the fourth century find that Firmicus is our chief and on some points our only source; his only rival is the Neoplatonist Sallustius. Although Firmicus is occasionally guilty of conspicuous factual error, other sources and documents corroborate his statements so often that readers need not question his general reliability. He gives accurate accounts of pagan rites and correct quotations of sacred formulas. Furthermore he fully comprehended the importance of the Oriental divinities in the paganism of his era in the West. And he noted the religious devolution that was consequent on the weakening of the critical spirit even among the educated classes.

It is proper to list Firmicus' chief misconceptions and errors. In a single chapter he referred first to Ganymedes and then to Catamitus, seemingly not realizing that they were one and the same.[135] He shares, but only to a small extent, the tendency of other Christian polemicists to beat a dead dog, such as the Greek myths.[136] His euhemeristic interpretation of several divinities was an anachronism, ill adapted to impress the pagans, for whom Stoic theology had long ago put euhemerism *hors de combat*.[137] He thought that the cult formulas (*symbola*) of the mysteries were passwords.[138] Stimulated by earlier Christian writers who had with some degree of plausibility interpreted certain scriptural mentions of wood, stone, horn, and spouse as allusions to Christ and His passion, Firmicus blindly added other passages which are completely malapropos: so he adduces Joel 2.16 on Christ the Spouse, though the passage is actually irrelevant.[139]

STYLE, VOCABULARY, LATINITY

Since the volumes of this series do not print the Greek or Latin text of the author being translated, and few readers will have an edition of Firmicus ready at hand for exact study of the Latin, a detailed discussion of his style and vocabulary seems impractical here. Interested persons will go to Ziegler's analysis of the clausulae, Groehl's survey of the syntax, Heuten's account of the style and vocabulary, and Pastorino's forty-two pages on syntax, orthography, morphology, word choice, and especially rhetorical figures.[140]

"The most conspicuous influence on the style and thought of the Latin apologetes and the fathers of the fourth century . . . comes from Cicero. Let us call it, then, the *Aetas Ciceroniana.*"[141] Firmicus, conformably to the trend of his time, endeavored to be a Ciceronian, *magni nominis umbra;* but, sad to say, he was as far beneath Cicero in ability as he was beyond him in time. In any case, he had no desire to be a fanatical Ciceronian, and was quite willing to adapt his Latin in a moderate degree to postclassical usages.[142] Thus postclassical words appear with some frequency, but postclassical abstracts less commonly than in most writers of the Empire. Firmicus has only seven non-Greek words that are the exclusive property of Christian writers, three of these being neologisms.[143] Among the loan words from the Greek, which he uses in considerable numbers, there is only one neologism, the hapax legomenon *ethopoeiacus* (8.4). In vocabulary Firmicus was no bold innovator. Since his primary subject was paganism, he was able to write with the use of only a couple dozen words from the technical terminology of the Bible and Christian doctrine: *gehenna, ecclesia, excommunicatio, diabolus, paradisus,* etc.

There are a few deviations from the classical norm in morphology and syntax. Instead of the standard form *fers,* we repeatedly have the uncontracted *feris, tranferis, proferis.* Compound verb forms appear with *fueram, fuissem,* and *fuerit.* There are seven instances of indirect questions using the indicative. For oratio obliqua we find mostly the infinitive or a *quod*-clause, never the widely popular *quia*-clause except in verbatim quotations from the Bible. *Vescor* is used once with the ablative; but where Cicero wrote "Est enim omne quo vescuntur homines penus" (*Nat. deor.* 2.68), Firmicus altered to the accusative, "Nam omne quod vescuntur homines penus vocatur" (14.2). In half a dozen sentences the sequence of tenses breaks down.[144]

Clausulae have been of value in proving that the same Firmicus wrote the *Mathesis* and the *De errore*, and in emending blurred or disputed passages of the MS. The favorite is a cretic followed by a trochee; next favored is a double cretic. Gerundives fit well into Firmician clausulae and are so used fourteen times: e.g., *metuendus* three times. But Firmicus avoids like the plague the verb *metuere* (except in biblical quotations) and uses the better-sounding *timere;* on this matter others agreed with Firmicus, and the long-term result was that no Romance language retains the verb *metuere*.[145]

Readers of Firmicus who are attentive to his style find it easy to believe that he was a Sicilian—passionate, hot, vehement, colorfully rhetorical. On this subject it is best to call to the witness stand an Italian critic, Moricca: ". . . con parola rovente, quale poteva venir dall'ardore di un'anima meridionale accopiata con l'entusiasmo del neofito battagliero."[146] Similarly a German critic: "His style is in keeping with his zealot mentality; he avoids calm discussion and speaks in an excited tone with unnatural pathos; he hounds the apostrophe quite to death."[147] "Firmicus has talent," said Heuten, and we may agree; but in truth it was a talent for overdoing things. Since he declined to admit that enough is enough, pleonasm issues from him in gushes. "Pleonasm is one of the figures most characteristic of the style of Firmicus, resulting in an excess and accumulation of terms, the frequent use of synonyms, the *genetivus inhaerentiae*, the etymological ablative, etc."[148] I quote a remarkable example which combines a redundant adjective with an etymological ablative (and homoeoteleuton): "festina celeritate properate" (21.6). As for the *genetivus inhaerentiae* ("construction très frequente dans les textes chrétiens de toutes les époques"[149]), we now have the dissertation of Weijermans, which shows that Firmicus in his two works used the construction 188 times, far more than any other Latin author, pagan or Christian. Take two treatises of almost exactly the same length, the *Octavius* of Minucius Felix and the *De errore*: the former contains six examples of the *genetivus inhaerentiae*, the latter twenty-six. This construction is a trademark of Firmicus just as much as the ablative absolute is of Caesar.[150]

Of the rhetorical figures, extensively studied by Pastorino in his Introduction, we may glance at only a few of the most obvious and striking. Of paronomasia, Pastorino cites thirty-seven examples: e.g., "Lugete mortuos vestros, et ipsi simili morte morituri" (8.3). Ciceronian anaphora appears in every one of the twenty-nine chapters and is well suited to the excited and overemphatic polemical style: "Lugete Liberum, lugete Proserpinam, lugete Attin, lugete Osyrin" (8.3). Alliteration, mostly of consecutive words, is sown not by the hand but by the sack: "Proficiscens peregre pater" (6.2). Rhetorical questions, often enhanced by anaphora, come in volleys: look at section 7 of Chapter 2, where the volley ends with "Cur plangitis fruges? Cur recrescentia lugetis semina?" Exclamations may come singly ("pro nefas!" 16.2) or they also in volleys, even artfully heightened by a quasi-rhopalic effect: "O flagitiosa confessio! O acerbi deflendique casus! O durae servitutis miseranda condicio!" (12.9). Irony comes in various guises, including exclamations: "Egregia erroris istius ac praeclara commenta!" (5.4). In apostrophe Firmicus cries out to the brother-emperors, Porphyry, Christ, the devil, but especially to pitiable mankind: "O misera et caduca mortalitas, O miser homo, O miseri, O miseri mortales, caduci homines," etc. (2.3, 2.8, 4.3, 7.9, 8.1).

We may conclude by translating some generalizations of Pastorino (xli). "Firmicus fails to perceive how his oratorical tumidity, his apostrophes, his abuse of rhetorical figures sensibly cool for the reader that passionate ardor which seems to have inspired the little book. He has talent and culture but is not an artist, even though sometimes his prose has a certain vigor, as in the apostrophe of the Sun (Ch. 8) and the attack on Mars (Ch. 9)." Not only because Firmicus was overshadowed by more important patristic writers, but also because his style was on the whole a failure, his Christian book went unmentioned and unnoticed (unless by Ambrosiaster) for twelve centuries, from the time of its publication until its rediscovery by Matthias Flacius Illyricus.

From the style, mannerisms, syntax, and vocabulary of Firmicus spring a number of difficulties for the reader or translator. Let those who discern flaws in this first English version blame the guilty translator as much as they will; but let them at least give heed to the authoritative words of a world-renowned expert on Latin syntax and stylistics, Alfred Ernout: "La traduction du traité de Firmicus est chose difficile; l'apparente clarté de la phrase dissimule souvent des ambiguïtés et des obscurités redoutables; la langue présente bien des tours déconcertants: les modes et les temps y sont souvent confondus, sans qu'il soit toujours possible de discerner si la faute en revient à l'auteur, ou au copiste—le choix de la clausule semble avoir déterminé certaines de ses fluctuations—; le sens des termes abstraits ne laisse difficilement préciser; les citations des textes scripturaires posent également des problèmes, la traduction latine citée par Firmicus présentant des divergences notables avec le texte de la version grecque des Septante, ou avec le texte de la Vulgate."[151]

TEXT AND TRANSLATIONS

The history of the text and editions of the *De errore* has been admirably written by Ziegler in the Introduction to his Teubner text of 1907, and only an abridged account is needed here.

Firmicus' book, overshadowed only a little later by the towering works of St. Augustine, unmentioned by any patristic or medieval writer, and demonstrably used only by Ambrosiaster, lay for more than twelve hundred years buried in oblivion, until the Reformation. Rummaging in German libraries to get material for the extensive century-by-century ecclesiastical history now popularly called the Magdeburg Centuries, the notable Slavic Lutheran Matthias Flacius (1520–75) found in Minden a minuscule codex mutilated at the beginning but designated at the end as *Iulii Firmici Materni V.C. de errore profanarum religionum*. Recognizing the book as an unpublished item that was worthy of being known, he brought it out at Strassburg in 1562, noting on the title page that it was "numquam antehac in lucem editus."[152] The codex, either purchased or purloined by Flacius from the monks of Minden,[153] next appeared in the library of Baron Ulrich Fugger in Augsburg in 1571.[154] Fugger's entire library passed by bequest to the Palatine Library of Heidelberg, and of course the latter in turn went to the Vatican in 1623. But during all this time and even for long afterwards editors and students of Firmicus knew nothing of the whereabouts of the codex.

In 1603 at Hamburg, Iohannes a Wower produced an edition wherein by common sense and shrewd conjecture he removed dozens of the errors perpetrated by Flacius. In 1826 at Copenhagen, Bishop Friedrich Münter brought out a passable edition with commentary, and this was re-printed in Migne's *Patrologia latina* 12 (1845). Münter simply took Wower's text, as indeed every editor since Wower had done. But Franz Oehler in 1847, by applying the real laws of textual criticism, made the first improve-ments in Wower's text (Leipzig, Vol. 13 of Gersdorf's *Bibliotheca patrum ecclesiasticorum latinorum selecta*).

Affairs now took a surprising turn through a happy chance. As Conrad Bursian was working in the Vatican Library, he took a look at the MS. designated as Vaticanus Palatinus Latinus 165. It proved to be not only a codex of Firmicus' *De errore,* but the very one studied by Matthias Flacius at Minden and subsequently lost to the world of scholarship for three centuries. Bursian recognized it to be of the ninth or tenth century, and he quickly saw that its reading had been repeatedly and grossly misrepresented by Flacius. It was partly blurred and hard to read, and lacked two folios at the beginning and two more after the present folio 4 (middle of Ch. 5). Bursian decided that a new edition was needed, and he brought one out at

Leipzig in 1856; Ziegler's comment (vii) on this is: "Si minus laudanda est, at tamen usum aliquem praebuit."

The Vienna Academy's *Corpus scriptorum ecclesiasticorum latinorum* was launched in 1866, and the preparation of both the first two volumes was entrusted to Karl Halm of Munich. The second volume in 1867 included Firmicus. For this edition Ziegler (viii) reserved his most withering superlatives of condemnation: "incredible carelessness, absolutely inexcusable frivolity, an edition that even the most lenient judge would have to pronounce the worst of all."[155]

The nineteenth century had failed to produce a satisfactory text of the *De errore*. But the Teubner series had never included a text of the *De errore*, and Ziegler, under the prompting of his teacher and mentor Skutsch, now set out to prepare for Teubner a text that should satisfy the standards of the twentieth century. This appeared in 1907, with a solid and lengthy introduction, an exceedingly accurate critical text, a complete *index verborum*, and other *subsidia*. The plaudits which greeted Ziegler's work are unabated, and Ernout in 1938 described it as "une des plus complètes et des plus soignées [éditions] de la bibliotheca Teubneriana."[156] It remains the best and most faithful textual edition that we have.[157]

Subsequently three more editions appeared. The Belgian Gilbert Heuten in 1938 reproduced Ziegler's text with a few changes, but added a valuable introduction, French translation, and commentary. Ziegler himself in 1953 brought out a sort of *editio minor* with some new textual readings, abridged *apparatus criticus*, full introduction, and German translation; the user of this discovers that he must still at all times refer to the 1907 edition. Finally, the

Sicilian Firmicus was elaborately edited in 1956 by the Sicilian Agostino Pastorino, with copious philological and religious commentary but with numerous misprints and errors.

No proper translation of Firmicus was possible from the bad texts that antedated Ziegler. Using Ziegler's text, Alfons Müller, one of the best experts on Firmicus, gave a faithful and almost too literal German translation in 1913. Next came the annotated Italian translation of Giuseppe Faggin in 1932, unknown outside of Italy. Heuten's notable French translation in 1938 is carefully compared with Müller's and corrects it at a few points. Ziegler in 1953 leaned freely on Müller, silently removing numerous errors. Firmicus has not hitherto appeared in an English version.

THE ERROR OF THE PAGAN RELIGIONS

[The first two leaves of the unique MS., containing about a hundred lines of text, are lost.[1] The recto of the first surviving leaf, f.1ʳ, is only partly legible. The following translation endeavors to convey the sense of such interrupted portions as can be read, with brackets enclosing whatever words are conjecturally restored in Ziegler's edition.]

God created the world from four elements, each of which is erroneously worshiped in certain countries.

Ch. 1] . . . What the Creator [God[2] did] in the making of man . . . we have said; in yearly [admonitions] of the children of perdition[3] . . . needs to be repeated in detail . . . by the manifest proofs of examples we shall show that [the divinization of the elements was the invention] of the devil, in order that by this means the spirit in unclean [thinking] . . . with the hope of [future] bliss [annulled] by distinctions set awry . . . unfortunate mankind [involved] in everlasting calamities. . . . Who could doubt that there are four elements, i.e., fire, water, air, and earth; and that these are found [in all corporeal things.] But these elements are diverse . . . with opposite potency.[4] Therefore the heathen are in error[5] [if to one of the] elements they assign pre-eminence . . . as the supreme deity, [as if] all the others had their substance from it . . . not knowing that all the elements are bound together by their very oppositeness, and that they too have God as their Creator,[6] who setting each severally in its due place and order [has fabricated] what

43

we either comprehend with our mind and thought or at any rate what we see with our eyes, [by the divine power] of His word[7] [having united] and put them together in a measured equilibrium[8] of material things.

Water-Cult in the Egyptian religion of Isis and Osiris

Ch. 2] The inhabitants of Egypt worship water,[9] supplicate water, venerate water with an everlasting series of superstitious vows. But in their cults which they call mysteries they add tragical funerals and [fear-inspiring struggles] which have a gruesome denouement:

[Here begins the verso of the first surviving leaf of the MS.; from this point forward, except in Ch. 5, the text is generally complete, though often hard to read.]

incest and adultery with a sister, and the drastic measures by which the husband exacted vengeance for this crime. Isis is the sister, Osiris the brother, Typhon the husband.[10] **2.** When Typhon learned that his wife Isis had been violated by the incestuous lust of his brother, he killed[11] Osiris, tore him limb from limb,[12] and scattered the still twitching members of the wretched corpse all over the banks of the Nile River.[13] Isis divorced Typhon, and for the purpose of burying her brother-spouse enlisted the aid of her sister Nepthus and the hunter Anubis;[14] and the reason why Anubis is assigned a dog's head is that he displayed the skill of a hunting hound in finding[15] the parts of the dismembered body. When Osiris was found in this manner, Isis gave him burial.[16] **3.** The fact is that these personages were kings[17] in Egypt, and tyrants as well; but Osiris was a just man except for the wrong that he did with his sister, whereas Typhon was a madman,[18] reckless, and haughty. That is why Osiris is worshiped and Typhon shunned.

The following is the gist of the cult of Isis. Buried in their shrines they keep an image of Osiris, over which they mourn in anniversary lamentations,[19] wherein they shave their heads[20] so that the ugliness of their disfigured polls may show their grief for the pitiful lot of their king. Also they beat their breasts,[21] tear their upper arms, and break open the scars of old wounds, so that the anniversary lamentations may ever renew in their hearts the memory of the death effected by gruesome and pitiable murder. And after performing these rites on set days, next they feign that they are questing for the remains of the mutilated corpse, and rejoice on finding them[22] as if their sorrows were lulled. **4.** O wretched mortals, soon to perish![23] In order to provide each year dismal rites of commemoration for your kings—neglecting the Supreme Deity,[24] who has set all things aright by the guidance of His divine skill—you are wasting both your hope and your life;[25] you are not converted by the splendor of the light revealed to you,[26] nor do you reach for the tokens of liberty regained, nor recognize the gifts to you of the hope of salvation, nor repent and ask pardon for past offenses. **5.** Vain is your supposition[27] that this water which you worship is at times of benefit to you. Quite another thing is the water by which human beings are renewed and reborn.[28] This water which you worship every year—why, a different power dries it up[29] by overheating the channels of its veins; or at any rate the calamitous blood of your king[30] befouls[31] it. That water which you scorn[32] is turned to fire and glorified by the power[33] of the Worshipful Spirit, so that from the water itself the healthiness of salvation, creeping through the old scars of conscience, is infused into those who believe. **6.** But in these lamentations and funerals, which in very truth are funerals that once took place, of a body whose remains are still extant today (for the tomb of Osiris[34] still exists in Egypt even today, and people see the remains of his cremated body[35]), their apologists insist on adding a Scientific Theory,[36] saying that Osiris is the seed[37] of growing things, Isis the earth,[38] Typhon heat.[39] And because growing things matured by heat are harvested to support the life of man, thus being separated and taken away from the companionship of the earth, and are sowed again as winter draws near, they maintain that it is the death of Osiris when they store away the produce, and it is the finding of Osiris when growing things, conceived by the fostering warmth of mother earth, again begin to be produced by the annual procreation. **7.** Suppose this is the true explanation of that cult, suppose it is because of growing things that vows are paid to those divinities: why add incest, why adultery,[40] why death by dreadful punishment? Why do you provide a bad example from your cult for human beings who go astray and are prone to sin anyway in their simplemindedness? Let the Scientific Theory which you allege be concealed in some other guise. Still, why conceal what everybody knows? Why do you mourn for the growing things? Why do you grieve for the seeds that germinate again? **8.** All these things are gifts for the sustenance of mankind, given by the divine generosity of the Supreme Deity. Thanksgiving for them is what we owe the Supreme Deity; we ought not to lament over His largess. Weep rather because you are in error, and bewail your error with mourning ever renewed. Don't go questing in anniversary cult-actions year by year for somebody else's dead body; rather make ready year by year consolations for your own death. **9.** Unhappy man, rejoicing that you have found something or other, when actually you are losing your soul every year as a result of those rites! You find there nothing but an idol which you yourself put there, nothing but an object to seek for and bewail again and again. Seek rather the hope of salvation, seek the beginning of light, seek what may either recommend you or restore you to the Supreme Deity; and when you have found the true way of salvation, rejoice and then cry out with exalted freedom of speech:[41] εὑρήκαμεν, συγχαίρομεν[42] ("We have found it! Together we rejoice!"), since your repentance has caused you to be saved from these calamities by the indulgence of the Supreme Deity.

Earth-Cult in the Phrygian Worship of Magna Mater and Attis

Ch. 3] The Phrygians who dwell in Pessinus[43] by the banks of the Gallus River assign the primacy over the other elements to the earth, and maintain that she is the mother of all things.[44] Then, desirous that they too should get themselves a set of annual rites,[45] they proceeded to consecrate with annual lamentations the love affair of a rich woman, their queen,[46] who chose to avenge in tyrannical fashion the haughty snub that she suffered from her young beloved. In order to satisfy the angry woman, or perhaps trying to find consolation for her after she repented, they advanced the claim that he whom they had buried a little while earlier had come to life again;[47] and since the woman's heart burned unbearably with overweening love, they erected temples[48] to the dead youth. Thereafter what the angry woman had done[49] to avenge the insult to her slighted beauty,[50] this they insist that the priests whom they ordain should suffer. Thus in annual rites[51] honoring the earth there is drawn up in array the cortege of the youth's funeral, so that people are really venerating an unhappy death and funeral when they are convinced that they are worshiping the earth. **2.** Here again, Most Holy Emperors, in order to hide such an error, they insist that this cult also is organized by a Scientific Theory.[52] The earth, they maintain, loves the crops, Attis[53] is the very thing that grows from the crops, and the punishment which he suffered is what a harvester with his sickle does to the ripened crops. His death they interpret as the storing away of the collected seeds, his resurrection as the sprouting of the scattered seeds in the annual turn of the seasons. **3.** Now I should like to have them answer me a question: Why did they combine this simple matter of seeds and crops with a funeral,[54] with death, with a haughty snub, with a punishment, with a love affair? Wasn't there really anything else which could be said? Wasn't there really anything else[55] which unhappy mortals could do in thanksgiving to the Supreme Deity for the crops? Do you howl[56] as a mark of thanksgiving for the new growth of the crops, do you mourn to show your joy? And when you do see the true explanation, do you still not regret your past behavior, but persist in busying yourself with annual lamentations, always running away from life and seeking death? **4.** Let them tell me what good it has done the crops to have them renew their laments annually with howlings, to have them groan over the woes of a corpse reborn—all this being organized, they say, by a Scientific Theory.[57] You grieve and mourn, and disguise your mourning under the cloak of a strange Theory. A farmer knows when to break the sod[58] with the plough, knows when to trust the seeds of grain to the furrows, knows when to harvest the crops ripened by the heat of the sun, knows when to thresh the dried ears. *This* is scientific theory, these are true sacrificial rites which are performed in yearly labor by right-minded men, this is the simple way that God wants, that men should obey the ordained laws of the seasons in bringing the harvest home. To explain this round of the seasons, why did they invent fictional tales about a dreadful death? Why is a matter disguised with tears which need not be disguised at all? Wherefore they necessarily must acknowledge that these rites were organized not in honor of the crops but in honor of an irrelevant death.[59] **5.** Now as for the claim that earth is the mother of all the gods (a claim asserted by those who assign primacy to this one of the elements)—why, truly she is the mother of *their* gods, and we do not object or deny, because they are forever making their gods out of stone or wood[60] gathered from the earth. All the earth is encompassed by the seas, and constricted again by the enfolding girdle of circumambient Ocean, roofed over too by the lofty vault of heaven, blown upon by the winds, besprinkled by the rains, and beset by fear which her constant quakings[61] manifest. You who worship such things, ponder what is in store for you, when your gods daily betray and acknowledge to you their impotence.

Air-Cult in the Syrian and Carthaginian
Worship of Caelestis

Ch. 4] The Assyrians[62] and part of the Africans[63] ascribe the primacy among the elements to the air, and worship it[64] in a shape which is the product of their imagination. For exactly this, the air, is what they have consecrated under the name of Juno or Venus the Virgin[65]—if virginity ever suited the fancy of Venus! As for Juno, they maintain (just to make sure that incest is not lacking in this quarter, too) that she progressed from being Jupiter's sister to being his spouse.[66] Animated by some sort of reverential feeling, they actually have made this element into a woman.[67] For,[68] because air is an intermediary[69] between sea and sky, they honor[70] it through priests who have womanish voices.[71] 2. Tell me, is air a divinity if it looks for a woman in a man, if its band of priests can minister to it only when they have feminized their faces, rubbed smooth their skin, and disgraced their manly sex by donning women's regalia?[72] In their very temples one may see scandalous performances,[73] accompanied by the moaning of the throng: men letting themselves be handled as women,[74] and flaunting with boastful ostentatiousness[75] this ignominy of their impure and unchaste[76] bodies. They parade their misdeeds in the public eye, acknowledging with superlative relish in filthiness the dishonor of their polluted bodies. They nurse their tresses[77] and pretty them up woman-fashion; they dress in soft garments; they can hardly hold their heads erect on their languid necks.[78] Next, being thus divorced from masculinity, they get intoxicated[79] with the music of flutes[80] and invoke their goddess to fill them with an unholy spirit so that they can ostensibly predict[81] the future to fools. What sort of monstrous and unnatural thing[82] is all this? They say they are not men,[83] and indeed they aren't; they want to pass as women, but whatever the nature of their bodies is, it tells a different story. **3.** Ponder too what sort of divinity it is which finds it such a delight to sojourn in an impure body, which clings to unchaste members, which is appeased by the contamination of a polluted body. Blush for Her Highness,[84] you poor wretches; God created you other than this. When the troop of you draws near the judgment seat of God, you will bring with you nothing that the God who created you can recognize. Reject this great and calamitous error, and abandon at last the inclinations of a heathen heart.[85] Do not take your body which God created and condemn it by the wicked law of the devil. While time still permits, go to the rescue of your disastrous situation.

The mercy of God is rich, and He forgives gladly. He leaves the ninety-nine sheep[86] and seeks the one that is lost, and to the prodigal son[87] who returns the father gives a garment and prepares him a feast. **4.** I do not want you to despair because of the multitude of your sins: the Supreme Deity through His Son Jesus Christ our Lord saves all who are willing and gladly pardons the repentant, nor is it much that He asks as the condition of pardon. Merely by faith and repentance you can redeem whatever you have lost through the wicked insinuations of the devil.

Fire-Cult in the Mithraic Religion of the Persians and Magi

Ch. 5] The Persians and all the Magi[88] who dwell in the confines of the Persian land give their preference to fire and think it ought to be ranked above all the other elements. So they divide fire into two potencies, relating its nature to the potency of the two sexes,[89] and attributing the substance of fire to the image of a man and the image of a woman. The woman they represent with a triform countenance, and entwine her with snaky monsters.[90] This they do so as not to disagree in any way with their sponsor, the devil; they want to have their goddess be sprouting all over with snakes and thus be adorned with the devil's polluted insignia. **2.** The male they worship as a cattle rustler,[91] and his cult they relate to the potency of fire, as his prophet handed down the lore to us,[92] saying: Μύστα βοοκλοπίης, συνδέξιε πατρὸς ἀγαυοῦ.[93] ("Initiate of cattle-rustling, companion by handclasp of an illustrious father"). Him they call Mithra, and his cult they carry on in hidden caves,[94] so that they may be forever plunged in the gloomy squalor of darkness and thus shun the grace of light resplendent and serene. O true[95] consecration of a divinity! O repulsive inventions of a barbaric code! Him whose crimes you acknowledge you think to be a god. So you who declare it proper for the cult[96] of the Magi to be carried on by the Persian rite in these cave temples, why do you praise only this among the Persian customs? If you think it worthy of the Roman name to serve the cults of the Persians, the laws of the Persians,

[Two folios of the MS are missing at this point.][97]

The Tripartite Division of the Soul

3. [the goddess] who, armed with a shield and protected by a cuirass, is consecrated on the pinnacle of the Acropolis.[98] Again another third is the one which in the wild and secluded forests obtains dominion over the beasts of the field. The last part of that threefold division is the one which makes known the pathways of the lusts, the base desires, the enticements of perverse concupiscence. Therefore they assign one part as the head's, so that it seems in some sort to embrace man's passion.[99] Another they fix in the heart, so that it seems, like the forests,[100] to embrace the variety of different thoughts which we conceive by manifold concentration. The third part is fixed in the liver,[101] whence spring libido and voluptuousness. For it is in the liver that the fecund genital semen gathers and by its natural stimuli stirs up concupiscence. **4.** So what does that division accomplish?[102] Observe closely how easy it is for the logic of truth to impugn a falsehood. If the soul is partitioned and its substance divided up according to the different kinds of functioning, through this organic disruption it begins to be[103] something that it was not, ceasing to be what it was. For the reason is one thing, passion another, libido another. Therefore this sundering disrupts the soul, which from such a partitioning sustains a heavy loss; it does not keep intact its own species and form when separated and distributed among three conflicting species,[104] and, to put it more accurately, it becomes mortal[105] by the very act of division. For everything that can be divided is material. Furthermore, what is material is necessarily mortal.[106] Therefore if the soul is divided, it is material; if material, it must likewise be mortal. What wonderful and splendid trumpery this error has fathered! From this deification[107] we are reaping a superlative benefit: yes, thanks to the trumpery and cult of those fellows the soul is proved[108] to be mortal!

The Euhemeristic Approach Proves the Nondivinity of the Cretan Liber and the Theban Liber

Ch. 6] Thus,[109] Most Holy Emperors, have the elements[110] been deified by the children of perdition. But there are still other superstitions[111] whose secrets must be revealed: those of Liber[112] and Libera, whose whole story[113] in detail must be made known to your sacred intelligence, to make you aware that in these pagan religions again it is the deaths of human beings that have been hallowed by worship.

Well then, Liber was the son of Jupiter[114]—I mean the Jupiter who was king of Crete. In spite of being the progeny of an adulterous mother,[115] Liber was reared under his father's eye with more zealous attention than was right and proper. Jupiter's wife, whose name was Juno, goaded by the fury of a stepmother's mentality,[116] plotted in every sort of way to encompass the murder of the child. **2.** When the father was on the point of going abroad, he took steps, since he was aware of his wife's concealed indignation, to keep the angry woman from any treacherous behavior, and entrusted his son to the protection of guards[117] whom he deemed suitable. Then Juno had just the right opportunity for her designs, and she was all the more violently infuriated because the father at his departure had handed over the throne[118] and scepter of the realm to the boy. First she corrupted the guards with bribes and gifts; then she stationed her minions, called Titans,[119] in the inner apartments of the palace. With a rattle and a mirror[120] of ingenious workmanship she so beguiled the fancy of the boy that he left his royal seat and let his childish desires lead him to the place of ambush. **3.** There he was intercepted and killed;[121] and to insure that no trace of the murder might be found, the gang of minions chopped his members up into pieces and divided them among themselves. Next, piling one crime upon another, as they were egged on by mortal terror of their despot's cruelty, they cooked the boy's members in various ways and devoured them, thus feeding on a human cadaver, a banquet unheard of up to that day. The boy's sister Minerva[122] (for she too was a party to the crime) saved his heart, which had fallen to her share; her double purpose was to have unambiguous evidence as she turned informer and likewise something to soften the brunt of her father's impetuous fury. When Jupiter returned, his daughter unfolded the tale of the crime. **4.** Thereupon the father, infuriated by the gruesome and calamitous act of butchery and by the anguish of his bitter grief, put the Titans to all manner of torture and killed them. In vengeance for his son he left untried no form of torment or punishment, but plunged madly through the whole gamut of penalties, thus avenging the murder of his so-called "son" with a father's affection but a despot's display of power. Then, unable longer to bear the pangs of paternal grief, and seeing that no solaces could assuage the sorrow caused by his bereavement, he had a statue[123] of the boy molded in plaster; and the artist placed the heart, whereby the crime had been revealed by the tattling sister, just in the spot where the contours of the breast were shaped. The next thing he did was to erect a temple in lieu of a tomb, and as priest he appointed the boy's *paedagogus*.[124] **5.** The latter's name was Silenus. Now the Cretans, wishing to allay the savage passion of their furious despot, established the anniversary of the death as a holyday, and arranged recurring sacred rites[125] celebrated every two years, wherein they rehearse seriatim all that the boy did or suffered at his death. They tear a live bull[126] with their teeth, representing the cruel banquet with this regular commemoration; and amid the forest fastness they howl with dissonant outcries, feigning the insanity of madmen to create the belief that the crime was not done in treachery but in madness. In front of them is borne the basket[127] in which the sister had secretly concealed the heart, and by the tootling of flutes and the din of cymbals[128] they counterfeit the rattle which was used to beguile the boy. So, by way of doing honor to a despot, a subservient rabble took a person who was unable to have any burial and made him into a god.

6. There was also another Liber in Thebes,[129] a tyrant famed for his magical powers. Gaining control of the women's wits by certain potions and charms, thereafter at his own sweet will he bade the frenzied creatures[130] commit atrocious deeds, so that he might have crazed women of noble rank as accomplices of his lusts and crimes. What sort of villainy he did, what a dreadful crime he bade a mother commit against her son and sisters against their brother, is daily represented on the stage by the tragic authors;[131] thus the criminal cruelty of the wicked tyrant is perpetually revived in the hearts of the audience by the gruesome representations. **7.** This Liber was stripped of his throne[132] and expelled from his fatherland by Lycurgus, who was backed by a conspiracy of soberly responsible men. The effeminate[133] Liber could not offer prolonged resistance to the united resolution of men. For it is common talk in the gymnasia[134] of Greece that he was a pervert and served the lustful desires of homosexuals. Lycurgus was not content merely with Liber's flight and exile, but fearing that the fugitive might be received by others where he might implant the seeds of his licentious crimes also in another region, girt on the sword and pursued this disgrace of his fatherland with a menacing edict. Then Liber threw away the fillets which he was wont to bind with encircling coronals of vine leaves[135] and fled with his halfmen lackeys[136] (for the only ones who accompanied him in flight were his associates in debauchery, shame, and lust). Over all the neighboring seacoasts he went wandering in the utmost trepidation and despair. **8.** There amid drunken girls and wine-soaked oldsters,[137] with all his scoundrelly cortege[138] still going on before, one hideous in a black garment, another spreading terror by displaying a snake,[139] a third with lips blood-flecked[140] from rending the limbs of a living animal, Liber was caught by Lycurgus and hurled into the sea over a nearby cliff which formed an immense precipice with impassable rocks. And this severe punishment was designed to let the mangled[141] corpse, long tossed by the waves of the sea, restore the errant wits of the populace to sanity and sobriety. Such was the end of Liber; and Homer exposes his panicky flight and indicates his death by saying: "Dionysus in terror dived down in the briny sea, where Thetis received him in her bosom; fearstricken he was, for a powerful shivering caught him at the man's bluster."[142] **9.** One who imitates you, Lycurgus, and follows your sober example with no swerving from your salutary laws, is even our consul Postumius.[143] For as we find in the books of the Annals,[144] the crimes of the Bacchanalia were made known by the report of a certain young man named Aebutius. There were still sound morals then in the city of Rome, and no one went chasing after dissolute foreign superstitions. On this occasion the senate did not fail[145] the consul, nor the laws the republic, nor the consul the laws; but all persons were investigated who were spreading the wicked inventions of this cult; and on the basis of a severe, or rather genuinely Roman,[146] judicial inquiry, capital punishment[147] was decreed for them all by vote of the senate. Nor did the avenging swords of the consul know any rest until their surgery had eradicated this mischief. O punishment worthy of the Roman name![148] O praiseworthy steadfastness of the old-time virtue! The consul would not spare even his fellow citizens when it was a matter of eliminating foreign vices in order to purge the fatherland.

The Folly of Apotheosizing Two Sicilian Women, Ceres and Proserpina

Ch. 7] Catching the contagion of this cult, and imitating it in the ritual of a funeral, is the consecration of her daughter's death by Ceres, a woman of Henna.[149] For whatever the father had done in Crete regarding his son, all this Ceres established as ritual in Henna when she was uncontrollably afflicted with maternal grief at the loss of her daughter. How this came about is a tale that I shall condense in a brief telling. The only daughter of Ceres, whom the Greeks call Persephone and we Proserpina (altering the form), was a girl whom many suitors were eager to espouse in marriage. Her mother conscientiously tried to form an opinion of the merits of each suitor, and everybody assumed that her decision was still in doubt. But a rich countryman (named Pluto on account of his

riches[150]) was so inflamed with rash desire that he could
not brook delay and, kindled with the flames of unseason-
able love, he kidnaped the girl near Percus[151] where he
found her. Now Percus is a lake in the territory of the
city of Henna, very lovely and pleasant, and its loveli-
ness[152] is due to its varieties of flowers. For all the year
long it wears coronals of flowers, one variety succeeding
another in turn. 2. There[153] you will find whatever hya-
cinth swells into its stalk, there the leafage of narcissus or
what paints the rose a golden hue above, there the pale
ivy[154] softly creeping along the ground; you find too the
sweetly blushing marjoram[155] along with purple violets,
nor are white lilies missing in the coronal. Truly a fitting
spot with its charm equally to lure and to hold the heart
of a girl.[156] In this spot Pluto found the maiden near the
twilight hour, seized her by force, placed her on his
chariot, and whirled her away while she rent her garments
and tore her hair. Her trimmed nails[157] were of no help
against her rustic lover; she shrieked and screamed in vain,
and vain were the confused cries of the other maidens. 3.
Then, as no one came to the rescue from the city, one of
the girls ran swiftly, with fear adding even more velocity
to her heels, and brought the mother word of the kidnaped
maid. Against the kidnaper the angry mother led out a
posse of armed men. Nor did Pluto fail to observe the
woman's approach, but glancing back[158] toward the city
and seeing countless swarms coming after him along with
the mother, he formed a dreadful counsel of despair.[159] He
drove the team of four, that was pulling his chariot,[160]
right into the middle of the lake, immense as it was,[161] with
abysmal depths. Swallowed up there together with his
beloved maiden, he provided for the eyes of a wretched

mother the melancholy spectacle of her daughter's death. **4.** The people of Henna, desirous of discovering solace in some quarter for the mother's grief, feigned that the king of the underworld had kidnaped the maid and, to add plausibility to this fiction, they claimed that he had reappeared with the maid out of another lake[162] near Syracuse. And in fact they erected a temple jointly for the kidnaper and the maid, diligently collecting the funds for the purpose, and decreed the annual payment of vows in the temple.[163] But in no wise was the mother's grief assuaged nor were the torments of her feminine resentment healed; but believing that her daughter had really been seen near Syracuse, she took Triptolemus,[164] the overseer of her property, as an escort and journeying by night arrived in mourning garb and disheveled squalor at the shore of Syracuse. There too without fail someone appeared to deceive the mother, whose woes made her credulous. Somebody named Pandarus[165] said that he had seen the kidnaper with the maid board a ship not far from Pachynus.[166] The woman believed this—eager as she was to hear that her daughter was alive, no matter how—and she rewarded the city with unstinted gifts. **5.** Stimulated by her generosity, the Syracusans made a cult out of the maid's kidnaping and, in an effort to mitigate the mother's grief, honored with temples[167] the tragic death and funeral. But not even this satisfied the mother; boarding a ship she went in quest[168] of her daughter on foreign shores. Thus wave-tossed and tempest-tossed, she came to the site of a city in Attica. Received hospitably there by the inhabitants, she distributed among them wheat, a grain thitherto unknown to them.[169] The place got its name from her homeland and her coming, for it was called Eleusis from the fact that Ceres had left Henna and come there.[170] **6.** So, because she had dispensed among them the grain which she had brought and had transmitted to them the lore of harvesting the crops, the people after her death buried her there and likewise deified her[171] for the benefit that accrued to them from the bountiful harvests, and she together with her daughter[172] was called by a divine name. For the frivolous Greeks[173] are fond of calling by divine names those who have bestowed some blessing upon them or helped them by counsel or noble deed. Such is their way of repaying gratitude for benefits: whatever persons have ever been helpful to them they call "gods" and believe in them as gods. Thus Nysa[174] has no doubts about Liber, nor does Sparta boggle over new stars,[175] while grieving Oeta[176] cremates and consecrates Hercules, and the foolish Cretans are still today adoring the tomb of the dead Jupiter.[177] **7.** To compound this pagan error, Most Holy Emperors, there is an additional circumstance which invests these two human beings,[178] Liber and Proserpina, as it were with greater prestige. For the inventive Greeks want to equate Liber with the Sun,[179] and Libera (whom they call Proserpina) they feign to be the Moon.[180] What a silly and pitiful notion this is we can gather from the very logic of the truth. The Sun as a little boy—who has ever seen that? Who deceived Him, who killed Him? Who tore Him asunder, who distributed the pieces, who feasted on His members? Who kidnaped the Moon, who hid Her away? Who made Her Pluto's wife? **8.** But this error also they want to defend by still one more Scientific Theory; for by this Theory they think they can worship the undivided and the divided intelligence,[181] i.e., τὸν ἀμέριστον καὶ τὸν μεμερισμένον νοῦν. **9.** Tell me, O

God's poor mortal creatures,[182] why do you link up funerals
with the phenomena of nature? Why do you pollute
the Divine Order with the atrocity of gruesome deaths?
What was the need for such harsh and cruel torture?
Why do you entertain the belief that divine affairs have
some connection with the story of a dreadful disaster,
that the nature of the stars, which the Supreme Deity
established with unalterable laws, is involved in the sorrows
over a human being's calamity? What is the good of what
you are doing? You are confounding the earthly with the
heavenly, the perishable with the supernal, the things of
darkness with the things of light, when you take human
griefs and woes and hallow them with honors divine.

The Sun Gives a Speech Deploring Heliolatry

Ch. 8] If the Sun[183] should call together all of humankind in an assembly and address them with a harangue,
perhaps he might stigmatize your hopeless behavior with
these words:

"Mortal men, rebellious in sundry ways every single day
against the Supreme Deity—who has impelled you to such
a height of wickedness as to assert wilfully in your pagan
error of sinful passion that I both die and live?[184] If the
figments of your insane thinking would just develop in an
ordinary way or in one fashion only! If the wickedness
of your scoundrelly thinking would just run riot without
insulting me! As it is, you who fling yourselves over precipices do not spare me either, nor does your speech evince
any reverence, but you are rushing to your own doom
and death, and dishonoring me in the process. 2. Some[185]
in obstinate frenzy of mind drown me in the waves and

rapid eddies of the Nile in Egypt,[186] others cut out my manhood[187] and mourn the loss, others kill me with a cruel death and either cook me[188] in a pot or fix the sundered limbs of my body on seven spits.[189] One who has flattered me a little[190] with winsome talk thereupon makes up the story that I am the driver[191] of a chariot and four. Reject at last such ruinous madness, and being admonished[192] by salutary persuasion, seek the true way of salvation. A foe of God[193] is he who either thought up or dreamed up these ideas, and no simple or ordinary punishment attends the crime of the person who pollutes [holy] secrets[194] by profane notions, making up such lies about the glorious work of God. 3. Mourn for your dead, you who are yourselves doomed to die by a similar death; bring grave-offerings to your kings as you please; and console their bereavement with remedies of another sort. Mourn for Liber, mourn for Proserpina, mourn for Attis, mourn for Osiris; but do so without heaping indignity upon me. I do not want you to drag me through their tombs and ashes, and I do not want my name to lend more support to your delusion. I was created by God to usher in the day, and that alone is enough for me. Why do you rob me of the dignity of an honorable task? God created me as something else, bade me be something else, and yet you men divide me up[195] to suit your passion and rend me to pieces to suit the caprice of your desire. I frankly show myself as just what I am, and I want you to understand of me nothing else but what you see. This is what pleases God, this is what He gladly welcomes, this is what leads you human beings to the way of salvation: that you should cast aside your errors and absorb the grace of God in simplicity and faith."

4. Let this much, Most Holy Emperors, be enough for me to say in a discourse spoken vicariously.[196] But now, speaking for myself, I who have been molded by the doctrine[197] of the Sacred Scriptures hereby admonish the children of perdition with a religious discourse. If they are gods whom you worship, why do you mourn for them?[198] Why do you weep for them in annual lamentations? If tears and grief are what they deserve, why do you load them with divine honors? So do one or the other of two things: either do not mourn for them if they are gods, or if you think them deserving of grief and tears, do not call them gods, lest your grief and tears should defile the majesty of the divine name. **5.** But since minds that are doomed to perdition and entangled in the snares of wicked desires cannot be won over by any rational plea, I will proceed with the rest of my treatise, hoping that when I have revealed and made known everything that pagan depravity has consecrated for worship, the mercy of God[199] in the name of our Lord Jesus Christ may raise up the fallen, call back to it those who flee, strengthen the wavering, correct those in error, and, what is most important, give life to the dying.

The Promiscuity of Venus, Beloved by Adonis, Mars, and Vulcan

Ch. 9] In most of the cities of the Orient (although this is a plague that has even crossed the sea to us), people mourn for Adonis[200] as the husband of Venus, and point out to bystanders his murderer and his wound. For Mars changed himself[201] into the shape and form of a wild boar and, in order to defend his claim to be first in Venus' affections, killed the youth, who heedlessly rushed against him. If Adonis was a god, why was he unaware of his rival's plot? If a man, why did he vie with a superior being? **2.** But I hear that another as well had marital partnership with Venus: Vulcan, if I mistake not, is said by these worshipers of the gods to be Venus' husband. O ridiculous belief of foolish men! An adulterer,[202] interposed between two husbands, conquers one of them but is entrapped by the other. But see what an embodiment the adulterous god chose for himself in order to conquer the husband: his preference was to be a boar, when he ought—since he had the power of metamorphosis—to have assumed rather the aspect and form of a lion.[203] But those who know the ways of animals say that the lion, for all his wild savagery of spirit, observes the virtue of chastity;[204] so it was right for the adulterer to spurn the shape of a lion and choose that of a lustful animal. **3.** Here let us now set forth the hidden meaning of the Gospel story. To the cast-out devil[205] the Lord turned over a herd of swine, and not without good reason, so that the unclean spirit, hurled along with the lustful animals down the cruel precipices into the waters, might meet the death that he deserved amid the welter of dying swine.

Cyprian Venus was a Human Harlot, Jupiter Sebazius a Devil-Sent Snake-God

Ch. 10] I hear that Cinyras[206] of Cyprus gave a temple to his harlot friend named Venus,[207] and even initiated many in the rites of the Cyprian Venus, and devoted them to her by senseless consecrations—yes, even stipulated that whoever wanted to be initiated, with Venus' secret con-

fided to him, should give the goddess one penny as pay.[208]
What sort of secret[209] it was we all must understand without telling, because its shameful character is such that we
cannot explain it in clearer detail.[210] The lover Cinyras
observed well the laws of whoredom: he bade the priests
of the consecrated Venus give her a piece of money, as if
to a whore.

The worshipers of Jupiter Sebazius[211] at their initiations
put a snake in their bosoms.[212] Still taking place are the
sinful acts of man's original error,[213] and the thing that
ruined mankind receives worship, and people adore the
cunning and malevolent cruelty of the deadly snake.

Corybantic Worship is Founded on Fratricide

Ch. 11] In the cult of the Corybantes[214] parricide is
the object of worship. For one brother was murdered by
two others; and as a precaution that no disclosure might
reveal the brother's violent death, the parricidal pair deified
him in the foothills of Mount Olympus. He is the same
person that the Macedonians worship in their fatuous
superstition. He is the Cabirus,[215] the bloody one to whom
the Thessalonians once offered supplications with bloody
hands.[216] Therefore one should reflect what kind of divinity it is that parricidal madness invented in order to conceal parricide.

The Sins of the Graeco-Roman Gods Are Used to Justify the Sins of Their Worshipers

Ch. 12] Therefore[217] whoever devoutly[218] observes these
cults, whoever takes pleasure in the dreadful contagion of
this superstition, is either seeking solace for his own

troubles or else is praising the gods' misdeeds[219] with an unspoken thought: what he wants, what he seeks, what he fervently craves is that he may have the same license of behavior as his gods had, and that resemblance to them in morals may bring him also to share in their way of life. **2.** One person is fond of adultery: well, he casts a glance at Jupiter and in that quarter finds encouragement for his passion. He approves, imitates, and glorifies the fact that his god was a deceiver in the shape of a swan,[220] a kidnaper in the shape of a bull, a hoaxer in the shape of a satyr, and (as if fain to cultivate the habit of generosity—but for debauched purposes) a briber who corrupted with lavishly flowing gold the princess maiden pent.[221] Another person is fond of the embraces of boys:[222] well, let him look for Ganymede in Jupiter's bosom, let him see Hercules questing after Hylas with the impatience of love, let him learn how Apollo was overcome with desire for Hyacinthus, let someone else look at the case of Chrysippus, and another at that of Pelops, so that he may declare that his gods authorize him to do whatever is today most severely punished by the laws of Rome.[223]

3. It is difficult to make the tally of all their adulteries, and to say who corrupted Amymone,[224] who Alope, who Melanippe, who Chione and Hippothoe. Your god, forsooth, is said to have done these deeds. That very god who, as they maintain, corrects with stern oracles the sins of erring mankind, loves Sterope,[225] kidnaps Aethyssa, ravishes Zeuxippe, woos Prothoe, and fondles Arsinoe in adulterous desire. But of that throng of corrupted women one girl vanished and thus vanquished[226] the amatory god: Daphne was one whom the god who divines and foretells the future could not find nor ravish. **4.** Another person lets himself be used as a woman, and then seeks consolation for his womanized body: well, let him consider Liber and how he repaid to his lover[227] even after death the libidinous reward he had promised, by an imitation of shameful coitus. If anyone in the heat of preternatural passion arms himself to encompass the murder of his father, let him take Jupiter as exemplar.[228] Whoever thirsts for his brother's blood may follow the pattern of the Corybantes.[229] Those who crave incest should look to the examples set by Jupiter:[230] he lay with his mother, wedded his sister, and, to round out to the full the crime of incest, approached his daughter also with the intent to corrupt her. **5.** Another persecutes weaker persons in a spirit of jealous violence and pants to torture an adversary with barbarous cruelty: well, let him learn the procedures of cruel torture from the torments visited upon Marsyas[231] by Apollo. Somebody covets[232] another's goods, and tries to attain his goal by causing the death of the owner: well, let him consider how Hercules killed Geryon[233] and drove off his Iberian cows. If anyone delights in the random massacre of human beings, he should diligently study the wild passions of Mars.[234] The multitude of sinners have collected from their gods the seminal ideas for almost all the types of crime; and to allow their doomed souls to commit misdeeds with impunity, they defend themselves with greater authority by the foregoing examples of wrongdoing. **6.** If a seducer wants to know the price of shame, if he desires to learn the method of seduction, let him look at Jupiter's gold[235] in the bosom of the seduced woman. If a public traitor wishes through wicked cupidity to betray the kingdom which was entrusted to his custody, let him take a look at those who betrayed Saturn[236] to his son. If anyone prone to do wrong wants to know how to flout the law of hospitality, or how to turn topsy-turvy the laws of friendship, or how to violate the sacred truce of the dinner table, why, look you, he may learn the procedure of these crimes from the tale of Tantalus' misfortunes.[237] **7.** Dismal comfort for criminal passion! Lamentable human delusion! Bloody meditation on unblest imitation![238] You have made a theatrical stage out of heaven,[239] and have led erring souls over headlong precipices into cruel disaster, by giving to human beings who are prone to sin a highroad to wrongdoing with the examples set by the gods as guideposts. But amid all this pattern of crime and avowal of misdeeds let us thank those who have revealed to us ignorant ones even the downfall and death of those gods,[240] thus letting us find out the whole story despite the many who try to stop us. For there existed even among men of old, though the worshipful grace of our Lord Christ had not yet illumined the earth, a scrupulous firmness in rejecting superstitions. **8.** Diomedes,[241] a chaste and temperate man, wounded Venus, worsted Mars and dealt him a stroke. By edict of Otus and Ephialtes[242] bellipotent Mars[243] was condemned to temporary exile and suffered the fetters of iron chains. Jupiter bemoaned his son Sarpedon[244] dead at Troy, and from the haughty king Neptune[245] got no pay for built walls. Apollo[246] pastured the kine of another king; and to the all-seeing Sun[247] another person brought the news of his cattle slain. Sparta buried the Castor-pair,[248] Hercules[249] went up in flames on Oeta, and elsewhere Aesculapius[250] suffered the lightning bolt. Vulcan,[251] flung headlong by his father, got a broken foot; Liber,[252] fleeing from Lycurgus, met his end. Venus[253] was caught in adultery and put on display; and after marrying a god she sought the bed of a

man, Anchises. Saturn[254] out of fear for his kingship devoured his sons, and then in flight from a son hid himself
as a fugitive in Italy. Juno was spurned to make way for a
love affair with Catamitus,[255] and the Moon came down
to Endymion;[256] and Jupiter involuntarily fell asleep[257]
when, counter to the wishes of his wife and daughter, he
was bearing aid to the Trojans. 9. What a shameful admission! What a dismal and deplorable set of happenings!
What a pitiable condition of harsh servitude! The power
of sacrilegious tyrants has driven holy men who devoutly
believe in God to worship these "gods," and (piling one
piece of wickedness upon another) has decreed death for
those who refused.[258] Better just move the temples over
to the theater[259] and turn the mysteries of those religions
into stage productions; yes, and to be sure that you don't
neglect any chance for disgusting behavior, turn the priests
into actors.[260] A more fitting place for those religions
couldn't be found. *There* let the vile throng croon about
the amours of the gods, *there* let them perform[261] the
story of their mischances and deaths. *There* a doomed
soul[262] can better learn adultery and crime from impure
and crime-smirched teachers, with the gods as exemplars.

Serapis Was Originally an Apotheosized Joseph, Sara's Child

Ch. 13] Learn further, Sacrosanct Emperors, what was
the origin of the worshipful deity of Alexandria,[263] so that
when I have exposed the inept flimsiness of this notion
also, my humble discourse may revert to the origin of
truth. In Egypt when the crops were parched by fiery
heat and famine threatened a dreadful doom, a youth

sprung from the seed of a God-fearing patriarch interpreted a dream of the king and revealed all that threatened.
It was Joseph,[264] son of Jacob, who had been cast into
prison because of his chastity, but who after his interpretation of the dream became a partner in the kingship. For
he had the harvests of seven years gathered and reserved,
and by this foresight of his divine intelligence mitigated
the scarcity of the next seven lean years. **2.** After his death
the Egyptians reared temples to him[265] in accordance with
the traditional custom of their race; and that posterity
might know of their gratitude for his just stewardship,
they represented him with his head bearing the measure[266]
with which he had apportioned the grain to the hungry.
Furthermore, to enhance the sanctity of his cult, they gave
him a name from the first author of his line. For because
he was the great-grandson of Sara, the nonagenarian[267] by
whom Abraham through God's favor had begotten a son,
he was called in Greek Serapis, i.e., Σάρρας παῖς—but
this took place through no wish of Joseph's, in fact
after his death. **3.** For his God-fearing spirit, dedicated as
it was to the Supreme Deity, could not have been swayed
to this crime of providing superstitious men with snares of
delusion from his very name, especially since he knew it
is one of the sacrosanct laws of God that no man should
venerate or worship any such thing. In Egypt this Joseph
is worshiped and adored; his statue[268] is guarded by a
throng of temple wardens, and in memory of old time the
misguided people with stubborn enthusiasm still today
clings to the liturgy of a cult established in honor of a
man most upright and most wise.

4. But at his statue too, just as at those of others, the
foul spirits of demons gather[269] by reason of the incessant

sacrifices. For the victims and the blood outpoured from the incessant slaughter of animals bring no effect save that the blood nourishes the substance of demons who are procreated by the devil. Manifest proofs that this is so have been given us by Porphyry,[270] the defender of the cults, enemy of God, foe of the truth, teacher of the arts of wickedness. In his book entitled *On the Philosophy of the Oracles*,[271] while he acclaimed Serapis' power he really acknowledged his weakness. For in the first part of the book, i.e., in the very introduction, he said: "Serapis, being invoked and being translated into a human frame, gave the following response."[272] **5.** Now let the children of perdition tell me which is more powerful, he who invokes and commands and causes a spirit to materialize, or he who is invoked and obeys and is materialized, directly upon his appearance, in a human frame that envelops him by the power of the commanding agent. We are grateful to your book, Porphyry: you have revealed to us the essence of your gods. Thanks to you we have learned how your gods are slaves at the bidding of men. Your Serapis[273] is invoked by a man, comes, and immediately upon arrival is materialized by a command, and the necessity to speak is perhaps enjoined upon him against his will.

6. So among us the lashes of exorcistic words[274] flagellate your gods when they start to do harm to men. So your gods, when they are materialized in human shapes, are afflicted[275] with the flames of spiritual fire through the word of God; and those who are worshiped as gods among you are through Christ's grace subject to human command among us, and must though reluctant undergo the healing of religious faith and the torments, and being vanquished must be subjected to avenging punishments.

The Penates and Vesta Are Only the Family Food and the Family Fire

Ch. 14] I shall also seek to explain what the Penates[276] are, lest I should seem to be omitting something. Those who believe that life is nothing more than an opportunity to eat and drink have fashioned themselves these gods out of their own low appetites, under this name of Penates deifying for the welfare of mankind the nourishments of the body which are provided by the daily meals. Merely because the meals serve to reinvigorate the weakened body, they have hallowed the foods as their only god, not knowing the truth of the divine word.[277] 2. For when the Lord Jesus Christ,[278] being anxious for our salvation, strove mightily in a divine wrestling with the devil and sought to rescue from his jaws the human nature which He had assumed, He nonplused him with the following response. When the devil said to Him: *If thou be the Son of God, command that these stones be made bread*,[279] answering the Lord said to him: *Not in bread alone shall man live, but in every word of God*. So, through not knowing the true nature of humanity they have deified the daily meals under this name of Penates. For everything that people eat is called *penus*;[280] hence comes the name of the larder (*cella penaria*), and hence the Penates as gods have been invented by the wretched imaginings of abject and prostrate mankind.

3. Learn moreover what Vesta is, so that you will not suppose her to be something ancient or discovered in circumstances of extreme religious awe. She is the household fire[281] which serves the daily needs upon the hearth. There-

fore let her have cooks as priests, and not unhappy virgins
who, since they scorn the coals of the very fire that they
tend, are either forced to sin by prostitution or else by per-
severing in their virginity waste the honor and esteem of
a glorious name.[282]

The Truth about the Palladium

Ch. 15] Listen also to what kind of divinity the Palladium[283] is. It is a statue made out of the bones of Pelops;[284]
and the Scythian Abaris[285] is supposed to have made it.
Now pray consider what kind of thing it is which a
barbarous Scythian hallowed. Is anything among the
Scythians devised by human reason, and could that un-
civilized race[286] which forever revels in cruel and inhuman
savagery discover anything right in the founding of religions? 2. This statue Abaris sold to the Trojans, making
empty promises to fools. A god was sold in order to be
useful to his buyer, and the buyer, now turned suppliant,
proceeded to adore an object which a bit earlier he had
seen put up for sale.

Moreover the material substance of the statue is from
the bones of Pelops! Abaris, if you want poor human
beings to worship human bones, at least gather up the
relics of a purer and chaster man than that! To the idol
which you make let some merit accrue from the virtues
of the man. Pelops was the boy favorite[287] of a lover, and
suffered the loss of his chastity[288] in a lengthy period of
prostitution. But not even when he was grown did he
refrain from crime: by a traitor's trick[289] he killed the man
whose daughter he wooed, and then false to his oath
attacked even the traitor himself, and hurled him down

over a steep cliff in order to avoid paying him the bribe he had promised. There is your fellow whose bones were chosen to make a god destined to preserve cities and kingdoms!

3. But he never did preserve them or do them any good, and from the disasters of the cities where he dwelt he could see what the future had for him.[290] Troy was burned by the Greeks, Rome by the Gauls; from both fires the Palladium was saved,[291] but saved by human help and not by its own powers. For human beings rescued it from both places, and carried it off so that it would not burn up in a human conflagration. Such a mighty divinity had to resort to human protection, and sought human aid to keep from being burned! What the Palladium won from fire was respite, not rescue.[292] The condemnation stands, the punishment waits, the fire threatens, the fire presses nigh, and there is no escape from it. **4.** Already the heavenly fire[293] is a-borning, already the approach of divine punishment is manifest, already the doom of coming disaster is heralded. In *this* fire the Palladium will be able to find no hiding place. *This* fire searches out the hidden, seeks the concealed,[294] and envelops in swift and flaming devastation whatever vain delusions have been the downfall of erring men. *For the day of the Lord comes*, it says, *like a burning furnace*.[295] You have heard what is to come, you have heard what is to come.[296] There will be nothing left of you to be gathered up and put in the barns of the Lord. You will burn like straw,[297] whose worthless cheapness is reserved to make cinders and ashes,[298] straw which rapacious fire[299] devours when fanned by the driving violence of the wind. **5.** This is your exit and end;[300] this is the punishment which God has ordained for the delusion of men, that whoever against God's will has either deluded or led astray an unfortunate man should burn in flames everlasting.[301]

I certainly wish to inquire carefully which Minerva they suppose this statue to represent. For it is a known fact that there were several Minervas, and on this point none disagrees. Therefore let us set forth the genealogy, outlook, skills, and interests of each Minerva, so that from all these data we may ascertain in honor of which Minerva the Palladium was consecrated.

Multiple Minervas

Ch. 16] As we read ancient lore, we find the tradition that there were five Minervas.[302] One, Vulcan's daughter,[303] is she who founded Athens, as a throng of country-folk followed her from the rural areas to inaugurate the urban mode of life.[304] Another, the daughter of King Nilus[305] in Egypt, was the teacher of the art of weaving. The third was the daughter of Saturnus,[306] it is true, but report has it that she was a virago. For she never confined herself within the bounds of feminine modesty, but always longed for arms and the din of battle and the bloody pursuits of war. The fourth was the daughter of Jupiter, the Cretan king,[307] and it was she who brought her father the news of the slaying of Liber. 2. The fifth was sprung from Pallas[308] as father and Titanis as mother, and men called her Pallas after her father's name.[309] She, instinct with the madness of parricidal frenzy and insane recklessness, slew her father Pallas in a cruel death and, not content simply with murdering him but wishing to prolong the fruits of her wickedness and to vaunt more gruesomely over the murder, arrayed herself[310] in the clothing stripped from his body, so as to advertise the crime of parricide by cruel ostentation. In her name was consecrated the Palladium (cry shame!), she is the Pallas who is worshiped, she is the one who is safeguarded by the law of the pontifices;[311] yes, and she whose crime deserves the severest condemnation has suppliants adoring her statue. Bring fire, multiply the flames, so that the Palladium may learn what it means to burn at your daily sacrifices. What else does a parricide deserve but to burn up daily in avenging flames,[312] on a fire that is kept forever ablaze—anticipating her sentence from God?

3. Call them tombs, Most Holy Emperors, not temples.[313] Rather call them the pyres of unhappy wretches. For in honor of children of perdition the pathetic servility of mankind has built temples instead of sepulchers. Here are kept the ashes of cremated bodies, here in accord with a godless law are laid away the ashes of the dead, so that the daily blood of victims may commemorate afresh their bitter end, so that the mournful lament for their doom may be revived in sad memorials year by year, so that a fresh wailing may awaken again the slumbering tears, so that from the rituals of cult the wretched mentality of human beings may learn to honor parricide and incest and murder—and learn to do them, too.

An Appeal to the Emperors to Smite Paganism

4. These practices must be eradicated,[314] Most Holy Emperors, utterly eradicated and abolished. All must be set aright by the severest laws of your edicts, so that the ruinous error of this delusion may no longer besmirch the Roman world, so that the wickedness of this pestilential usage may no longer wax strong, and so that whatever aims at the downfall of the man of God[315] may no longer prevail upon the earth. Some people object and resist, and passionately crave their own ruin. But rescue these poor fellows, and deliver them from perishing! The Supreme Deity entrusted to you the sovereignty precisely that through you the affliction of this wound may be healed. We know the dangerous nature of their crime, and we know what punishments are appropriate for delusion; but it is better for you to save them against their will than to let them follow their wishes into perdition.

5. Sick persons[316] like what is not good for them, and when ill health takes control of the human frame the sufferers make perverse demands, counter to their own welfare. The mind, preyed upon by the languor of affliction, incessantly craves what will merely aggravate the disease, spurns with contempt the healing arts, and hastens with impatient desire to its own downfall. Then if the mischief of the disease grows worse, stouter remedies are invoked; the medical art, solicitous for the patient's welfare, resorts to sterner measures. Disagreeable foods and bitter potions are forced upon the unwilling sufferer, and if the trouble worsens both cautery and knife[317] are tried. So when the patient recovers his health and has his well-being restored, he acknowledges with a revival of sound judgment that whatever was done to him against his will for the infirmity of his sick body, was all done for his own good.

Putative Gods and the Etymology of Their Names

Ch. 17] Hear also, Sacrosanct Princes, how the names of the gods were formed. This luminary which at God's command puts the darkness to rout and restores to mankind the day, and which directs its orderly course through the span of twelve hours, people elected to call the Sun (*Sol*),[318] not because it is solitary, as some argue, for up yonder are also the sky and moon and very many other stars which are visible (of which some as if fixed[319] and belonging together keep shining forever in the spot which they have occupied once and for all, while others in dispersion all over the heavens follow wandering courses in fixed planetary orbits), but it is called Sol because at its rising it dims the other stars and shines solitary.

2. Also Luna (identical with Lucina)[320] derived her name from being a luminary of the night. Some have also chosen to call her Diana,[321] because by shining through the night she almost makes for man a second day (*diem*). Those who swim in the sea maintained that Neptune[322] is named from the word "swimming" (*natando*); they constructed the substance of his name from their own favorite activity. People call the entire essence and nature of the earth Father Dis,[323] because the nature of the earth is such that all things sink into it and again emerge from it in birth, a fact that has made manifest the earth's opulence and riches (*divitias*).

3. People choose to call the substance of grain Proserpina[324] for the reason that grain is beneficial (*prosunt*) to mankind once it is sown (*seri*).[325] The earth itself they call Ceres,[326] borrowing this name from her bearing (*gerendis*) the crops. Mavors[327] got his name from the chances of war,

as if he overturned great things (*magna vortat*). Minerva[328] likewise is a warlike name, as if she either diminishes (*minuat*) or menaces (*minetur*). The beauty (*venustas*) of mankind was named Venus.[329] The name of Apollo[330] was formed in Greek from human misfortunes, as if he either lost or destroyed everything entrusted to him. Some also call the sun Apollo, because every day at sunset it loses the splendor of its light, and the Greek word to "lose" is *apollin*.

4. You see how topsy-turvy delusion thinks up these imaginary and fictitious gods, how old wives' superstitions fashion for us their shapes and names.[331] But truth has detected all these impostures, and sane reason has found them out, so that when everything that sacrilegious delusion had concealed was investigated and uncovered, the truth might shine reborn. Once all these notions were mischievously concocted, they first terrorized mortals;[332] then, as the novelty wore off, people convalesced as it were from a long sickness, and admiration gave way to a sort of contempt. So the intellect was gradually emboldened to examine with care what caused its awe, and immediately deployed its keen talent to plumb the mysteries of false and foolish superstitions. Then, after drawing rational conclusions from assiduous mulling over of hidden enigmas, the intellect penetrated to the causes, so that the human race first learned, then scorned, and finally rejected the pitiful falsehoods of the pagan religions.[333]

Pagan Symbols: the Cult of Attis vs. the Eucharist

Ch. 18] Now I should like to explain[334] what signs or symbols[335] the wretched human throng uses for purposes of recognition in the superstitious cults themselves. For they have special signs, special responses, which the teaching of the devil[336] has transmitted to them in the meetings sponsored by those impious cults of theirs.

In a certain temple a person (doomed to perdition![337]) says when seeking admittance to the inner chambers: "I have eaten from the tambourine, I have drunk from the cymbal, and I have mastered the secrets of religion"[338]— the Greek words being ἐκ τυμπάνου βέβρωκα, ἐκ κυμβάλου πέπωκα, γέγονα μύστης Ἄττεως. 2. A sorry confession of the wicked thing you have done, unhappy man! You have quaffed the virus of deadly poison, and under the stimulus of guilty frenzy you taste the cup of doom. The sequel of that food is always death and punishment. This drink which you boast you have taken fatally chokes the vein of life[339] and by the prolongation of contaminating evils wreaks havoc in the seat of the soul.

Different is the food which bestows salvation and life, different is the food which both commends and restores man to the Supreme Deity, different is the food which revives the languishing, recalls the straying, lifts up the fallen, and gives the tokens of eternal immortality to the dying. Seek the bread of Christ,[340] the cup of Christ, that the substance of man, scorning the frailty of earth, may be sated with immortal nourishment. 3. And what is this bread, or what the cup which Wisdom proclaims with mighty voice in the books of Solomon? For it says: *Come, eat my bread, and drink the wine which I have mingled.*[341] And Melchisedech,[342] king of Salem and priest of the Supreme Deity, bestowed on the returning Abraham the grace of benediction with bread and wine. Also, when Isaac[343] had blessed Jacob, and Esau with supplications en-

treated his father for the same favor, the father replied:
*I have appointed him thy lord, and have made all his
brethren his servants; I have established him with wheat
and wine.* Then Esau wept with woeful lamentation for
his plight, because he had lost the blessing of wheat and
wine, that is, of future bliss.

4. Now the Holy Spirit declares through Isaias[344] that
this divine bread is tendered by God to consecrated men:
*Thus saith the Lord: Behold, my servants shall eat and you
shall be hungry. Behold, my servants shall rejoice and you
shall be confounded; the Lord shall slay you.* Not only is
this bread denied by the Supreme Deity to sacrilegious
and impious men, but also punishment is promised them
and the doom of bitter death decreed, the upshot being
that divine chastisement is visited upon their hungry
throats.

5. To the same effect, furthermore, are the worshipful
statements of the thirty-third Psalm. For the Holy Spirit
says through David: *Taste, and see that the Lord is
sweet.*[345] Sweet is the heavenly nourishment, sweet the
food of God, and in it resides no dire torment of grievous
hunger; in fact it expels from the marrow of man the
venom of earlier poison. And the following oracular statements declare that this is so, for these are the words: *Fear
the Lord, ye His saints; for there is no want to them that
fear Him. The rich have wanted and have suffered hunger;
but they that seek the Lord shall not be deprived of any
good.*[346]

6. You who stalk thus toga-clad in the temple, resplendent in purple, your head weighed down with a crown
either aureate or laureate—loathsome want is what is to
follow your present self-delusion, and the onerous weight

of poverty is imminent for your shoulders.[347] That poor
man whom you flout is well-to-do and rich; Abraham[348]
is preparing him a seat in his bosom. Then you, across the
intervening gulf of flames, will implore him for a tiny
drop of running water to soothe the pangs of your conscience; but Lazarus will not be able, though willing, either
to give you or to beg for you any palliative for your
pain. And this is because everyone receives recompense
on a parity with his deserts. To Lazarus life is awarded
because of his troubles in this world; for you the penalty
of everlasting torments is decreed because of your blessings
in this world.

7. Moreover, in order to insure a plainer understanding
of what that bread is which overcomes the doom of dismal
death, the Lord Himself with His holy and worshipful lips
defined it, lest human hopes might be deceived by misguided interpretations arising from divergent treatises. For
He says in the Gospel according to John: *I am the bread
of life. He that cometh to me shall not hunger: and he that
believeth in me shall never thirst.*[349] Likewise, continuing
in His discourse, He signifies the same fact in a similar
way, for He says: *If any man thirst, let him come and
drink, whoever believeth in me.*[350] And again He Himself
says, to bring home to believers the real nature of His
greatness: *Except you eat the flesh of the Son of man and
drink His blood, you shall not have life in you.*[351]

8. Therefore have no part in the food of the tambourine,
God's poor mortal creatures![352] Seek the grace of the food
of salvation, and drink of the immortal cup. Christ by
His banquet calls you back to the light, and quickens[353]
your dull members and limbs rotting with grievous poison.
Renew the child of perdition with heavenly food, so that

what is dead in you may be reborn through the divine goodness. You have learned what it behooves you to do; choose what you will. Yonder the outcome is death;[354] here is offered the gift of immortal life.[355]

Mithraism vs. Christ the Light and the Bridegroom

Ch. 19] . . . δε νύμφε, χαῖρε νύμφε, χαῖρε νέον φῶς. (O bridegroom hail, O bridegroom hail, new light).[356] O disastrous delusion, why do you thus plunge unhappy man over the precipice? Why do you promise him the trappings of a false hope? With you there is no light, nor anyone who deserves to be called[357] bridegroom. There is one light, one bridegroom: the honor of these names has been taken by Christ. You will not be able to transfer to yourself the glory of another's good fortune, nor adorn yourself with the splendor of the heavenly light. You are flung forth into darkness and squalor. There reign filth, squalor, gloom, darkness, and the horror of perpetual night.[358]

2. If you want at least a pale shimmer of light to shine upon you, lift up your countenance[359] and open your downcast eyes, and abandoning the darkness[360] betake yourself to Him who has said: *I am the light of the world.*[361] Among His divine precepts is this, that every day in this earthly round our work should radiate light. Now it cannot radiate light unless the adornment of a spotless conscience protects us and unless a sound and sterling life commends us. Then shall arise for us the grace of true light, then the Author of light enters[362] within us, then we can both receive and behold the true light.

3. But to checkmate the wickedness of the voice of sacrilege, I shall demonstrate from the oracular statements of the Sacred Scriptures who the bridegroom truly is, to prove that the bridegroom is Christ and the Church is His bride,[363] from whom every day spiritual sons[364] are begotten by the worshipful Father. In this essay of proof let the venerable arcana of the prophets be revealed, and let the faithful word of holy revelations stand by me. Thus speaks Joel at the prompting of the Divine Spirit: *Blow the trumpet in Sion: sanctify a fast, proclaim a healing, gather together the people, sanctify the church, welcome the ancients, gather together the little ones that suck at the breasts. Let the bridegroom go forth from his bed-chamber and the bride out of her bridechamber.*[365] **4.** Jeremias signifies this same idea in a similar way. For he says, threatening Jerusalem with a grim prophecy: *And I will take away out of the cities of Juda and out of the streets of Jerusalem the voice of those rejoicing, the voice of the bridegroom and the voice of the bride.*[366] The Holy Spirit also in the Psalms proclaims the going forth of the bridegroom. This prophecy is found in the eighteenth Psalm, for it says: *And he, as a bridegroom coming out of his bridechamber, hath rejoiced as a giant to run the way; his going out is from the end of heaven, and his circuit even to the end thereof, and there is no one that can hide himself from his heat.*[367]

5. Let arcana of a more secret kind be revealed: in the Apocalypse, that is, in Revelation, we find who the bridegroom is. For so it is written: *Come and I will shew thee the new bride, the wife of the Lamb. And he took me up in spirit to a great mountain and shewed me the holy city Jerusalem coming down out of heaven.*[368] I must also communicate what the Gospel teaching transmits to us on this very topic. For we find in the Gospel according to John this statement: *You yourselves are witnesses that I said to those who were sent from Jerusalem to me that I am not Christ, but that I am sent before Him. For he that hath the bride is the bridegroom: but the friend of the bridegroom is he who standeth and heareth him and rejoiceth with joy because of the bridegroom's voice.*[369]

6. This mystery is revealed;[370] this is the bridegroom whose coming the band of the wise virgins[371] awaits; it is before Him that the holy troop of virgins bear their lamps with wakeful care.[372] To the servants who await the bridegroom the gift of blessed rewards is promised, for we find in the Gospel according to Luke: *Let your loins be girt and your lamps burning and you yourselves like to men who wait for their lord, when he shall come from the wedding; that when he cometh and knocketh they may open to him. Blessed are those servants whom the Lord, when He cometh, shall find watching.*[373] Lo, the bridegroom's identity is revealed by the prophetic and worshipful sayings.

7. Why do you, in sorry case as you are,[374] award yourself the name of happy? If you wish to be saved and to follow the light of the Bridegroom, cast away your delusions and in the anxiety of wakeful care atone with religious devoutness for the sins of your past life. Then when the Bridegroom finds you watching in His name, when He recognizes the merits of your faith, He will give you the greatest reward, He will give you the perfect gift: you shall enter with Him the marriage chamber of heaven, you shall behold the universe's royal hall, and in order that you may be a true sharer therein, the boon of immortality will be conferred upon you by the most holy and most just Lord.

Rock-born Mithra vs. Christ the Rock

Ch. 20] Another pagan sacrament[375] has the key word θεὸς ἐκ πέτρας, "god from a rock."[376] Why do you adulterate the faith and transfer this holy and worshipful mystery to pagan doings? Different is the stone[377] which God promised He would lay in making strong the foundations of the promised Jerusalem. What the symbol of the worshipful stone[378] means to us is Christ. Why do you with the knavery of a thief transfer to foul superstitions the dignity of a worshipful name? Your stone is one that ruin follows and the disastrous collapse of tumbling towers;[379] but our stone, laid by the hand of God, builds up, strengthens, lifts, fortifies, and adorns the grace of the restored work with the splendor of everlasting immortality.

For Isaias says of this at the behest of the Holy Spirit: **2.** *Thus saith the Lord: Behold, I lay a stone for the foundations of Sion, a precious stone, elect, a chief cornerstone, honored, and he that shall believe in it shall not be confounded.*[380] Also in the Psalms there is a similar declaration, for the Holy Spirit says in the 117th Psalm: *The stone which the builders rejected: the same is become the head of the corner. This is the Lord's doing: and it is wonderful in our eyes.*[381] Through many prophets the Holy Spirit shows us the meaning of that name, for the prophet Zacharias says: *Behold, I bring my servant, the Orient is his name; for the stone that I have laid before the face of Jesus; upon the one stone there are seven eyes.*[382]

3. But to establish the point more manifestly, let us unfold still more ancient mysteries of the worshipful Scriptures. It is expressed in Deuteronomy in these words: *And thou shalt write upon the stone all this law.*[383] Also Josue the son of Nun[384] by divine command specifically expresses it, for he says: *And he took a great stone and set it before the Lord. And Josue said to the people: Behold, this stone shall be a testimony unto you, that it hath heard all that was said by the Lord when He hath spoken to you. And it shall be a testimony unto you in the last of days when you shall have departed from your Lord.*[385]

4. Now that through this "stone," that is, through our Lord Jesus Christ, both these gods will fall and the multitudinous temples with them, is clearly explained by Daniel in worshipful prophecies. For he said, interpreting the king's dream: *And behold, a statue, a statue exceeding great, and the look of the statue itself was terrible, and it stood raised up before thee. Its head was of fine gold, but its breast and arms of silver, and the belly and thighs of brass, and the feet part of iron and part of clay. Till a stone was cut out of a mountain without hands of men cutting; and it struck the statue upon the feet of iron and clay and broke them in pieces. And it came to pass that the iron, the clay, the brass, the silver and the gold were broken to pieces together like chaff, like the dust of a summer's thrashing floor. And the wind fanned them away so that nothing of them remained. And the stone that struck the statue became a great mountain and filled the whole earth.*[386]

5. What spot is there on the earth that the name of Christ has not possessed? Where the sun rises and where it sets, where the North Star[387] lifts and the South slopes low, all is filled with the majesty of His worshipful name;[388] and while in some regions the dying limbs of idolatry still palpitate, yet we have arrived at the stage where all lands may be purged and this pestilential evil drastically amputated.[389]

What oracular utterance of the prophets issues any statement concerning the stone of the idolaters, whereof people say "the god from a rock"? And for whom has the stone been an obstacle, for whom a help? **6.** But this holy stone (that is, Christ) either supports the foundations of faith or, being set in the corner, unites[390] with balanced control the two lines of wall (that is, it gathers into one the strength of the Old and the New Testament), or at any rate brings into accord the disparity of body and soul by conferring immortality upon man, or promulgates the law, or gives testimony against sinners, or, what is better, smites the statue of the devil, so that when he is overcome and prostrate and turned into ashes and cinders,[391] Christ may lift up His sublime head and attain[392] the pure realm of His sovereignty.

7. It is to you, Most Holy Emperors Constantius and Constans, and to the strength of your worshipful faith that we must now appeal. A person who to the best of his ability follows in all of his actions the will of the Supreme Deity is elevated above mankind, freed from terrestrial frailty,[393] and linked in the fellowship of celestial beings.[394] Only a little is lacking that the devil should be utterly overthrown and laid low by your laws,[395] and that the horrid contagion of idolatry should die out and become extinct. The venom of this poison[396] has vanished, and every single day marks a weakening in the hard core of godless passion. Up with the banner of faith! For *you* the divine will has reserved this task. Through the favor of the God of victory[397] you are victors over all your foes, who were a blot on the escutcheon of the Roman Empire. Hoist the ensign of the reverend law; confirm and promulgate what will redound to our good. Be it a fortunate and blessed thing for the commonwealth that amid the heaps of enemy slain you have overthrown the host of heathendom.[398] Happy you whom God has made partners in executing His purpose and His will.[399] For your hands the benevolent Godhead of Christ has reserved the extermination of idolatry and the overthrow of the pagan temples. *He* has resisted the evils of the spirit;[400] *you* have conquered the evils of earth. Erect the trophies of victory, and cause to be borne before you the imposing record of your triumphs. Rejoice in the destruction of paganism, exult all the more vehemently, exult confidently. Your good fortune is interlinked with the power of God; with Christ fighting at your side you have won a victory for the salvation of mankind.

Tauriform and Bicorn Dionysus vs. the Cross

Ch. 21] Let us review in order all the symbols of paganism, so that we may prove that mankind's most wicked foe has borrowed them from the holy and worshipful sayings of the prophets[401] for the contaminated crimes of his madness.

2. Now we find that there is the following cry: αἰαῖ δίκερως δίμορφε ("Alas, bicorn and biform one!").[402] That god of yours is not biform but multiform, for the shape of his poisonous visage undergoes many mutations of aspect. He is the basilisk[403] and scorpion who is trampled upon by the fearless footsteps of the faithful; he is the malicious serpent whose head is the object of deceived mortality's quest;[404] he is the sinuous snake who is drawn out with a hook,[405] who is caught and confined. That god of yours is adorned with the hair tufts of the Lernaean hydra.[406] Do you see how a throng of dying serpents succeeds their stricken lord?[407] Why do you sprout thus with hydras that keep being born? Why do you make yourself a composite of fecundating crimes?

3. We have learned the road leading to your death; we know by what remedies your artful poisons may be overcome. We drink the immortal blood of Christ, and Christ's blood is united with our own. This is the salutary remedy against your crimes, a remedy which daily keeps the deadly poison from the tainted people of God.[408]

That god whom they bewail,[409] who has seen him wearing horns? What are those horns which he boasts he possesses? Something different are the horns which the prophet mentions at the behest of the Holy Spirit, and which you, Sir Devil, think you can appropriate for your maculate face. 4. But where, Sir, are you going to get yourself adornment and glory in this matter? The horns signify nothing else but the worshipful sign of the cross.[410] By one "horn" of this sign, the one which is elongated and vertical, the universe is held up and the earth held fast; and by the juncture of the two horns which go off sidewise the East is touched and the West supported; hence the whole world is stabilized on a solid footing in three parts, since its foundations are held firm by the immortal root of the steadfast work.[411]

This is the secret that the worshipful declaration of the prophet transmitted to us. For we find the following written in Habacuc: *His glory covered the heavens; and the earth is full of His praise; and His brightness shall be as the light. Horns shall be in His hands, and there the strength of His glory is confirmed and He shall establish His love. The word shall go and advance before His steps.*[412]

5. Behold the worshipful horns of the cross, behold the immortal pinnacle of sacred strength, behold the divine architecture of a glorious work! You, O Christ, with your outstretched arms support the universe and the earth and the kingdom of heaven; on your immortal shoulders rests our salvation; you, O Lord, carry the token of life everlasting;[413] you through worshipful inspiration proclaim this to us by the prophets. For Isaias says: *Behold, a Son is born to you, and the government is upon His shoulders; and His name is called Messenger of Mighty Counsel.*[414]

6. These are the horns of the cross, which support and likewise embrace all things; and these horns the life of man uses to its advantage. To conquer Amalec,[415] Moses stretched out his arms and imitated these horns; the more easily to attain the object of his desire, he made himself a cross from a rod. To these horns hasten with hurrying speed,[416] to these horns flee with humble veneration, to these horns let yourself be nailed by justice, equity, modesty, mercy, patience, and faith, so that bearing before you the worshipful emblems, and rejoicing in the majesty of a consecrated brow, you may be sharers of Christ's burial and likewise of His life.

The Ointment of Osiris vs. the Ointment of Christian Confirmation

Ch. 22] We adduce also another symbol, in order to lay bare the crimes of polluted thought. It is needful to give a complete and systematic account of it, so that all may be led to agree that the law of the divine dispensation has been corrupted by the devil's crooked imitation.[417]

On a certain night a statue is laid flat on its back on a bier, where it is bemoaned in cadenced plaints.[418] Then when the worshipers have had their fill of feigned lamentation, a light is brought in. Next a priest anoints the throats[419] of all who were mourning, and once that is done he whispers in a low murmur:[420]

Θαρρεῖτε μύσται τοῦ θεοῦ σεσωσμένου·
ἔσται γὰρ ἡμῖν ἐκ πόνων σωτηρία.

("Rejoice, O mystai! Lo, our god appears as saved!
And we shall find salvation, springing from our woes.")[421]

2. Why do you exhort unfortunate wretches to rejoice? Why do you drive deluded dupes to exult? What hope, what salvation do you promise them, convincing them to their own ruination? Why do you woo them with a false promise? The death of your god is known, but his life is not apparent, nor has a divine prophecy ever issued a statement about his resurrection,[422] nor has he manifested himself to men after his death to cause himself to be believed. He provided no advance tokens of this action, nor did he show by prefiguring symbolic acts[423] that he would do this.

3. You bury an idol, you lament an idol, you bring forth

from its sepulture an idol, and having done this, unfortunate wretch, you rejoice. You rescue your god, you put together the stony limbs that lie there, you set in position an insensible stone. Your god should thank you, should repay you with equivalent gifts, should be willing to make you his partner. So you should die as he dies, and you should live as he lives![424]

4. Now as for the throat being anointed with scented stuff,[425] who would not despise[426] the folly of this business and hold it in scorn? Therefore the devil has his anointed ones ("Christs"),[427] and because he himself is Antichrist,[428] he reduces unfortunate wretches into an unholy alliance with the infamy of his own name. Save this ointment for the dead,[429] save it for the dying, that you may besmear with the poisonous stuff those whom you have entrapped with your snares, and plunge them forever in a sorrowful and deadly doom.

Ch. 23] A different thing is the ointment[430] which God the Father gave over to His only Son, which the Son in the divine power of His godhead gives freely to those who believe. Christ's ointment is made with an immortal composition and mixed from the perfumes of spiritual ingredients. This ointment frees the decaying limbs of mankind from the snares of death, so that when the first man is buried, straightway from the same person another man may be born in happier case.[431] And to explain this more manifestly, we must unfold the mysteries of the Sacred Scriptures.

2. For David says, to convey to us the grace bestowed by this ointment: *Thou art beautiful above the sons of men; grace is poured abroad in thy lips; therefore hath He blessed thee forever. Gird thy sword upon thy thigh, O*

*thou most mighty. With thy comeliness and beauty set
out; proceed prosperously and reign because of strength*[432]
*and meekness and justice; and thy right hand shall conduct
thee wonderfully. The arrows are sharp, O thou most
mighty; under thee shall people fall, in the heart of the
king's enemies. Thy throne, O God, is for ever and ever;
the scepter of thy kingdom is an upright scepter. Thou hast
loved justice and hated iniquity; therefore thy God hath
anointed thee with the oil of gladness above thy fellows.
Myrrh and stacte and cassia from thy garments, from the
ivory houses, out of which they have affected thee with
delight.*[433]

3. We have seen through the secrets of the immortal
ointment, and the order of the divine dispensation has
been revealed to us. An everlasting kingdom and heaven's
diadem have been conferred upon our Lord with the
power of the ointment. Moreover, who it is that is vested
with the authority to rule the world and that is honored
with the majesty of the worshipful name, another prophecy
shows us. For this same David says: *Why have the Gentiles
raged, and the peoples devised vain things? The kings of
the earth stood up, and the princes met together, against
the Lord and against His Christ.*[434] Why do you thus
vaunt yourself, O sacrilegious creed? Why with unbridled
audacity do you beguile unfortunate men? Christ's ointment gives the kingdom of heaven; your ointment awakens
the flames of Gehenna.[435]

The Triumph of Christ the Savior

Ch. 24] But I should like to discuss in a careful inquiry
what that priest fellow asserts with his unclean lips and

words polluted with foulness. He invites the mystai[436] to
be of good cheer because their god is saved, and tells them
to have the confidence of good hope.[437] Oh in what pathetic,
what grievous snares this ephemeral cunning gets itself
involved! Who saves your god? That suffering of his—
whom has it done any good? Learn, learn what you do
not know, learn what you do not see.

2. Christ, the Son of God, in order to rescue humankind from the snares of death, truly endured all His passion in order to take away the yoke of harsh captivity to
sin, to restore mankind to the Father, to mitigate man's
offense and thus bring him into harmony with God in a
happy reconciliation, and to show by His own example the
realization of the promised resurrection. The Son of God
did what He had promised beforehand: He shut the doors
of the infernal abode and overthrew the stern law of
necessity by trampling upon death. For three days[438] He
mustered and passed in review the throng of the just, so
that the malice of death should no longer have dominion
over them, and that the merit of the just might not sink
in ruins through long despair. He broke the everlasting
barriers, and the iron gates[439] tumbled at Christ's command.
Lo, the earth quaked and its steadfast foundations were
shaken when it recognized the godhead of the present
Christ. Before the preordained time the whirling spin of
the universe hastened the day to its end, and the sun without completing the span of the daylight hours accelerated
its course and sloped low to night.[440] Behold, the topmost
edges of the veil are rent,[441] and the gloom of night hides
the world in darker shadows. All the elements were confounded[442] while Christ struggled—at the time, that is,
when He first armed man's body against the tyranny of

death. For three days that conflict was fought, until death was crushed and the strength of its malice was overcome.

3. Why do you, O man of religion, man of Christ, with your usual impatience give way to despair and faintness of heart? Can you not bear three days' delay? Do you betray your anxiety and despair by voicing novel prayers? Just that is what you are going to do on the Day of Days, as the Holy Spirit indicates in awesome words, saying through the mouth of David: *We are counted as sheep for the slaughter. Arise, why sleepest thou, O Lord? Arise, and destroy us not even to the end. Why turnest thou thy face away? Dost thou forget our want and trouble? For our soul is humbled down to the dust; our belly cleaveth to the earth. Arise, O Lord; help us and save us for thy name's sake.*[443]

4. Lo, after three days the day arises brighter than is its wont, the sun regains the glory of its quondam luster, and Christ Almighty God is adorned with the rays of a more resplendent sun. The Godhead of salvation exults, and the throng of the just and the saints attends His triumphal car.[444] Then in a transport of joy jubilant mortality cries out: *O death, where is thy sting?*[445] Then the Godhead of salvation, hastening on before, bids the heavenly doors swing wide for Him: "Open, open and tear down the immortal barriers: Christ God has trampled upon death and recalls to heaven the man whom He has saved." This is foretold by the holy voice of the worshipful prophet, and from his prophetic lips is heard the voice of One who commands. For the Holy Spirit says, to show us the power[446] of Christ's command: *Lift up your gates, O ye princes, and lift yourselves up, O eternal gates, and the King of Glory shall enter in.*[447] **5.** This command is addressed to the uncomprehending angels, for they could not know when the Word of God descended to earth. And that is why they respond with an anxious question: *Who is this King of Glory?*[448] To their questioning Christ replies in the manifest majesty of His godhead: *The Lord strong and mighty, the Lord mighty in battle.*[449] Immediately the Son of God is recognized by heaven's warders, and they know what escaped their ken before. They see the spoils of the foe overthrown, and recalling the order of the primal cosmos they too join their cries with those who mount, echoing again: *Lift up the gates, O ye who keep them,*[450] *and lift yourselves up, O eternal gates, and the King of Glory shall enter in.*

6. To His Son returned the Father restores the promised scepter of the kingdom, and grants the throne of the kingdom in parity of power, that He may command, rule, possess, and hold dominion in the everlasting majesty of His godhead. Hear what the Holy Spirit bade Daniel say of Him: *I beheld in a vision at night, and lo, one like the Son of man, coming in the clouds of heaven, came even to the Ancient of days and stood in his sight, and those who attended presented him. And royal power was given him, and all the kings of the earth by their generations and all nobility shall serve him. And his power is an everlasting one which shall not be taken away, and his kingdom shall not be destroyed.*[451]

7. These same facts are shown us by holy revelation, for we find written in the Apocalypse the following: *And I turned and looked back to see the voice that spoke with me. And I saw seven golden candlesticks, and in the midst of the candlesticks one like to the Son of man, clothed with a garment down to the feet, and he was girt over the paps*

*with a golden girdle. And his head and his hairs were white,
as white wool, as snow. And his eyes were as a flame of
fire; and his feet like unto fine brass, as from a burning
furnace. And his voice as the sound of many waters. And
he had in his right hand seven stars. And from his mouth
came out a sharp two-edged sword. And his face shone as
the sun in his power. And when I had seen, I fell at his
feet as dead. And he laid his right hand upon me, saying:
Fear not. I am the First and the Last, and alive, who was
dead. And behold I am living for ever and ever and have
the keys of death and of hell.*[452]

8. Also after His resurrection, when He was giving His
disciples definite mandates, He concluded the series of
deathless mandates with this injunction: *All power is given
to Me in heaven and in earth. Go ye therefore and teach
all nations, baptizing them in the name of the Father and
of the Son and of the Holy Spirit, teaching them to observe all things whatsoever I have commanded you.*[453]
Moreover that God the Father, making Him a partner of
His kingdom, granted Him a seat on the royal throne is
shown by this prophecy: *The Lord says to my Lord: Sit
thou at my right hand until I make thine enemies the foot-
stool of thy feet. The Lord will send forth the scepter of
thy power from Sion, and thou shalt rule in the midst of
thine enemies. With thee is the principality in the day of thy
strength, in the brightness of the saints. From the womb
before the daystar I begot thee. The Lord hath sworn and
He will not repent.*[454]

9. The enemies of God,[455] Most Holy Emperors, are
these: men who confound the orderliness of the truth by
contrariety, men who under the impulse of perverse passion formulate sacrilegious vows, men who in the madness

of their pagan hearts are forever venerating either a stock
or a stone.

Under the existing circumstances, we have a duty to dis-
close the plan of the sacred dispensation. In our purpose
of refuting the foulness of pagan error we aim to explain
in detail whatever the teaching of the prophets has handed
down to us who search the holy word of God. Let it not
be needful to inquire anxiously from us about the sequence
of the truth when we have told what fictions[456] have been
devised by those who passed on sacrilegious ideas to erring
mortals. Therefore let us briefly hold all else in abeyance
and turn the discussion to the task of explaining what is
true.

The Purpose of the Incarnation: to Undo the Evil Effects of the Fall

Ch. 25] Do you, Lord Emperors, patiently lend me
your sacred ears,[457] that I may unfold to your clemency the
whole story which I promise.[458] The reason why God, i.e.,
the Son of God, suffered Himself to become man shall be
briefly and truthfully explained to your piety.

God, creating after His own image the first man,[459] i.e.,
Adam, gave him a definite set of commands. He, being deceived by the devil's persuasions through the woman, i.e.,
Eve, lost the dignity of the glory that had been promised
him. There was a tree in Paradise[460] which caused him to
lose the boon of the rewards promised him by God. **2.**
Man was created from the slime of the virgin earth[461] (for,
as Scripture says, it had not yet rained upon the earth[462]).
By scorning God's commands, this man ensnared the human race in the affliction of mortality.[463]

This whole matter called for reformation and correction, and the reformation was obliged to reform the very first beginnings. Adam, created from the slime of the virgin earth, by his own transgression[464] lost the promised life. Christ,[465] born of the Virgin[466] Mary and the Holy Spirit, recovered[467] immortality and the kingdom. A tree of wood[468] supplied to the victims of deceit a pestilential fruit; the wood of the cross by its immortal construction restored life. Adam scorned God, Christ obeyed Him.[469] So, by the divine plan, Christ regained what Adam lost.[470]

3. For after long ages, in the last reaches of time, that is, almost at the end of the week of the centuries,[471] the Word of God commingled Itself with human flesh, to save mankind, to conquer death, to link the frailty of the human body with divine immortality. Else what could the mighty throng of saints have done?[472] What hope of salvation could they have had? What reward for their merits if they too, subject to one and the same lot and condition, were held fettered in the ineluctable[473] noose of mortality? From God's mercy and power should Abel have promised himself nothing? Henoch nothing? Noe nothing? Sem nothing? Abraham nothing? Isaac nothing? Jacob nothing? They too, after earning so much merit by their faith, would have departed, bound over equally with all the rest, and one doom of death would have encompassed all the saints of God, nor would their piety have met any reward with God, did one and the same condition of death devour them all. **4.** But God had promised Abraham a rule more resplendent than the stars of heaven.[474] Therefore Mary, the Virgin of God, a descendant from the family of Abraham, conceived, that the posterity of the men named above might be united in the bond of an immortal society, and that thus the human race, linked in an equal pact of union through a man who was likewise God, should by the merit of obedience attain to the realm of immortality.

And so, Most Holy Emperors, since we have satisfied the ears of curiosity, let us proceed with the sequel, in case[475] that even by this means a cleansing discourse may avail to purge the maculate ears of pollution.[476]

Denunciation of the Serpent-Devil

Ch. 26] There follows still another symbol, which is conveyed to the credulous ears of wretched men as something of great importance: ταῦρος δράκοντος καὶ ταύρου δράκων πατήρ. ("The bull was father of the serpent, and the serpent father of the bull.")[477] At last, Sir Devil,[478] you have betrayed to us the telltale signs of your bespotted name; at last with your own lips you have acknowledged your infamous name. I know who you have been, what you have dared; I know what the malicious persuasiveness of your rascality has wrought. This was the meaning of your extravagant promise to Eve when you were corrupting her: you said, *You shall be as gods*.[479] Already at that moment you were preparing temples for yourself and yours,[480] and making shrines, and consecrating with nefarious ceremonies the filth of your venom-filled mouth.[481]

2. You crawl about in temples[482] and feed on the miserable blood of slain victims; your poisons have felt no lack of gore, no lack of half-burned parts of cremated bodies; you have even bloodied yourself many a time with the blood of human victims,[483] and the rabies and venom of your thirsty jaws have been fed by the gore of Latiaris'

temple[484] or the altar of Carthage.[485] You, you behaving thus, boast that you help wretched men—all that you may slay them by your cruelty, deceive them by your persuasions, and overthrow them by your promises. That is the way you look out for your own, you parricide! Flee, unhappy men, flee and abandon that pesthouse with all the speed you can. The object of your worship is a serpent; he cannot hide it; he himself has confessed the appropriateness of his name, and punishment attends the guilty one who has confessed.

3. Listen to what the holy prophet proclaims by the divine prompting. The authority of Isaias transmitted this prophecy to us, for he says: *In that day God shall brandish His holy and great and strong sword over the snake, a serpent great and crooked, and shall slay the snake.*[486] The will of God is the substance of the completed work.[487] The serpent's death sentence has been pronounced. Whatever God has said is done. The doomed serpent has this comfort, that a numerous throng of the children of perdition accompanies his downfall. If you want to know the day of his death: he was struck down at the moment when he saw the God-man, when the godhead of Christ appeared to us.

4. Since that day whoever has followed the teachings of this serpent, with the serpent must die. *He* invented, *he* devised those gods whom you worship. If your minds remain obstinate in this error, you too shall burn equally with your gods,[488] so that what your first parents deserved by God's punishment may be extended also to your doom by the sharing of a common deed. Believe me, the devil has overlooked nothing whereby he might either weaken or destroy wretched man. For this reason he has changed himself into all kinds of forms with manifold diversity; for this reason he has provided himself with different sorts of cunning, that with varied and manifold deceits he may ensnare men and slay them.

Pagan vs. Christian Symbolism

Ch. 27] The accursed butcher schemed (oh the wickedness of it!) to have his cult always renewed by something wooden, because he foreknew that man's life, once nailed to the wood of the cross, would thereby be clasped in the embrace of everlasting immortality, and he wanted to fool doomed men by a counterfeit of the wood.[489] In the Phrygian cult of her whom they call the Mother of the Gods, a pine tree[490] is cut every year, and an image of a youth is fastened on the middle of the tree. In the cult of Isis the trunk of a pine tree is cut away. Its center is skilfully hollowed out, and an effigy of Osiris made of seeds is buried there.[491] 2. In the cult of Proserpina a tree is felled and shaped into the form and look of a virgin, and when it has been carried into the city there is mourning for forty nights and on the fortieth night it is burned.[492] But a similar fire consumes also those other wooden things which I have mentioned, for after a year flames devour a pyre made precisely of these wooden objects. Unhappy man! You are wrong and emphatically wrong. That fire will not be able to do you any good. Vainly you flatter yourself about these flames; vainly you always renew the fire with your fablings.[493] The fire which exacts the penalty for your misdeeds rages in a continuation of torment forever.

3. Learn an orderly account of the divine wood, the wood that saves,[494] so that you will realize there cannot

be succor for you in any other way.[495] An ark of wood[496] saved the human race from the flood; Abraham laid wood on the shoulders of his only son; a wooden rod protected God's people in their exodus from Egypt; wood restored a sweet taste to the bitter waters of Merra (Mara);[497] by a wooden rod the life-giving water was drawn from the spiritual rock; that Amalec might be conquered Moses stretched out his hands which were folded round the rod; the patriarch dreamed of an angel leaning on a wooden ladder, and saw other angels ascending and descending[498] by it; and the law of God was entrusted to a wooden tabernacle—and all these things were done so that man's salvation might come step by step, as it were, to the wood of the cross.

Therefore the wood of the cross supports the fabric of heaven,[499] confirms the foundations of earth, and leads into life the men who cling thereto. The wood of the devil always burns and dies, and along with its embers leads men who believe in it down to the abysses of hell.

4. Now what sort of ceremony that is should be carefully explained.[500] The devil by way of consecrating his tree has a ram immolated in the dead of night on the roots of the felled tree.[501] Scoundrel, who gave you this idea? Where did your ruinous passion learn it? Must you in your villainous passion be everlastingly ranging yourself against the Supreme Deity? The reason why the stern divine judgment flings you down from heaven in broken humiliation, why everlasting punishment is decreed for you by God's sentence, is that to your record of crimes a new crime is added every day, that by your crafty persuasiveness you seek to deceive the man of God.[502] See what the mocking adversary has devised for himself!

When Abraham was on the point of sacrificing his son, a ram was substituted at God's behest and fastened to the roots of a nearby tree.[503] **5.** When about to deliver His people from the tyranny of the Egyptians, the Supreme Deity bade a ram be slain at night and the doorposts be marked with its blood. He ordained that the ram be consumed by a fixed number of persons in a nighttime meal, and gave the sacrifice the name of Pasch.[504] But this was something that the providence of God's power devised as a prefiguring of things to come, that we might be shown symbolically the true Pasch. That is why the prophet said, when at the behest of the Divine Spirit he foretold the passion of our Lord: *He was led as a sheep to be a victim; and as a lamb before his shearer, so he opened not his mouth. In humility his judgment was taken away. His nativity who has declared, for his life shall be taken from the earth?*[505] **6.** Another prophet too proclaimed the same thing in a similar prophecy: *Lord, show me and I shall know. Then I saw their thoughts. Like a lamb without malice I was led to be a victim. They devised a counsel against me, saying: Come, let us put wood on his bread and erase his life from the earth.*[506]

7. Moreover it is shown us by sacred revelation that our Lord is called a lamb. For in the Apocalypse we find the following written: *And I saw in the midst of the throne and of the four living creatures, and in the midst of the ancients, a Lamb standing, as it were slain, having seven horns and seven eyes: which are the seven spirits of God, sent throughout the earth. And he came and took the book out of the right hand of him that sat on the throne. And when he had taken the book, the four living creatures and the four and twenty ancients fell down before the Lamb,* *having every one of them golden harps full of odors of supplications, which are the prayers of saints. And they sang a new canticle, saying: Thou art worthy to take the book and to open the seals thereof, because thou wast slain and hast redeemed us to God, in thy blood, out of every tribe and tongue and people and nation, and hast made them to our God a kingdom and priests. And they shall reign on the earth.*[507] **8.** John also[508] calls the Son of God by the name of Lamb, so that he too is in harmony with the prophetic promise. For he says in the Gospel: *The next day John sees Jesus coming to him, and he saith: Behold the Lamb of God. Behold Him who taketh away the sins of the world.*[509]

For the salvation of mankind the hallowed blood of that Lamb is shed, that by the outpouring of the precious blood the Son of God may redeem His saints, that those who are saved by the blood of Christ may first be sanctified by the potency of the blood of immortality. Let the blood outpoured before idols find no one present,[510] and let not the gore of sacrificed cattle befool wretched human creatures or bring them to perdition. That blood pollutes, it does not redeem, and by various vicissitudes[511] it destroys[512] a person in death. Unhappy are they who are drenched by the outpouring of sacrilegious blood. That sacrifice of a bull or a ram[513] pours out upon you the stain of wicked blood.

Biblical Condemnation of Idolatry, to Be Supported by the Secular Arm

Ch. 28] And so[514] let that filth which you are accumulating be washed away. Seek the native springs,[515] seek the clean waters, so that there Christ's blood with the Holy Spirit may wash you white[516] after your many stains.

But a higher authority[517] is needed to enable full conviction to restore wretched human creatures to sound thinking, so that in minds cured and renewed in health there may remain no vestige of the quondam pestilential disease. **2.** So through the mouth of the prophets and by the divine utterance of God we are informed what idols are[518] and what reality they possess. All the particulars must be given here so that it will not look as if an idea were being advanced on the basis of my own temerity, when the idea is really transmitted to me by divine magisterium[519] and certified by the voice of heaven.

What is the reality of idols is shown by the worshipful voice of Wisdom, for it says in the books of Solomon: *They had esteemed all the idols of the heathens for gods, which neither have the use of eyes to see, nor noses to draw breath, nor ears to hear, nor fingers of hands to handle, and, as for their feet, they are slow to walk. For man made them, and he that borroweth his own breath fashioned them. But no man can make a lord for himself. For, being mortal himself, he formeth a dead thing with his wicked hands. But he is better than those whom he worshipeth, because he indeed hath lived, but they never.*[520] What more do we ask? Wisdom with voice divine has admonished us, and taught us what it had seen in the secrets of God, and shown us what was salubrious, so that frail and perishable mortality[521] might not rush to its own doom and death.[522]

3. The Holy Spirit gives us this same forewarning in the Psalms; for we find this written in the 134th Psalm: *The idols of the Gentiles are silver and gold, the work of men's* *hands. They have a mouth and speak not, they have eyes and see not, they have ears and hear not, for neither is there any breath in their mouth. They are like to them that make them.*[523] If the sculptor who, by way of showing off his talent, has carved or cast an idol is struck with the divine punishment of a curse, think what a person must expect who salutes as a god what the sculptor sold.

4. Jeremias too, giving precepts to the people at God's behest,[524] admonished them with this discourse:[525] *Say you moreover in your hearts: Thou oughtest to be adored, O Lord. Moreover my angel is with you, and I myself will demand an account of your souls. Their tongue is polished by a craftsman and themselves too, laid over with gold and silver, are false things, and they cannot speak. And as if it were for a maiden that loveth to go gay, so do they take gold and make up crowns upon the heads of their gods. But there are times when the priests will convey away from their gods gold and silver and bestow it on themselves. Yea, and they will give thereof even to prostitutes and harlots, and they adorn the gods with clothing like men, the gods of silver and gold and wood.*[526] He also adds later,[527] to remove every fret of doubt: *Owls and swallows and birds in like manner fly upon its body and head, whereby you will know that they are no gods. Therefore you will not fear them. It is gold for show that they have about them; except a man wipe off the rust, it will not shine. For neither when they were molten did they feel it.*[528] *They were bought for a price, whereas there is no breath in them; having not the use of feet, they are carried upon shoulders.* He adds also by way of further confirming our mind in its assurance: *Knowing therefore by these things that they are not gods, fear them not.*[529] And to make manifest the

despicable behavior of their priests he adds: *Priests sit in their temples, having their garments rent and their heads and beards shaven and nothing upon their heads. And they roar and cry before their gods, as men do at the feast when one is dead.*[530]

5. And that both kings and nations will make such pronouncements about the gods, the same prophet indicates with presageful utterance, for he says: *It shall be known hereafter that they are false things by all nations and kings, because it is manifest that they are no gods and that there is no work of God in them. They will not set up a king over the land nor give rain to men. Also they will determine no causes nor deliver the land from oppression, because they can do nothing. And when fire shall fall upon the house of gods of wood and gods laid over with gold and with silver, their priests shall be saved; but they themselves shall be burnt in the midst like beams. And they will not withstand a king and war. How is it to be supposed or admitted that they are gods? Neither will these gods of wood and laid over with gold and with silver deliver themselves from thieves or robbers. They that are strong take from them the gold and silver wherewith they are clothed.*[531]

6. Take away, yes, calmly take away, Most Holy Emperors, the adornments of the temples. Let the fire of the mint or the blaze of the smelters melt them down, and confiscate all the votive offerings to your own use and ownership.[532] Since the time of the destruction of the temples you have been, by God's power, advanced in greatness.[533] You have overthrown your enemies,[534] enlarged the Empire, and, to add greater luster to your exploits, altering and scorning the fixed order of the seasons you have done in the winter what was never done before or will be again: you have trodden upon the swollen and raging waters of the Ocean.[535] The wave of a sea already become almost unknown to us has trembled[536] beneath your oars, and the Briton has quailed before the unexpected visage of the Emperor. What more would you have? Vanquished[537] by your exploits, the elements have bowed to you.

7. Moreover, the ordinances of the sacrosanct Law declare that God commands men not to make idols. For in Exodus we find this written: *You shall not make to yourselves gods of silver nor gods of gold.*[538] And again in the same book I find the voice of God commanding: *Thou shalt not make to thyself an idol nor the likeness of anything.*[539] The Holy Spirit pronounces shame on the wretched persons, because He desires to retrieve and not destroy those in error, and He says through Isaias: *You will be confounded with confusion that trust in graven things, that say to molten things: You are our gods.*[540] He also gives a law for the consecrated people to keep devoutly in perpetuity, and this is His commandment: *Thou shalt adore the Lord God, and shalt serve Him only.*[541] And in Deuteronomy similar commandments of God are made known, for He says: *Thou shalt not have other gods apart from me.*[542] He adds also by way of driving home to their hearts the weight of His power: *See, see that I am, and there is no god besides me. I will kill and I will make to live. I will strike and I will heal; and there is none that can deliver out of my hands.*[543]

8. In the Apocalypse also this same fact is demonstrated by holy revelation, for this is the Scripture: *And I saw another angel flying in the midst of heaven, having the* *eternal gospel to preach upon the earth through all nations and tribes and tongues and peoples, saying with a loud voice: Rather fear the Lord and give Him glory, because the hour of His judgment is come. And adore ye Him that made heaven and earth, the sea and all that is therein.*[544] Also our Lord Jesus Christ, safeguarding the ordinances of His Father's law, promulgates this same teaching in a worshipful commandment, for He says: *Hear, O Israel: the Lord thy God is one God, and thou shalt love the Lord thy God with thy whole heart, and with thy whole soul, and with thy whole strength. This is the first thing. And the second is like to it: Thou shalt love thy neighbor as thyself. On these two precepts dependeth the whole law and the prophets.*[545]

9. And following this divine and worshipful precept comes the Lord's immortal and holy conclusion. For by way of pointing out more clearly the way of salvation, He adds these words: *Now this is eternal life, that they may know thee, the only true Lord, and Jesus Christ, whom thou hast sent.*[546]

You know the series of the holy commandments: what you must follow and what you must shun you have learned from the worshipful and immortal voice. Hear on the other hand what destruction is in store for the scorners, and in what calamities the stringency of the worshipful law has bound them fast. **10.** For the conclusion of the worshipful commandments is gathered up in these words: *He that sacrificeth to gods shall be destroyed root and branch, save only to the Lord.*[547]

If the fearful penalty smote only the sacrilegious man, if the law's severity menaced only the sinner, he well might be confirmed in sacrilege by the rashness of his obstinate madness; but as it is, it menaces his line and posterity, and aims at leaving no portion of his most wicked seed, at seeing that no vestige of his unholy progeny shall remain. *He that sacrificeth to gods shall be destroyed root and branch.* Think what you are about, wretched and afflicted victim of delusion! Your wickedness condemns a multitude, will destroy a multitude, and the proliferating punishment is parceled out through all the substance of your line.

And why the authority of the ordained law is so ruthless towards sacrificers is shown by clear indications in Deuteronomy, for we find written there: *They sacrificed to devils and not to God.*[548] Do not give yourself over to contaminated and polluted spirits, do not hope for help from inferior beings,[549] do not supplicate those whom by God's grace you already ought to be dominating. 11. Lo, that demon whom you worship, when he hears the names of God and His Christ, trembles and can hardly put together stammering words to answer our questioning; clinging to the man he is torn, burned, and flogged, and straightway confesses the crimes he has committed.[550] Not to worship him, not to supplicate him, not to prostrate yourself and genuflect to him, is commanded by an interdict of the worshipful law. Hence the severity of the penalty, hence the fearful sentence of punishment, because being granted freedom of choice by God's indulgence, you rather choose the yoke of slavery. The Supreme Deity with the voice of salvation unceasingly upbraids this crime, and His mercy makes haste with the use of frequent threatenings[551] to set erring mankind on the right path. Hear what the divine voice says through the prophet

Isaias: *They have adored the gods which their own fingers have made. And man hath bowed down, and man hath been debased. And I will not forgive them.*[552]

12. The angry Deity is addressing you too, O pagan men, and with His sacred voice is still admonishing your errors. For He speaks as follows through the same prophet: *You have poured out libations to them and have placed sacrifices for them. Shall I not be angry at these things? saith the Lord.*[553] The God of salvation[554] still postpones His severity and suspends His anger, in case you might perhaps repent of your sins and somehow abandon the ruinous course of your sacrilegious will. Behold, in the very onrush of anger He again pleads in the accents of moderation and represses the goadings of His wrath. For He says through the prophet Jeremias: *Walk not after strange gods to serve them, and do not adore them nor provoke me by the works of your hands to destroy you.*[555]

13. Why are you so prone to sacrilege, and why do you stop up your ears? Why in the heat of obstinate madness do you rush like this to your own doom and death? God made you free; it is in your power either to live or perish. Why do you hurl yourself over the precipice? Since you are on a slippery path and on the very point of falling, do at last plant carefully your faltering steps.[556] Lo, the sentence is pronounced; lo, the penalty is decreed. Long has the divine leniency spared your crimes, long has it pretended to overlook your wickedness. You are coming to the critical point where hope and prayers fail; and that you may be more plainly instructed, learn the upshot of the punishment. On this topic there is a complete and systematic pronouncement in the Apocalypse, for it is written as follows: *If any man adores the beast and his*

image and has received a mark on his forehead and on his hand, he also drinks of the wine of the wrath of God mingled in the cup of his wrath, and shall be punished with fire and brimstone before the eyes of the Lamb. And the smoke of their torments shall ascend up for ever and ever; neither shall they have rest day nor night, whoever adore the beast and his image.[557]

Let the Emperors Stamp Out
Paganism and Be Rewarded by God

Ch. 29] But on you also, Most Holy Emperors,[558] devolves the imperative necessity to castigate and punish this evil, and the law of the Supreme Deity enjoins on you that your severity should be visited in every way[559] on the crime of idolatry. Hear and store up in your sacred intelligence what is God's commandment regarding this crime.

In Deuteronomy this law is written, for it says: *But if thy brother, or thy son, or thy wife that is in thy bosom, or thy friend who is equal to thy own soul, should ask thee, secretly saying: Let us go and serve other gods, the gods of the Gentiles; thou shalt not consent to him nor hear him, neither shall thy eye spare him, and thou shalt not conceal him. Announcing thou shalt announce about him; thy hand shall be first upon him to kill him, and afterwards the hands of all the people; and they shall stone him and he shall die, because he sought to withdraw thee from thy Lord.*[560] **2.** He bids spare neither son nor brother, and thrusts the avenging sword[561] through the body of a beloved wife. A friend too He persecutes with lofty severity, and the whole populace takes up arms to rend the bodies of sacrilegious men.

Even for whole cities, if they are caught in this crime, destruction is decreed; and that your providence may more plainly learn this, I shall quote the sentence of the established law. In the same book the Lord establishes the penalty for whole cities with the following words, for He says: *Or if in one of the cities which the Lord thy God gives thee to dwell in, thou hear men saying: Let us go and serve other gods which you know not: killing thou shalt slay all who are in the city with the death of the sword, and shalt burn the city with fire. And it shall be without a habitation, nor shall it be built any more forever, that the Lord may turn from the indignation of His wrath. And He shall give thee mercy, and pity thee, and multiply thee, if thou shalt hear the voice of the Lord thy God and observe His precepts.*[562]

3. To you, Most Holy Emperors, the Supreme Deity promises the rewards of His mercy and decrees a multiplication on the greatest scale. Therefore do what He bids; fulfil what He commands. Your first efforts have been crowned abundantly with major rewards. While in the status of neophytes in the faith you have felt the increase of the divine favor. Never has the worshipful hand of God abandoned you; never has He refused you aid in your distress. The ranks of your foemen have been laid low, and always the arms that warred against you have been dropped at sight of you. Proud peoples have been subjugated and the Persian hopes have collapsed.[563] Cruelty in its evil array has been unable long to stand against you. You have seen God's power, both of you, each by a different event;[564] on you has been conferred a celestial crown of victory, and by your happy success our troubles are relieved.

4. These rewards, Most Holy Emperors, the Supreme Deity has given you in recognition of your faith; as you are repaid for the time being with these distinctions, He invites you in to the secrets of the worshipful law. With a pure heart, a devout conscience, and incorrupt mind let your clemency ever fix its gaze upon heaven, ever look for help from God, implore the worshipful godhead of Christ, and offer spiritual sacrifices to the God of salvation for the welfare of the world and your own. So will all things come to you in happy success: victories, riches, peace, plenty, health, and triumphs, so that borne forward by the power of God you may govern the world in fortunate sovereignty.[565]

NOTES

LIST OF ABBREVIATIONS

AC	F. J. Dölger, Antike und Christentum (Münster i. W. 1929–50)
ACW	Ancient Christian Writers (Westminster, Md.–London 1946–)
ARW	Archiv für Religionswissenschaft (Berlin–Leipzig 1898–1942)
Blaise-Chirat	A. Blaise and H. Chirat, *Dictionnaire latin-français des auteurs chrétiens* (Strasbourg 1954)
BphW	Berliner philologische Wochenschrift (Berlin 1881–1944)
Christ-Schmid	W. von Christ and W. Schmid, *Geschichte der griechischen Litteratur*, Zweiter Teil (Munich 1920–24)
CSEL	Corpus scriptorum ecclesiasticorum latinorum (Vienna 1866–)
Cumont	F. Cumont, *Les religions orientales dans le paganisme romain* (4th ed. Paris 1929)
DA	Dictionnaire des antiquités grecques et romaines (Paris 1873–1919)
DACL	Dictionnaire d'archéologie chrétienne et de liturgie (Paris 1907–53)
DB	Dictionnaire de la Bible (Paris 1895–)
Dessau	H. Dessau, *Inscriptiones latinae selectae* (Berlin 1892–1916)
DTC	Dictionnaire de théologie catholique (Paris 1903–)
HSCP	Harvard Studies in Classical Philology (Cambridge 1890–)
Leumann-Hofmann	M. Leumann and J. B. Hofmann, *Lateinische Grammatik* (Munich 1928)
LM	Ausführliches Lexikon der griechischen und römischen Mythologie (Leipzig–Berlin 1884–1937)

Löfstedt, PKPer	E. Löfstedt, *Philologischer Kommentar zur Peregrinatio Aetheriae* (Uppsala–Leipzig 1911)
LSJ	Liddell-Scott-Jones, *A Greek-English Lexicon* (Oxford 1940)
ML	J. P. Migne, Patrologia latina (Paris 1844–55)
Moore	C. H. Moore, *Julius Firmicus Maternus der Heide und der Christ* (Diss. Munich 1897)
Nilsson	M. P. Nilsson, *Geschichte der griechischen Religion* (2nd ed. Munich 1955–61)
RAC	Reallexikon für Antike und Christentum (Stuttgart 1950–)
RE	Realenzyklopädie der classischen Altertumswissenschaft (Stuttgart 1893–)
REA	Revue des études anciennes (Bordeaux 1899–)
REG	Revue des études grecques (Paris 1888–)
RHLR	Revue d'histoire et de littérature religieuses (Paris 1896–1922)
RMP	Rheinisches Museum für Philologie (Bonn, later Frankfurt, 1827–)
RVV	Religionsgeschichtliche Versuche und Vorarbeiten (Giessen, later Berlin, 1903–39)
Schanz	M. Schanz, C. Hosius, and G. Krüger, *Geschichte der römischen Litteratur* 4/1 (2nd ed. Munich 1914)
Souter	A. Souter, *A Glossary of Later Latin to 600 A.D.* (Oxford 1949)
VC	Vigiliae christianae (Amsterdam 1947–)

BIBLIOGRAPHY

EDITIONS OF THE LATIN TEXT

Flacius Illyricus, Matthias (Strassburg 1562). The *editio princeps*.

Wower, Ioannes a (Hamburg 1603).

Oberthür, C. (Würzburg 1783). In his *Opera omnia sanctorum patrum latinorum* 5. First edition to contain the chapter divisions subsequently adopted by all editors.

Münter, Friedrich (Copenhagen 1826). Reprinted in ML 12.971-1050 (Paris 1845).

Oehler, Franz (Leipzig 1847). In E. G. Gersdorf, *Bibliotheca patrum ecclesiasticorum selecta* 13.57-120.

Bursian, Conrad (Leipzig 1856). Bursian was the first editor since Flacius who had access to the unique manuscript.

Halm, Karl (Vienna 1867). In CSEL 2, with Minucius Felix.

Ziegler, Konrat (Leipzig 1907). In *Bibliotheca Teubneriana. Index scriptorum, Index nominum, Index verborum*.

Heuten, Gilbert (Brussels 1938). In *Travaux de la faculté de philosophie et lettres de l'Université de Bruxelles* 8. Ziegler's text, with a few modifications; valuable introduction and commentary; careful translation into French.

Ziegler, Konrat (Munich 1953). In *Das Wort der Antike* 3. Practically an *editio minor* of the Teubner edition of 1907, with diminished critical apparatus and no indices; separate German translation, with nine pages of notes.

Pastorino, Agostino (Florence 1956). In *Biblioteca di studi superiori* 27. Has the fullest commentary ever published on Firmicus.

TRANSLATIONS

Anon. of 17th century, in Bibliothèque Nationale MS. 1340. Printed in J.-A. Buchon, *Choix de monuments primitifs de l'église chrétienne* (Paris 1837). Heuten 29: "Fort libre, elle se contente souvent de résumer ou de paraphraser, et, la base solide d'un texte bien établi lui faisant défaut, elle ne donne de l'oeuvre qu'une idée d'ensemble."

Kempfer, G. (1718). Münter, ML 12.982: "Belgice vertit

notisque illustravit G. Kempfer 1718." Heuten was unable to find a copy of this in the libraries of Holland and Belgium.

Müller, Alfons, *Des Firmicus Maternus Schrift vom Irrtum der heidnischen Religionen, aus dem Lateinischen übersetzt*, in *Bibliothek der Kirchenväter* 14 (Kempten-Munich 1913).

Chiriac-Dimaneea, N. (Pitesti 1927). A Rumanian translation, called incomplete and unsatisfactory by the Rumanian scholar J. Coman.

Faggin, Giuseppe, *Giulio Firmico Materno, L'errore delle religioni profane (prima versione italiana), con introduzione e note* (Lanciano 1932).

Heuten, Gilbert, *Julius Firmicus Maternus De errore profanarum religionum, traduction nouvelle avec texte et commentaire*, in *Travaux de la faculté de philosophie et lettres de l'Université de Bruxelles* 8 (Brussels 1938).

Ziegler, Konrat, *Julius Firmicus Maternus, Senator, Vom Irrtum der heidnischen Religionen, übertragen und erläutert*, in *Das Wort der Antike* 3 (Munich 1953).

DISCUSSIONS OF FIRMICUS: SUBSIDIA

Bauer, J. B., "Textkritisches zu Firmicus Maternus de errore profanarum religionum," *Wien. Stud.* 71 (1958) 153–60. On Ziegler's edition of 1953.

———, "Zu Firmicus Maternus, De errore profanarum religionum 5, 4," *Eranos* 57 (1959) 73–75.

Becker, A., "Julius Firmicus Maternus und Pseudo-Quintilian," *Philologus* 61 N.F. 15 (1902) 476–78.

Blaise, A., *Manuel du latin chrétien* (Strasbourg 1955).

Boissier, Gaston, *La fin du paganisme* (Paris 1891).

Boll, F., "Firmicus," RE 6 (1909) 2365–79.

Brakman, C., *Miscella tertia* (Leyden 1917) 23–28 ("Ad Firmicum Maternum").

———, "Firmiciana," *Mnemosyne* 52 (1924) 428–48.

Chatillon, Fr., "L'Eau baptismale dans les perspectives de Firmicus," *Mélanges offerts à M. Andrieu, Rev. des sciences religieuses*, vol. hors série (Strasbourg 1957) 95–101 (on 2.5).

Clemen, Carl, "Zu Firmicus Maternus," RMP 73 (1920–24) 350–58.

Coman, J., "Essai sur le 'De errore profanarum religionum' de Firmicus Maternus," *Revista clasica* 4/5 (1932–33) 73–118.

Cumont, Franz, "La polémique de l'Ambrosiaster contre les païens," RHLR 8 (1903) 417–40.

——, *Les religions orientales dans le paganisme romain* (4th ed. Paris 1929).

Dibelius, Martin, "Die Isisweihe bei Apuleius und verwandte Initiations-Riten," *Sitzungsb. d. Heidelberger Akad. d. Wiss., phil.-hist. Klasse* 8 (1917) no. 4, 1–54. Esp. 8–13 on Firmicus 18.1.

Dieterich, Albrecht, *Eine Mithrasliturgie* (3rd ed. Leipzig 1923).

Dölger, F. J., "Nilwasser und Taufwasser. Eine religionsgeschichtliche Auseinandersetzung zwischen einem Isisverehrer und einem Christen des vierten Jahrhunderts nach Firmicus Maternus," AC 5 (1936) 153–87.

——, "Die Bedeutung des neuentdeckten Mithrasheiligtums von Dura-Europos für die handschriftliche Überlieferung der heidnischen Mysteriensprache bei Firmicus Maternus und Hieronymus," AC 5 (1936) 286–88.

Dombart, Bernhard, "Über die Bedeutung Commodians für die Textkritik der Testimonia Cyprians," *Zeitschrift f. wiss. Theologie* 22 (1879) 374–89.

——, "Zu Julius Firmicus Maternus," *Jahrb. f. Class. Phil.* 125 (1882) 592.

Ellis, Robinson, "On the Octavius of Minucius Felix and Firmicus De errore profanarum religionum," *Journ. Phil.* 26 (1899) 197–202. Textual notes.

Engelbrecht, August, "Lexikalisches und Biblisches aus Tertullian," *Wien. Stud.* 27 (1905) 62–74 at 72. On the Biblical text used by Firmicus.

Ernout, Alfred, Review of Heuten's edition, *Rev. de philol.* 64 N.S. 12 (1938) 239–50.

Festugière, A. J., Review of Heuten's edition, REG 52 (1939) 643–47.

Flacius Illyricus, Matthias, *Quarta centuria ecclesiasticae historiae* (fourth volume of the "Magdeburg Centuries"; Basel 1562). Ch. 10, columns 1117–21; a good résumé of the *De errore* by its discoverer.

Forbes, Clarence A., "Firmicus Maternus and the Secular Arm," *Class. Journ.* 55 (1959–60) 146–50.

——, "Critical Notes to Firmicus Maternus, *De errore,*" VC 21 (1967) 34–38.

———, "Firmicus Maternus, Julius," *New Catholic Encyclopedia* (New York 1967) 5.935f.

Franses, D., O.F.M., "J. Firmicus Maternus en de Canon der H. Mis.," *De Katholiek* 160 (1921) 247–60, 384–97.

Friedrich, Theodor, *In Iulii Firmici Materni de errore profanarum religionum libellum quaestiones* (Giessen diss. Bonn 1905).

Groehl, F., *De syntaxi Firmiciana* (Diss. Breslau 1918).

Haupt, M., "Analecta," *Hermes* 2 (1867) 8f.; "Coniectanea," *ibid.* 8 (1874) 249. Textual notes.

Henry, Paul, S. J., *Plotin et l'occident. Firmicus Maternus, Marius Victorinus, Saint Augustin et Macrobe,* in *Spicilegium sacrum Lovaniense* 15 (Louvain 1934).

Hertz, J. M., *De Julio Firmico Materno eiusque imprimis de errore profanarum religionum libello* (diss. Copenhagen 1817).

Heuten, Gilbert, "Primus in orbe deos fecit timor," *Latomus* 1 (1937) 3–8. On 17.4.

———, "Une variante de la Bible latine pré-hiéronymienne," *ibid.* 3 (1939) 261–63. On 28.4.

Kroll, Wilhelm, Review of Moore, BphW 17 (1897) 1479–81.

Lana, Italo, Review of Pastorino's edition, *Riv. fil.* 86 N.S. 36 (1958) 203–11.

Laurin, Joseph-Rhéal, O.M.I., *Orientations maîtresses des apologistes chrétiens de 270 à 361,* in *Analecta Gregoriana* 61 (Rome 1954).

Martin, E. J., "The Biblical Text of Firmicus Maternus," *Journ. of Theol. Stud.* 24 (1922–23) 318–25.

Michels, P. Thomas, "The *symbolum* in Firmicus Maternus De errore profanarum religionum," *Folia* 2 (1947) 50–54.

Mommsen, Theodor, "Firmicus Maternus," *Gesammelte Schriften* 7 (Berlin 1909) 446–50, from *Hermes* 29 (1894) 468–72.

Moore, Clifford Herschel, *Iulius Firmicus Maternus, der Heide und der Christ* (diss. Munich 1897).

Müller, Alfons, *Zur Überlieferung der Apologie des Firmicus Maternus* (diss. Tübingen 1908).

Norden, Eduard, *Agnostos theos* (Leipzig-Berlin 1912, reprinted 1923). Pp. 233–39: "Doxologien bei Firmicus."

Pastorino, Agostino, "Note Firmiciane," *Siculorum Gymnasium* 6 (1953) 120–26.

Prindle, Lester M., *Quaestiones de libello quem Iulius Firmicus Maternus scripsit de errore profanarum religionum* (unpub. diss. Harvard 1922, summarized in HSCP 33 [1922] 181f.).

——, "Toleration and Persecution in the Age of Constantine: Tradition, Fact, and Theory" (unpub., abstracted in *Proc. Amer. Phil. Assoc.* 55 [1924] xxxi).

Quacquarelli, A., "La parentesi negli apologeti retori latini da Tertulliano a Firmico Materno," *Orpheus* 4 (1957) 63–75.

Richard, Gaston, "Les obstacles à la liberté de conscience au iv⁰ siècle de l'ère chrétienne," REA 42 (1940) 499–507.

Riedinger, Utto, "Θαρρεῖται Θεοῦ τὰ μυστήρια. Ein Beitrag des Pseudo-Kaisarios zu den Symbola des Firmicus Maternus," *Perennitas. Beiträge zur christlichen Archäologie und Kunst*, ed. H. Rahner and E. von Severus (Münster 1963) 19–24.

Rostan, Carlo, "Il cristianesimo del IV. secolo: il primo appello al braccio secolare," *Nuova riv. stor.* 12 (1928) 384–403.

Schanz, M., *Geschichte der römischen Litteratur* 4/1 (2nd ed. Munich 1914) 129–37.

Setton, Kenneth M., *Christian Attitude towards the Emperor in the Fourth Century* (New York 1941) 57–67.

Skutsch, F., "Cuias fuerit Firmicus," *Hermes* 31 (1896) 646f.

——, "Firmicus De errore profanarum religionum," RMP 60 (1905) 262–72.

——, "Ein neuer Zeuge der altchristlichen Liturgie," ARW 13 (1910) 291–305.

Spiegelberg, W., "Das Isis-Mysterium bei Firmicus Maternus," ARW 19 (1916–19) 194f.

Thomas, Paul, "Ad Firmicum Maternum," *Mnemosyne* 49 (1921) 64f.

Thorndike, Lynn, "A Roman Astrologer as a Historical Source," *Class. Phil.* 8 (1913) 415–35.

——, *A History of Magic and Experimental Science* 1 (New York 1923) 525–38.

Vahlen, Johannes, "Varia III," *Hermes* 10 (1876) 459. On 13.4.

Van der Leeuw, G., "The Σύμβολα in Firmicus Maternus," *Egyptian Religion* 1 (1933) 61–72.

Vecchi, Alberto, "Giulio Firmico Materno e la 'Lettera agli Ebrei,'" *Convivium* 25 (1957) 641–51.

Weyman, Carl, "L'astrologie dans le 'De errore' de Firmicus," RHLR 3 (1898) 383f.

———, Review of Ziegler's Teubner text and Müller's diss., BphW 29 (1909) 775–81.

Wikström, Tage, "Zum Texte der sog. Apologie des Firmicus Maternus," *Eranos* 53 (1955) 172–92.

Wölfflin, Eduard, "Firmicus Maternus," *Archiv f. lat. Lex.* 10 (1898) 427–34.

Ziegler, Konrat. "Neue Firmicus-Lesungen," RMP 60 (1905) 273–96.

———, "Zur Überlieferungsgeschichte des Firmicus Maternus De errore," *ibid.* 417–24.

———, "Zur Überlieferung der Apologie des Firmicus Maternus," BphW 29 (1909) 1195–1200. Partly a review of Müller's diss.

———, "Zur neuplatonischen Theologie," ARW 13 (1910) 247–69.

Zucker, Fr., "Euhemeros und seine ἱερὰ ἀναγραφή bei den christlichen Schriftstellern," *Philologus* 64 N.F. 18 (1905) 465–72.

INTRODUCTION

[1] C. H. Moore, *Iulius Firmicus Maternus, der Heide und der Christ* (diss. Munich 1897).

[2] The view that Firmicus was an African rhetor antedates the proof that he was identical with the astrologer Firmicus. It is distressing to see this misinformation repeated in recent decades, as by G. Richard, REA 42 (1940) 502.

[3] *Math.* 6.30.26, convincingly emended (from *quis meus* to *civis meus*) by F. Skutsch, "Cuias fuerit Firmicus," *Hermes* 31 (1896) 646f.

[4] So think numerous scholars, cited by Pastorino (99): e.g., F. Boll in RE 6 (1909) 2365. Pastorino, though admitting the strong possibility of autopsy, claims that the passage about the rape of Proserpina from Enna is a pastiche of recollections from Ovid (*Met.* 5.390–413, *Fast.* 4.427–42) and Cicero (*Verr.* 4.48.107). Heuten (in his Appendix 2, p. 194) by a tabulation of parallelisms made it seem probable that Firmicus had at any rate read Ovid and Cicero, though this need not exclude the additional influence of autopsy; Heuten observed that Firmicus exhibited unusual pleasure in giving a lengthy account of Enna and its myth. Be it also noted that Firmicus, devotee of rhetoric, was using the rhetorical τόπος of the *locus amoenus*, and indeed uses the words *amoenus* and *amoenitas*, whereas Cicero and Ovid do not.

[5] In the explicit of *Math.* 4, Urbinas (263) erroneously expands V.C. to *vir consularis;* this misled the Aldine editor.

[6] L. M. Prindle, in an unpublished paper, abstracted in PAPA 55 (1924) xxxi.

[7] Moore 47. The supposition that he studied in Athens is gratuitous guesswork: "Il savait le grec, qu'il avait peut-être étudié à Athènes; sa patrie, la Sicile, était du reste un des grands foyers de l'hellénisme" (Coman 111).

[8] See Ziegler (2nd ed.) 10–12, 14.

[9] Greek loanwords in the *De errore* are listed by Heuten 195f.

[10] 7.5: Eleusis from the root ἐλευσ-, to "come"; 13.2: Serapis from Σάρρας παῖς; 17.3: Apollo from ἀπόλλειν.

[11] W. Kroll, BphW 19 (1897) 1480. Besides, the ghost of "African Latin," conjured up by Wölfflin and his followers in

the early volumes of the *Archiv für lat. Lexicographie und Grammatik*, was laid by Kroll and others; so Leumann-Hofmann 817: "Von einem africanischen Latein . . . redet man heute nicht mehr."

[12] Firmicus does not reveal where he practiced law; Coman conjectured Rome, but this guess was rebuked by Heuten, *L'Ant. class.* 6 (1937) 177.

[13] All this is from the prooemium to Book 4 of the *Mathesis*, sects. 1–3.

[14] Mavortius' career, summarized by Otto Seeck, RE 13 (1927) 1371–73, *s. v.* Lollianus nr. 10, is rather well known to us from several inscriptions (Dessau 1223–25, 1232, 8943) and from Ammianus Marcellinus.

[15] Mommsen, *Gesammelte Schriften* 7.446–50, a revised printing of his article in *Hermes* 29 (1894) 468–72. Mommsen thinks Mavortius received from Constantine no formal and public designation for the consulship, since the inscriptions which record his *cursus honorum* are silent on the matter; rather it was an "adulatory" designation. Friedrich (53) quarrels with the word "adulatory" and, despite the *argumentum ex silentio*, maintains that Mavortius was formally consul designate until the designation was invalidated by Constantine's death. Friedrich points to the confused *Vierkaiserjahr* 69, when Vitellius rejected some of the consuls designate of his predecessors.

[16] Mommsen, misled by an unsound edition of Firmicus, referred to *Math.* 8.15.4 as another allusion to the proposed rank of consul ordinarius for Lollianus Mavortius; but in that passage all the MSS. and the *editio princeps* have *Tullianus* and only the deplorable Aldine edition of 1499 has *Lollianus*. Tullianus was consul in 330 (W. Ensslin, RE 7 A [1939] 798), and this date fits well with the other evidence for dating the *Mathesis*.

[17] See Franz Boll's complete chronological list of eclipses known from ancient sources: "Finsternisse," RE 6 (1909) 2352–64.

[18] Eclipse: *Math.* 1.4.10; the three joint rulers: *ibid.* 1.10.14. The correct deductions as to date were drawn by Mommsen in his article of 1894. Lynn Thorndike, "A Roman Astrologer as a Historical Source," *Class. Phil.* 8 (1913) 415–35, at 419 n. 2, disputed Mommsen's dating, arguing that there might easily be a scribal confusion between Constantinus and Constantius—in which case the terminal date of 337 would disappear. No one has cared to follow Thorndike in defying Mommsen and the MSS.

[19] *Math.* 2.29.10.

[20] Dessau 1222: *Rufius Volusianus bis consul ordinarius;* Mommsen, *Gesammelte Schriften* 7.449f.

[21] Otto Seeck, "Ceionius nr. 21," RE 3 (1897) 1860. Ziegler (2nd ed. 5) gives September 30 instead of December 30, but this appears to be a mere oversight.

[22] *Mathesis* to mean "astrology," the science of the *mathematici,* is a non-Greek usage which occurs frequently in Late Latin after Tertullian (Souter).

[23] All the foregoing is from the prooemium to Book 1.

[24] M. W. L. Laistner, "The Western Church and Astrology during the Early Middle Ages," in his *The Intellectual Heritage of the Early Middle Ages* (Ithaca 1957) 57–82, at 82, arguing against Cumont, RHLR 8 (1903) 436.

[25] *Math.* 5.1.38, 6.2.8, and 8.1.10 on the promise regarding the *Myriogenesis;* 8.4.14 on Nechepso. All the pertinent words are carefully quoted by Schanz 4.1.133.

[26] *Math.* 4.20.2: *in singulari libro quem de domino geniturae et chronocratore ad Murinum nostrum scripsimus;* 7.7.4: *ex eo libro qui de fine vitae a nobis scriptus est.*

[27] Friedrich 55, citing Cumont, *Mon. Mithr.* 2.535, on the aristocratic propensity for becoming initiates.

[28] Carl Clemen, RMP 73 (1920–24) 351; Coman 107; Heuten 5. Clemen supported Friedrich's case by noting that Firmicus often (6.9, 12.9, 19.5, 26.1) used *tradere* to indicate the transmission of religious beliefs or secrets or verbal symbols. Coman observed that Mithraic theology rested on an astrological basis (Cumont 136), and of course Firmicus was a devotee of astrology. Heuten thought Friedrich's view unproven but not unlikely. For further discussion see notes on 5.2.

[29] *Math.* 2.30.10, quoted by Boll, RE 6 (1909) 2365.

[30] *De errore* 8.4; so interpreted by Heuten, Ziegler, Pastorino, and others.

[31] F. Skutsch, "Ein neuer Zeuge der altchristlichen Liturgie," ARW 13 (1910) 291–305, esp. 293 and 303f.

[32] R. Reitzenstein and P. Wendland, "Zwei angeblich christliche liturgische Gebete," *Nachr. d. Gött. Ges. d. Wiss.* (1910) 324–34, at 331 (Wendland); Eduard Norden, *Agnostos Theos* (Leipzig 1912, repr. 1923) 233–39: "Doxologien bei Firmicus."

[33] R. E. Witt, *Albinus and the History of Middle Platonism* (Cambridge 1937) 130.

³⁴ *Asclepius* 8, in the *Corpus Hermeticum* of Nock–Festugière. The date of this Latin opus is uncertain, but Norden puts it in the early lifetime of Firmicus.

³⁵ Heuten 3.

³⁶ The attribution to Firmicus by Dom G. Morin of the anonymous Christian treatise called *Consultationes Zacchaei et Apollonii* (*Flor. patr.* 39, 1935) was erroneous and has been rejected: Altaner, *Patrology* (New York 1960) 422.

³⁷ Cumont 13.

³⁸ Eutropius, *Brev.* 10.9.

³⁹ 28.6; for the expedition see Amm. 20.1.1.

⁴⁰ Boll, RE 6 (1909) 2377, referring to the earthquake which destroyed Neocaesarea in Pontus in 344 (Jerome, *Chron.* Ol. 280.4) and that which destroyed Dyrrhachium and shook Rome and Campania in 345 (Jerome, *ibid.* Ol.281.1). Heuten (6 n. 2) and Pastorino (xix–xx) falsely ascribed Boll's hypothesis to Mommsen, but rejected it, largely because earthquakes are a common τόπος in Christian-pagan polemics.

⁴¹ *Cod. Theod.* 16.10.4; Pastorino xx.

⁴² *Cod. Theod.* 9.7.3; for a full interpretation of this matter, see below, note on 12.2.

⁴³ J.-R. Palanque, in the Fliche-Martin *Histoire de l'église* 3 (Paris 1936) 20–24.

⁴⁴ Cumont, RHLR 8 (1903) 421f., shows that the cults of Isis, Mithra, etc. were still maintained in Rome about 375 A.D., according to Ambrosiaster, *Quaest. Vet. et Nov. Test.* 114.11–12. See also A. Alföldi, *A Festival of Isis at Rome under the Christian Emperors of the Fourth Century* (diss. Pannonicae ser. 2, fasc. 7, Budapest 1937). Augustine (*Conf.* 8.2.3) spoke of the pagan sympathies, still in his time, of *tota fere Romana nobilitas*.

⁴⁵ Date when paganism became a minority: F. Lot, *La fin du monde antique* (rev. ed. Paris 1951) 47. Proportion of pagans in early fourth century: A. Bouché-Leclercq, *L'Intolérance religieuse et la politique* (Paris 1917) 333. A. D. Nock, *Sallustius* (Cambridge 1926) cii, thinks that the tone of Sallustius, about the year 363, "suggests that paganism has waned, but still possesses a not inconsiderable following."

⁴⁶ *Cod. Theod.* 16.10.2, trans. by Clyde Pharr.

⁴⁷ *Ibid.* 3.

⁴⁸ J. Geffcken, *Der Ausgang des griechisch-römischen Heiden-*

tums (Heidelberg 1920) 97, maintained that Constantius' law of 341 dealt a mortal blow to paganism. But see Prindle, ch. 1, p. 26: "Leges certe Constantii et Constantis sacris antiquis haud multum nocuisse et per multos annos postea deos falsos fere impune cultos esse multa indicia demonstrant."

[49] *Vir egregiae tranquillitatis, placidus* (Eutrop., *Brev.* 10.15.2). Cf. Carlo Rostan on the religious policy of Constantius: *Nuova riv. storica* 12 (1928) 385.

[50] 28.6 (to the emperors): *Post excidia templorum in maius dei estis virtute provecti.*

[51] *Expositio totius mundi* (mid-fourth century) pp. 159f. in the edition of G. Lumbroso (1898).

[52] E. Gibbon, *The History of the Decline and Fall of the Roman Empire* (Bury's ed.) 3.200.

[53] Symmachus, *Relationes* 3.7 (MGH 6, ed. Seeck).

[54] *Cod. Theod.* 16.10.6, trans. by Clyde Pharr.

[55] W. W. Hyde, *Paganism to Christianity in the Early Roman Empire* (Philadelphia 1946) 207.

[56] F. Martroye, "La répression de la magie et le culte des gentils au ive siècle," *Rev. hist. de droit franç. et étranger* 9 (1930) 669–701. Heuten, in his Addenda 211, states that he first disagreed with Martroye but later was convinced. De Labriolle, in the Fliche–Martin *Histoire de l'église* 3.182, thinks that Martroye's view can no longer hold true for Constantius' repressive legislation of 356.

[57] Rostan, *art. cit.* 387: "La legislazione del principe ariano (Constantius) . . . doveva, agli occhi degli eccessivi, sembrare singolarmente temperata."

[58] E. Renan, *L'Église chrétienne* (Paris 1879) 300.

[59] Paul Allard, *Le christianisme et l'empire romain* (Paris 1896) 183.

[60] Heuten 2. Similarly G. Boissier, *La fin du paganisme* (Paris 1891) 67.

[61] Rostan, *loc. cit.*

[62] Earlier Christian apologies had been addressed to Hadrian and the Antonines, seeking to appease or convince them: Quadratus and Aristides to Hadrian (Eus., *Hist. eccl.* 4.3), Justin to Antoninus Pius (*ibid.* 4.26), Athenagoras to Marcus Aurelius and Commodus.

[63] *Op. cit.* 68. Schanz 4.1.134 pillories Firmicus with these phrases: "der Geist der Fanatismus . . ., die Stimme der Intol-

eranz . . ., der Fanatiker." Gibbon (Ch. 28) characteristically sneered that Firmicus was "piously inhuman."

[64] E. K. Rand, *Founders of the Middle Ages* (Cambridge 1928) 41.

[65] Alberto Vecchi, "Giulio Firmico Materno e la 'Lettera agli Ebrei,'" *Convivium* 25 (1957) 641–51, at 642.

[66] Coman (77), approved by Heuten, *L'Ant. class.* 6 (1937) 178.

[67] Compare *De errore* 13.4 with *Math.* 7.1.1.

[68] Porphyry, *De abst.* 2.38.

[69] *De errore* 13.4, with Pastorino's note.

[70] G. Richard, "Les obstacles à la liberté de conscience au ive siècle de l'ère chrètienne," REA 42 (1940) 499–507, at 505.

[71] Prindle, Ch. 1, p. 3.

[72] *De errore* 16.4, 28.10, 6.9, 29.1. Firmicus quotes Exod. 22.20 and other passages from the Pentateuch.

[73] G. Richard, *op. cit.* 502: "Fanatisme aveugle . . ., d'inspiration juive plutôt que chrétienne, puisqu'il invoquait le Deuteronome, cette loi que saint Paul jugeait abolie par la passion du Christ."

[74] P. de Labriolle, *History and Literature of Christianity from Tertullian to Boethius* (trans. by H. Wilson, London 1924) 236.

[75] Tertullian, *Ad Scap.* 2: *nec religionis est cogere religionem;* cf. *Apol.* 24.6 for another defense of freedom of religion. Said Lactantius (*Div. inst.* 5.20.9) in the early part of the century of Firmicus: *Non expetimus ut deum nostrum colat aliquis invitus, nec si non coluerit irascimur.*

[76] Cassiodorus, *Variae* 2.27 (an imperial letter to the Jews of Genoa, about A.D. 507–11): *Religionem imperare non possumus, quia nemo cogitur ut credat invitus.*

[77] S. Butler, *Hudibras* 3.3.547f.

[78] The so-called Cebes (*Tabula* 19) drew a somewhat similar medical analogy, showing the beneficial effects of *paideia* and the disastrous consequences of refusing the medicine.

[79] This quotation and the accompanying analogy are from Ch. 16.4–5.

[80] P. 6 of the Introduction to his translation of Firmicus, *Bibliothek der Kirchenväter* 14 (1913). A. Piganiol, *L'Empire chrétien* (Paris 1947) 79, leans toward Müller's opinion.

[81] *Perditi* or *perditi homines* (or the same in the singular) seven

times in Firmicus: 1, 6.1, 8.4, 13.5, 16.3, 18.8, 26.3. Likewise, *gladius ultor* of the decree may be influenced by Firmicus' *gladius vindex* (29.2) and *vindices gladii* (6.9), in passages soliciting imperial vengeance on the pagans.

[82] J. Geffcken, *Zwei griechische Apologeten* (Leipzig 1907) 316.

[83] L. M. Prindle, summary of dissertation, HSCP 33 (1922) 181f.

[84] Alfred Ernout, review of Heuten, *Rev. de philol.* 12 (1938) 239. Cf. Nilsson 2.683: "die Hauptquelle unserer Kenntnis der spätantiken Mysterien."

[85] Heuten 11.

[86] Theophilus, *Ad Autol.* 1.11; Tertullian, *Apol.* 28–36.

[87] 3.2, 6.1, 7.7, 8.4, 13.1, 16.3, 16.4, 20.7, 24.9, 25.4, 28.6, 29.1, 29.3, 29.4.

[88] Cumont (167f.) observes that consistent believers in astrology, such as the Emperor Tiberius, logically neglected religion because of their acceptance of Fate as omnipotent; but Firmicus in the *Mathesis* illogically implored the gods for help against ineluctable astral influences.

[89] Cumont, RHLR 8 (1903) 431. Cf. also, especially for references to Greek polemics against astrology, Cumont 289 n. 61.

[90] Ambrosiaster, *Quaestiones Vet. et Nov. Test.* 115.1 and 83.

[91] Lynn Thorndike, "A Roman Astrologer as a Historical Source," *Class. Phil.* 8 (1913) 415–35, at 418.

[92] Ps.-Quintilian, *Decl. mai.* 4.13. See Carl Weyman, "L'Astrologie dans le *De errore* de Firmicus," RHLR 3 (1898) 383f.

[93] Quoted by Heuten (12) from an unpublished work on Firmicus by H. Cavelier d'Esclavelles.

[94] G. van der Leeuw, *Egyptian Religion* 1 (1933) 62.

[95] G. van der Leeuw, *op. cit.* 63.

[96] See above, pp. 6–7.

[97] Heuten, *L'Ant. class.* 6 (1937) 178, objecting to the view of Coman (90) that Firmicus depicted exclusively contemporaneous paganism.

[98] Firmicus' admiration for Cicero as a stylist was voiced twice in the *Mathesis:* 2 praef. 2: *Marcus vero Tullius, princeps ac decus Romanae eloquentiae;* 8.5.3: *decus eloquentiae Tullius.*

[99] Boll, RE 6 (1909) 2368.

[100] *Cat.* 1.3: *Non deest rei publicae consilium neque auctoritas huius ordinis: nos, nos, dico aperte, consules desumus,* reworked

in 6.9: *Tunc nec senatus consuli, nec leges rei publicae nec consul legibus defuit.* The phrase in *Cat.* 2.23, *impuri impudicique*, favored by assonance, was picked up by Firmicus 4.2 and four times in the *Mathesis* (Moore 49). The rare epic word *bellipotens* (12.8) was found by Firmicus not in Ennius himself but in Cicero's quotation of Ennius, *De div.* 2.116.

[101] Cicero, *Verr.* 4.48.107; Ovid, *Met.* 5. 385–95 and especially *Fasti* 4.427–42. Heuten (194) gives a careful table of verbal parallelisms in these descriptive passages, and indeed they had been often noted by earlier scholars, as by Fr. Zucker, *Philol.* 64 N.F. 18 (1905) 465–72.

[102] Heuten 20 and *passim* in his notes.

[103] G. E. McCracken, *Arnobius, The Case against the Pagans* 1 (ACW 7; Westminster, Md. 1949) 39.

[104] Ziegler (2nd ed.) 10–13; Pastorino, notes on 7.7 (p. 107), 8.1 (p. 111), 12.8 (p. 140), and 14.2 (p. 158). In half a dozen reviews of Heuten's book I find no commendation of his "discovery" of Labeo as a source except from the ill-informed pen of Léon Herrmann, a person with whom one may always safely disagree: *Rev. belge de philol. et d'hist.* 17 (1938) 930f. Italo Lana, *Riv. fil.* 36 (1958) 205, in a learned review of Pastorino, approves his rejection of Labeo.

[105] Schanz-Hosius 2.755–8; Teubner text by G. Lehnert (1905).

[106] Actually in 1897, *Compte rendu du IV. Congrès scientifique international des catholiques tenu à Fribourg (Suisse)*, "Misc. Critica 11"; more accessibly printed in RHLR 3 (1898) 383f.

[107] Ps.-Quint., *Decl. mai.* 4.13.

[108] Ps.-Quint., *Decl. mai.* 4.14 = *De err.* 17.4; 10.4 = 18.2; 5.6 = 19.2 (*erige vultus*); 2.24 = 20.1; 5.20 = 28.10 (*in verba colligere*); 9.19 = 28.11; 7.3, 7.12, and 16.9 = 28.11 (companion use of *urere* and *lacerare*). A. Becker, *Philologus* 61 N. F. 15 (1902) 476–78.

[109] On the Bacchanalia compare *De errore* 6.9 with Livy 39.14f. Here Firmicus referred to his source by saying *sicut in libris annalibus invenimus;* Heuten at once thought of Labeo, but others will agree with Pastorino (*ad loc.*) that Firmicus was capable of going directly to Livy, with whom the *Mathesis* shows some acquaintance (Moore 40ff.). Ziegler in his critical apparatus (Teubner) calls favorable attention to an emendation proposed in

1651 by Gronovius, but never adopted by any editor: *in Livii annalibus.*

[110] Plotinus: *Math.* 1.7.14–22; Porphyry: *ibid.* 7.1.1.

[111] Franz Boll, *Sphaera* (Leipzig 1903) 7.2; Christ-Schmid 2.853.

[112] 26.2, based on Porph. *De abst.* 2.56.

[113] Fr. Zucker, "Euhemeros und seine Ἱερὰ ἀναγραφή bei den christlichen Schriftstellern," *Philologus* 18 (1905) 465–72. Zucker's view was promptly supported by F. Jacoby, "Euemeros," RE 6 (1909) 955.

[114] L. M. Prindle, *Quaestiones de libello quem Iulius Firmicus Maternus scripsit de errore profanarum religionum* (unpub. diss. Harvard 1922) Ch. 2, p. 3.

[115] *FGrHist* 63 F25, from Lactantius, *Div. inst.* 1.17.10.

[116] W. Kroll, BphW 17 (1897) 1480, rejected Moore's contention (p. 31) that Firmicus might have read Ennius' version of Euhemerus. Moore's dissertation, though famed for its proof that there was only one Firmicus, is unsatisfactory in its discussion of sources. J. W. Schippers, *De ontwikkeling der Euhemeristische Godencritiek in de Christelijke Latijnse literatuur* (Groningen 1952) 89, lists eight arguments for believing that Firmicus did not directly use Euhemerus.

[117] J.-R. Laurin, *Orientations maîtresses des apologistes chrétiens* (Rome 1954) 444.

[118] B. Dombart, "Über die Bedeutung Commodians für die Textkritik der Testimonia Cyprians," *Zeitschr. f. wiss. Theol.* 22 (1879) 374–89. The two treatises which Firmicus used are the *Testimonia* and *Ad Fortunatum.*

[119] E. J. Martin, "The Biblical Text of Firmicus Maternus," *Journal of Theological Studies* 24 (1922–23) 318–25, discussed closely the citations which diverge in wording from Cyprian's version. He held that they indicated the use by Firmicus of a Spanish text of the Old Testament—a text concerning which only sketchy information is available. On this shaky platform he rested the hazardous view that Firmicus spent the Christian portion of his life in Spain. This ill-founded view was rejected by Heuten (6 n. 3) and Ziegler (1953 ed., 19). Dom B. Capelle, *Revue bénédictine* 36 (1924): *Bull. d'anc. litt. chrét. lat.*, p. [114] no. 237, reviewed Martin's article with corroboration of the

Spanish nature of the OT codex used by Firmicus, but said this merely pointed to a Spanish scribe for the codex, not necessarily to a Spanish residence for Firmicus.

[120] Teubner ed., 84, "Index scriptorum."

[121] Festugière, REG 52 (1939) 643: "Le *de err. pr. rel.* est un méchant ouvrage, plein de lieux communs de l'apologétique (culte des éléments, mythes scandaleux des dieux, etc.)." Geffcken, *Zwei griechische Apologeten* (Leipzig 1907) 317: "Er hat im wesentlichen die alten Gemeinplätze von der Göttern wiederholt."

[122] The three parallel passages are: 2 (Min. Fel. 22.1), on Isis; 12.8 (Min. Fel. 22.7, 23.3–7, 30.3), on misbehavior or humiliation of the gods; 14.3 (Min. Fel. 25.10), attack on the vestal virgins. The interesting verbal parallels occur only in 12.8, but this is just the passage where Kroll denies that the more ample Firmicus has borrowed from the less informative Minucius: BphW 17 (1897) 1480.

[123] Clem. Al., *Protr.* 4.58.4; *De err.* 12.7.

[124] *Op. cit.* 2.28.2. Boll, RE 6 (1909) 2379, and Pastorino, on *De err.* 16.1, agree that Clement (rather than Cicero, Arnobius, or Ampelius) is the most likely source. Pastorino presents a table of parallel passages and a review of scholarly opinions about them.

[125] *Op. cit.* 2.16.3. Firmicus gives a slightly different word order.

[126] Cinyras: Clem. Al., *Protr.* 2.13.4, and 2.14.2, cf. Firm. 10.1. Sebazius: *ibid.* 2.16.2, cf. Firm. 10.1. Divine pederasty: *ibid.* 2.33.5, cf. Firm. 12.2 (the same five instances in each author). Loves of Poseidon: *ibid.* 2.33.2 (seven women), cf. Firm. 12.3 (five women, all from the list in Clement). Dionysus and Prosymnus: *ibid.* 2.34.3–4, cf. Firm. 12.4 (the story is elsewhere recorded only in Arnob. 5.28).

[127] Actually Arnobius used *summitas* five times: 1.25, 2.19, 3.28, 3.31, and 7.36 (Ziegler noted only the first and last of these passages). The word is exceedingly rare before the fourth century: Cens. 13.5, Tert., *Adv. Valent.* 23. Heuten and Pastorino have retained the word in their editions of Firmicus, but Ziegler in his second edition has substituted *insanitatem* (following Oehler).

[128] C. Brakman, *Miscella tertia* (Leyden 1917) 25–28: "Quae ratio intercedat inter Firmicum Maternum et Arnobium."

[129] F. Gabarrou, *Le latin d'Arnobe* (Paris 1921) 102.

[130] Cf. below, p. 36.

[131] G. E. McCracken, *op. cit.*, ACW 7, 52.

[132] John Lawson, *The Biblical Theology of Saint Irenaeus* (London 1948) 30.

[133] A. Vecchi, "Giulio Firmico Materno e la 'Lettera agli Ebrei,' " *Convivium* 25 (1957) 641–51, at 650 n. 1. W. S. Reilly, S.S., "L'Inspiration de l'Ancien Testament chez saint Irénée," *Rev. bibl.* 26 (1917) 489–507, states that Irenaeus, Justin, and some other early writers exaggerated the role of the Holy Spirit in composing the Old Testament, but the Church has never condemned their theory of verbal dictation.

[134] Cumont, "La polémique de l'Ambrosiaster contre les païens," RHLR 8 (1903) 417–40, offered hints of this influence but did not dwell upon it. Heuten, Appendix 1, pp. 191–93, presented a table of comparisons, all from *Quaestiones* 82, 88, and 114; the points of contact are data on the cult of the elements, Anubis, and the Galli, and certain phrases which are repeated word for word.

[135] 12.2 and 12.8.

[136] Cumont (187, E. T. 203): "The Christian polemics, therefore, frequently give us an inadequate idea of paganism in its decline. When they complacently insisted upon the immorality of the sacred legends, they ignored the fact that the gods and heroes of mythology had no longer any but a purely literary existence."

[137] Christ-Schmid 2.1.232f., on the neglect and disrepute of euhemerism in this period.

[138] 18.1, with Pastorino's digest of many discussions of the passage.

[139] 19.3. P. J. Morris, in *A Catholic Commentary on Holy Scripture* (London 1953) 656, does not see any allegory in Joel's reference to *sponsus*.

[140] Ziegler's Teubner edition, xxiii–xxxi; F. Groehl, *De syntaxi Firmiciana* (diss. Breslau 1918); Heuten 8–11, 195f. (with criticisms by Ernout, *Rev. de philol.* 12 [1938] 249); Pastorino xxxv–lxxvi.

[141] E. K. Rand, *Founders of the Middle Ages* (Cambridge 1928) 255.

[142] For Heuten (10) to call Firmicus a purist is an exaggeration: Pastorino xxxv.

[143] Heuten (195, Appendix 3 h-i) lists these words with errors:

the verb *adimplere* (4.2) is neither a neologism nor exclusively Christian; cf. *Thesaurus* or Pastorino's note; *collapsio* (20.1), a neologism, is not peculiar to Firmicus but reappears in another sense in a fifth-century anonymous treatise (ML 41.844). But *artuatim* (2.2; *Math.* 7.2.8) and *immaculare* with intensive *in-* (2.5, 16.4, plus six occurrences in *Math.*) are not found outside of Firmicus. Delete from Heuten's list of exclusively Christian words *incandido, intimo, parricidalis, spiritalis, vivifico.*

144 See Ziegler's Teubner edition, Index IV, *Syntactica*, for all the points in this paragraph.

145 Ziegler xxviii.

146 U. Moricca, *Storia della letteratura latina cristiana* 2.1 (Turin 1928) 60.

147 Schanz 4.1.134.

148 Pastorino li.

149 Christine Mohrmann, VC 3 (1949) 99.

150 L. H. Weijermans, *De genetivus inhaerentiae in het Latijn* (diss. Nijmegen 1949) 30f., 35ff. This treatise, exhaustive in its narrow subject, can serve to correct some misstatements about Firmicus. Moore (48), following the views of Wölfflin, held that the abundant use of the *genetivus inhaerentiae* was a mark of African Latin—flatly denied by Weijermans (61 and 108) and disproved by his statistics. C. Brakman, *Arnobiana* (Leiden 1917) 17f., declared that Firmicus learned the *genetivus inhaerentiae* from Arnobius; had he read Arnobius before he used the construction 161 times in the *Mathesis?*

151 Ernout (rev. of Heuten), *Rev. de philol.* 12 (1938) 244f.

152 Half a century after the MS. was rediscovered, Theodor Friedrich (*In Iulii Firmici Materni de errore profanarum religionum libellum quaestiones* [Bonn 1905] 5) examined it closely and declared that it could not have been the one that Flacius used; but Friedrich did not allow for the unmethodical madness of Flacius as an editor. Ziegler incontrovertibly recognized corrections on the MS. in the handwriting of Flacius.

153 Paul Lehmann, in a letter quoted by Ziegler (xii), suggested these as being probable methods of acquisition by Flacius.

154 Alfons Müller, *Überlieferung* 12f.

155 Serious flaws in Halm's edition had been discovered by F. Skutsch, RMP 60 (1905) 262–72. Dieterich, as he tried to make sense of Firmicus while preparing the first edition of his

Mithrasliturgie (1903), was so mystified by Halm's text that he concluded the MS. used by Flacius must not have been the one found by Bursian. Dieterich was led to make some excellent emendations, which he published in the dissertation of Friedrich, *In Iulii Firmici Materni libellum quaestiones* (Bonn 1905).

[156] A. Ernout, reviewing Heuten in *Rev. de philol.* 12 (1938) 244f. Similarly, A. F. Norman, reviewing Pastorino in *Class. Phil.* 53 (1958) 50, acclaimed Ziegler's "masterly exposition of the technique of textual criticism."

[157] "Ancora oggi il migliore," said Pastorino in 1956 (Prefazione vii).

TEXT

[1] We can only conjecture what introductory matter Firmicus wrote to occupy the opening two folios, which have been lost. Ziegler in his translation (6 n.) reasonably supposes that the brother-emperors Constantius and Constans were respectfully and ceremoniously addressed. Other possibilities (raised by Müller in his translation, p. 16): Firmicus' conversion to Christianity, references to his astrological writings, introduction of the topic of the four elements.

[2] Skutsch, ARW 13 (1910) 291–305, observed that even when Firmicus wrote on astrology, he already uttered Christian sentiments and quasi-Christian prayers. So we read in the *Mathesis* (3 prooem. 2) words that closely resemble those translated here: *et ita hominem artificio divinae fabricationis composuit (deus).*

[3] The eleven occurrences of *perditus* in the *De errore* all allude to the lost souls of the pagans, a concept that haunted Firmicus.

[4] Similar thought and language in *Math.* 7 prooem. 2: *Qui ad fabricationem omnium quattuor elementorum diversitate composita ex contrariis et repugnantibus cuncta perfecit.* Christian and pagan alike were willing to accept the Empedoclean doctrine of the four elements.

[5] The Latin word *error* appears twenty-two times in our treatise, once (17.1) in reference to the "wandering" of planets but elsewhere always designating the false beliefs to which the book's title alludes. The pagan error of worshiping one or more of the four elements (or "elements" in a wider sense to include sun, moon, and stars) was widely recognized and rebuked by Christian apologists: J. Geffcken, *Zwei griech. Apologeten* (Leipzig 1907) 49ff. Cf. Ambrosiaster, *Quaest. Vet. et Nov. Test.* 82 (p. 139.11 ed. Souter, CSEL): *Paganos elementa colere omnibus cognitum est;* other references in Cumont 298 n. 16–18. Against worshiping the spirits of these elements, which he calls τὰ στοιχεῖα τοῦ κόσμου, St. Paul warns the Galatians (4.3) and Colossians (2.8 and 20): Fr. Pfister, "Die στοιχεῖα τοῦ κόσμου in den Briefen des Apostels Paulus," *Philologus* 69 N.F. 23 (1910) 411–27.

[6] *Fabricatorem deum*, only here in the *De errore*, but four times in the *Math.: deus ille fabricator hominis* (3 prooem. 2),

fabricatorem mundi deum (7 prooem. 2), *fabricator hominis deus* (4.1.3), *fabricatorem nostrum deum* (8.1.3). Cf. Moore 9.

[7] Firmicus here uses *verbum* to represent the Johannine concept of the Logos; so most Latin versions of the Bible except the African, which used *sermo:* C. Mohrmann, VC 4 (1950) 206. Though he never employs the words *trinitas* and *persona*, Firmicus seems to allude to the Trinity both here and 25.1 (*Deus, id est filius dei*).

[8] *Aequata moderatione*, a pet expression, again in 20.6, but already used five times in the *Math.:* 2.10.3, 3.6.26, 5.2.14 (Ziegler's emend.), 5.7.4, 7.1.2.

[9] In systematic fashion Firmicus now begins four successive chapters with the names of the four nations which originated the worship of each of the four elements: Egyptians, water; Phrygians, earth; Syrians and Carthaginians, air; and Persians, fire. Firmicus is the first writer to associate in a systematic way four peoples and four great religions with the four elements. On the Egyptian worship of water Pastorino cites numerous Greek writers, e.g., Lucian, *Iupp. trag.* 42. That both Osiris and Isis were occasionally identified with water appears from the magical papyri: Preisendanz, *Pap. graec. mag.* 2.12.234 and 4.2982. The lost words at the beginning of Ch. 2 may actually have voiced the thought supplied by Flacius in the *editio princeps*, that the reason why the Egyptians worshiped water is that they reaped endless benefits from the Nile: so Ziegler and Pastorino.

[10] Firmicus errs. All other sources represent Osiris as both brother and husband of Isis, while Typhon married his sister Nephthys; cf. Plut., *De Iside et Osiride* 12. The adultery, according to Plutarch (*ibid.* 14), took place when Osiris mated with Nephthys under the mistaken impression that she was his wife Isis. On Osiris in general, see W. Helck, "Osiris," RE Suppl. 9 (1962) 469–513.

[11] *Occidit.* Though this verb is conjoined with *lacerare* here and 7.7, Firmicus did not intend it to be a colorful synonym of *interficere*. Postclassical Latin prefers *occidere* in vulgar usage, reserving *interficere* for an elevated style. The *Itinerarium* of Egeria shows only *occidere*. In the *De errore* we find ten examples of *occidere*, none of *interficere* except in four biblical quotations. Cf. E. Löfstedt, *Phil. Komm. zur Peregr.* 256f.

[12] The adverb *artuatim* is a neologism of Firmicus, already used

in *Math.* 7.2.8; derived from *artuare*, a neologism in *Math.* 6.31.75.

[13] No other source states that the dismembered body of Osiris was scattered over the banks of the Nile. Firmicus wished to lead up to his claim (2.5) that this fratricide polluted the Nile water, by contrast with baptismal water: cf. Heuten 133.

[14] Pagan Romans and Christians alike looked with some disfavor on the *latrator Anubis* (Verg., *Aen.* 8. 698), *Anubis canina cum facie* (Arnob. 6.25), whose head was really that of a jackal, not of a dog. See H. Herter, "Anubis," RAC 1 (1950) 480–84.

[15] *Invenit.* The verb *reperire* loses favor in late Latin. The *De errore* has forty examples of *invenire*, none of *reperire*. Cf. E. Löfstedt, *Phil. Komm. zur Peregr.* 234.

[16] Of the contradictory versions reported by Plutarch (*De Iside et Osiride* 18 and 20) that Isis 1) buried the members separately in many different places and 2) reassembled and then buried the body, Firmicus follows the latter.

[17] Firmicus now commences his euhemeristic interpretation of pagan deities. Euhemerism was particularly easy of application to a country which held its Pharaohs divine. Osiris in Egyptian bas-reliefs appears as a king; among the dead he reigned as king; and his resurrection at the climax of his festival was that of a dead king. Some modern religionists believe that in reality Osiris was, as Firmicus says, an actual Pharaoh: J. Vandier, *La rel. égypt.* (Paris 1944) 43.

[18] In Egypt the cult of Set (Typhon) lost favor from the time of the XXII dynasty, and Set's reputation suffered by comparison with Osiris: see J. Garnot, *La vie relig. dans l'anc. Égypte* (Paris 1948) 20–24.

[19] The annual festival called the *Inventio Osiridis*, described in this and the following sentence, took place from Nov. 1 to 14: see N. Turchi, *Le relig. misteriche del mondo antico* (Milan 1948) 65.

[20] For reasons of ritual cleanness (not as a sign of mourning, as Firmicus states) the priests of Isis were required to shave their heads, and sometimes the lay worshipers did so by choice, e.g., the emperor Commodus, *Script. hist. Aug., Comm.* 9.4. See Th. Hopfner, *Plutarch über Isis und Osiris* (Prague 1941) 2.62f.

[21] Min. Fel. 22.1: *Isiaci miseri caedunt pectora;* other references in Pastorino. Here Firmicus is trying to write with strong effects

of alliteration and assonance: *dehonestati defleant . . ., lacerant lacertos, veterum vulnerum,* etc.

[22] Min. Fel. 22.1: *Mox invento parvulo gaudet Isis, exultant sacerdotes.*

[23] Cf. the similar phrase *fragilis et caduca mortalitas,* reproduced verbatim in 28.2 from *Math.* 1.7.4. Cicero in his philosophical writings rather often used *caducus* in the sense of "perishable, ephemeral"; Firmicus the Ciceronian used the word six times in the *De errore,* always in this sense. *Caducus* was a favorite word also of Arnobius (McCracken, ACW 8.562, n. 168), a writer whom Firmicus probably read. *Mortalitas* as a substitute for *mortales* is frequent in Christian Latin, with the usual fondness for the abstract instead of the concrete: Leumann-Hofmann 792; Blaise-Chirat, *s.v.*

[24] Firmicus' favorite epithet for *deus* is *summus:* twenty-two times in the *De errore,* occasionally also in the *Mathesis.* The *De errore* shows only three occurrences of *summus* not attached to *deus.* Arnobius, in his much longer work against paganism, has *deus summus* only twice, 4.36 and 7.35.

[25] The proverbial correlation of hope and life is known from Cicero, *Att.* 9.10.3: *dum anima est spes esse dicitur.*

[26] Pastorino reviews several variant interpretations of the "light" and concludes that it means "baptism." More persuasive is the view of Italo Lana in his learned review of Pastorino, *Riv. fil.* 36 (1958) 206f., that *lumen* refers to Christ as the Light of the World. In 19.1 we read: *Unum lumen est, unus est sponsus: nominum horum gratiam Christus accepit;* and in the following sentence of the same passage the words *luminis splendore* (repeated exactly from here) are seen by the context to refer to Christ. In 19.2 *splendor luminis* occurs for the third time, followed at once by Christ's words, *Ego sum lux mundi* (John 8.12). Firmicus means that the pagan worshipers of Isis are unwilling to be converted, even though the Light, i.e., Christ in human form, is displayed before them.

[27] The following attack on the worship of Isis and Serapis seemed imperative to Firmicus because these Egyptian deities had long since become firmly entrenched in Rome and the West, where they were worshiped continuously for five centuries, even for a few decades after Firmicus wrote. See Cumont 79f.; Min.

Fel. 22.2: *Haec Aegyptia quondam nunc et sacra Romana sunt.*

[28] The water of baptism; see John 3.5.

[29] The allusion is to the sun's partially drying up the Nile when it is not in flood: see F. J. Dölger, "Nilwasser und Taufwasser," AC 5 (1936) 153–87, at 165f.

[30] Osiris.

[31] The verb *immaculare* with intensive *in-* occurs nowhere outside of Firmicus (2.5, 16.4, and in six passages of the *Math.*).

[32] *Illam (aquam) ignita.* John the Baptist baptized with water, but prophesied that the coming baptism would be *in Spiritu sancto et igni* (Matt. 3.11, Luke 3.16). Firmicus is trying to say that Nile water, used in Isiac worship, is nothing more than plain, natural water; but baptismal water contains the potency of fire and the Holy Spirit, as John prophesied. Such is the interpretation of this vexed passage by J. B. Bauer, *Wiener Studien* 71 (1958) 153f., and Festugière, REG 52 (1939) 643f. Most of the other interpretations are listed and discussed by Pastorino. T. Wikström, *Eranos* 53 (1955) 173–75, proposed the reading *ignotam* in the sense of "petty, low, worthless." Preferable is *ignita*, nominative: so Festugière, *loc. cit.*, and F. Chatillon, *Mélanges Andrieu* (1956) 97–99.

[33] *Venerandi spiritus maiestate decoratur.* Firmicus liked to repeat a resonant phrase of his own invention, and in 23.3 we find *venerandi nominis maiestate decoratur.* Bauer (see previous note) holds that *maiestas* in Firmicus frequently means "power, potency," as in 13.4, where it has the antonym *infirmitas.*

[34] The tomb of Osiris was claimed by Busiris, Memphis, Abydos, Philae, and Taphosiris: Plut., *De Iside et Osiride* 20f.

[35] A cremation of Osiris is unknown in Egyptian tradition; Firmicus is here making an unfounded statement, as suggested by H. J. Rose, *Class. Rev.* 71 (1957) 234.

[36] *Physica ratio,* Cicero's Latinization of λόγος φυσικός. Since Firmicus was a student of Cicero's *De natura deorum,* it may be inferred that he learned the phrase there from one or more of its five occurrences: 2.23, 2.54, 2.63, 2.64, 3.92. The first philosophic school to give a physical interpretation of the gods was the Stoa: M. P. Nilsson, *Harv. Theol. Rev.* 36 (1943) 257f. The Ciceronian Lactantius attributes the method of *physica ratio* exclusively to the Stoics: *Inst. div.* 1.12.3. But the Neoplatonists also adopted the method, and Firmicus was thinking of them as

much as of the Stoics. He parrots the phrase with mockery in 2.7, 3.2, 3.4 (bis), and 7.8; and by capitalization the translator has sought to draw attention to the mockery. Augustine, *De civ. Dei* 4.11, carried on the disparagement of the *physica ratio*.

[37] Ad. Erman, *Die Religion der Ägypter* (Berlin-Leipzig 1934) 40.

[38] Chiefly a Greco-Roman rather than an Egyptian equation. Serv., *Ad Aen.* 8.696: *Isis autem lingua Aegyptiorum est Terra, quam Isim volunt esse.* This may be based on a Stoic etymology, deriving Isis from Egyptian *is-t*, "place."

[39] An equivalence corroborated by Plut., *De Iside et Osiride* 33, and Sallustius, *De diis* 4. But Typhon-Set was reputed to be maleficent, representing the torrid and damaging desert-heat; thus Firmicus in the following sentence errs in attributing to him the beneficial warmth that makes crops grow and mature.

[40] Indignation at the many instances of incest and adultery in the record of the pagan deities was a stock theme of Christian apologists. The indignation rings true in Firmicus, who had a high moral code even when he wrote the *Mathesis*.

[41] *Erecta sermonis libertate.* Cf. Min. Fel. 37.1: *Christianus . . . libertatem suam adversus reges et principes erigit.* The apologists are glorifying Christian παρρησία.

[42] The two Greek words were shouted by the worshipers as the culmination of the *Inventio Osiridis:* Cumont 90f. In Rome the culminating day was Nov. 14, a festival called the *Hilaria.* Juv. 8.29f.: *Exclamare libet populus quod clamat Osiri invento* (the scholiast on this passage cites the two Greek words). The two liturgical words appear also in Seneca, *Apoc.* 13.4 (with the second verb altered to the subjunctive), and Athenagoras, *Suppl.* 22. All the references are collected by A. Dieterich, *Eine Mithrasliturgie* (3rd ed. Leipzig 1923) Anhang, no. 11. That Greek was the liturgical language of the foreign cults in Rome is clear from inscriptions, from several passages in Firmicus, and from Dieterich's "Reste antiker Liturgien," *op. cit.,* Anhang.

[43] This city, really a temple-state, was the chief seat of the worship of Cybele: copious references in David Magie, *Roman Rule in Asia Minor* (Princeton 1950) 2.769f. Strabo, 12.3.7, p. 543, states that it is near the Sangarius River and its small tributary the Gallus. The name of the latter is unrelated to the Galli, the priests of Cybele.

[44] Firmicus nowhere names Cybele. She was worshiped as the source of life, the goddess of Nature, therefore easily identifiable as Terra Mater or the Great Mother of everything. Well known is the episode of Rome's reception of her cult, symbolized by a black meteoric stone, in 204 B.C.: Livy 29.10 and 14.

[45] The familiar Roman festival called the Megalesia.

[46] That Cybele was a wealthy woman and queen of Pessinus is a tendencious euhemeristic interpretation, unattested outside of Firmicus. There are many versions of the Cybele-Attis story, collected by A. Rapp in LM 1.715–8. Firmicus' version of the love affair is most nearly paralleled in Min. Fel. 22.4: "Adulterum suum infeliciter placitum, quoniam ipsa et deformis et vetula, ut multorum deorum mater, ad stuprum inlicere non poterat, exsecuit."

[47] The resurrection of Attis is unmentioned except by Firmicus: Nilsson, 2.649f. L. Deubner, *Gnomon* 4 (1928) 439f., thinks this late addition to the Attis story was an effort to make him rival Osiris and Adonis. M. J. Lagrange, *Rev. bibl.* 28 (1919) 449, repudiates any possibility that a resurrection cult of Attis, feebly attested by Firmicus in the fourth century, should have helped in the first century to make believable the resurrection of Christ.

[48] Temples strictly for Attis are unknown; but a Metroon, i.e., a temple honoring Cybele, might honor Attis also. In Rome a temple called the Phrygianum, honoring Cybele and Attis, was located almost in the spot where St. Peter's now stands: H. Graillot, *Le culte de Cybèle* (Paris 1912) 337.

[49] By contrast with Arnobius, Firmicus habitually speaks of delicate matters in delicate terms. In the ordination of the priests of Cybele, the so-called Galli, "la consécration suprême est l'éviration, véritable sacrement de l'ordre. On y voyait un symbole; elle figurait le mystère de la douleureuse Passion d'Attis" (Graillot, *op. cit.* 293).

[50] Firmicus' *pro iniuria spretae formae* is an obvious echo of Verg., *Aen.* 1.27: *spretaeque iniuria formae.*

[51] In honor of Attis a festival at the time of the vernal equinox was established in Rome by the emperor Claudius. The ceremonies, lasting from March 15 to 27, are described by Cumont 52–54. On the 24th the funeral of Attis was commemorated with self-inflicted flagellation and bloodshed on the part of the Galli.

[52] Again, as in 2.6, Firmicus introduces the *physica ratio* of the

Stoics and Neoplatonists. The naturalistic interpretation of the
Attis myth appears in the Neoplatonists Julian, *Or.* 5.161Cff., Sallustius 4 (cf. pp. l–lv in Nock's ed.), and Marinus, *Vita Procli*,
ch. 33.

[53] Frazer has a short chapter on Attis as a god of vegetation:
Golden Bough, Part 4 on "Adonis, Attis, Osiris."

[54] Similarly Minucius Felix (22.1) complains of the Oriental
cults and mysteries: *Invenies exitus tristes, fata et funera et luctus
atque planctus miserorum deorum.*

[55] Accepting Skutsch's addition of *aliud* to the text in the
second question, whereby each question will begin with the
identical words, *Itane non erat aliud quod.*

[56] The verb is *ululas*, repeated almost immediately in the noun
form *annuis ululatibus*. Cf. Claudian, *In Eutrop.* 2.302f.: *patriam
sacris ululatibus Attis personat.* During their frenzied dances the
Galli gave out savage shrieks and howlings: Graillot, *op. cit.* 124
and 302. Vergil and others use the verb to designate the howling
of wolves.

[57] Almost a verbatim quotation from 3.2; the *physica ratio*
again.

[58] *Novit agricola quando terram aratro dimoveat*, from Verg.,
Georg. 2.513: *Agricola incurvo terram dimovit aratro.* The other
parallels adduced by Ziegler, Lucr. 6.869 and Ovid, *Met.* 5.341,
are less close and less likely to have haunted Firmicus' mind.

[59] Firmicus' line of argument is that no symbolic interpretation
(*physica ratio*) should be attached to the death of Attis; the true
physica ratio declares that the death of Attis was the death of an
ordinary mortal, irrelevant to crops, vegetation, and the cycle
of the seasons. The laws of nature, governing the development of
the crops, were stabilized and not to be affected in the least by
Phrygian cult-usages. Cf. E. M. Pickman, *The Mind of Latin
Christendom* (Oxford 1937) 15.

[60] In the present context Firmicus is alluding to the black
meteoric stone, holy symbol of Cybele, which had been ceremoniously brought to Rome from Asia Minor in 204 B.C. (Livy
29.10 and 14), and to the cut pine, "wrapped like a corpse in
woolen bands and garlands of violets," which represented Attis
dead (Cumont 52). But the allusion is, of course, meant to be
understood also in a wider sense, as the usual Christian protest
against idolatry: cf. Arnob. 7.49–51 (against the black stone of

Cybele); Min. Fel. 24.6; Clem. Al., *Protr.* 4.46.1; Geffcken, *Zwei griech. Apologeten*, Index *s.v.* "Götterbilder."

⁶¹ To be rejected is Boll's view that Firmicus here alludes to the contemporary earthquakes of 344 and 345: see Introduction, p. 9.

⁶² The Roman confusion between Assyrians and Syrians was frequent, and naturally Firmicus meant the latter: Festugière, REG 52 (1939) 645.

⁶³ The Carthaginians and, in general, the Punic residents of North Africa.

⁶⁴ The etymological theory equating Ἥρα and ἀήρ by an anagram can be traced back to Empedocles (Diels, *Vorsokr.* 1.289 lines 17 and 36) and Plato (*Crat.* 404C), but was especially beloved by the Stoics: copious citations (including Arnob. 3.30) in Pease's ed. of Cic., *Nat. deor.* 2.66. The Ciceronian passage reads, in part: *Aer autem, ut Stoici disputant, interiectus inter mare et caelum Iunonis nomine consecratur.* The chief goddess of Carthage, called Tanit in the Punic language, was called Caelestis in Latin and early equated by the Romans with Juno Caelestis, who might be considered vaguely as a goddess of the air. See Cumont, "Caelestis," RE 3 (1899) 1247–50; Preisendanz, "Tanit," RE 4A (1932) 2178–2215; Gilbert Charles-Picard, *Les religions de l'Afrique antique* (Paris 1954) 105. The Carthaginian Tertullian (*Apol.* 23.6) speaks of *ista ipsa Virgo Caelestis pluviarum pollicitatrix*, and a North African inscription (CIL 8.16810) equates Juno with the air.

⁶⁵ Cumont (RE 3.1249) says that Tanit in Africa was a goddess of fertility, and as such was equated with Venus. A North African inscription (CIL 8.9796) is dedicated to the Great Virgin-Goddess Caelestis. Many writers held that there was more than one Venus, and that one Venus was a virgin. References in Pease's ed. of Cic., *Nat. deor.* 3.59, especially Aug., *De civ. Dei* 4.10: *An Veneres duae sunt, una virgo, altera mulier?*

⁶⁶ Ziegler's note (trans., 55): "Mit Iuppiter hat die Caelestis nichts zu tun. Die Beziehung zu ihm hat Firmicus, weil sie gelegentlich auch der Juno angeglichen wurde, willkürlich aus der griechisch-römischen Religion auf sie übertragen, um wieder ein incestum konstatieren zu können." Arnobius (3.30) commented on the tradition that Juno was the sister-spouse of Jupiter.

⁶⁷ Firmicus' words, *Effeminarunt sane hoc elementum*, are

modified from Cicero's *Effeminarunt autem eum Iunonique tribuerunt* (*Nat. deor.* 2.66). Cicero was referring to the masculine gender of the word *aer*.

[68] The MS. reads *nam*, accepted by Ziegler (Teubner ed., Addenda et Corrigenda, p. 120) because the combination *nam quia*, though most unusual, recurs at the beginning of a sentence in 13.2. Firmicus never uses the word *num* (Wower's emendation, adopted by Halm and by Ziegler in his 1953 ed.). Pastorino reads *nam*.

[69] *Aer interiectus est inter mare et caelum*, words unchanged from the Ciceronian model (*Nat. deor.* 2.66), *aer . . . interiectus inter mare et caelum.*

[70] Heuten rightly denies that *prosecuntur* can mean "invoke" (*anrufen*, Müller). The meaning "honor" is frequent in both classical and Christian Latin (Blaise-Chirat); Heuten needlessly introduces the idea of a cortege of priests.

[71] The priests of Tanit-Caelestis were not eunuchs, but the Galli of the Syrian goddess were: Lucian, *De dea Syria* 27; Cumont, "Syria Dea," DA 4 (1918) 1595. Firmicus has inaccurately attributed to Caelestis features of the worship of the Syrian goddess: so Pastorino and Festugière, REG 52 (1939) 645. Less likely is the view of Cumont and Graillot that Firmicus erroneously had in mind the Galli of Cybele.

[72] Attested for the Galli of the Syrian goddess by Lucian, *De dea Syria* 51.

[73] Immorality in the temples, with those of Isis in the lead, was common: L. Friedländer, *Sittengeschichte Roms* (10th ed., Leipzig 1922) 1.303f. Naturally this provoked Christian complaints: Min. Fel. 25.11, Tert., *Apol.* 15.7.

[74] *Muliebria pati*, an expression borrowed from Sallust, *Cat.* 13.3, and used again by Firmicus in 12.4 (and twice in the *Mathesis*). In Apuleius, *Met.* 8.24, a Gallus is called a *cinaedus*, and Cumont, "Gallos," RE 7 (1912) 675, cited two obscure Greek sources equating Galli with *cinaedi*. In his chapter of attack on paganism Ambrosiaster, imitator of Firmicus, complained of effeminacy and transvestitism in Oriental cults and used three times the phrase *muliebria pati: Quaest. Vet. et Nov. Test.* 114.7 and 11. Cf. Cumont, RHLR 8 (1903) 422f.

[75] A verbatim borrowing from Cic., *pro Flacco* 22.52: *gloriosa ostentatio.*

⁷⁶ *impuri et impudici*, from Cic., *Cat.* 2.23: *impuri impudicique;* the same synonymous pair appears four times in the *Mathesis.*

⁷⁷ The long hair of the Galli is mentioned by several writers, e.g., Apul., *Met.* 8.27.

⁷⁸ *Lassa cervice* is a phrase with a poetical ring and indeed appears in a poetical fragment of Maecenas, quoted by Seneca, *Ep.* 114.5; same phrase in prose, Sen., *De vita beata* 25.2; cf. *laxa cervice* in Pers. 1.98. But there is no probability that Firmicus had read these authors. Norden, *Ant. Kunstprosa* 1.294, interpreted the phrase in Maecenas as referring to the Galli, but most scholars have thought otherwise: cf. Beltrami on Sen., *Ep.* 114.5, and Lana, *Riv. fil.* 36 (1958) 209.

⁷⁹ Heuten (195) erroneously listed *adimpletus* as a word found only in Firmicus; Blaise-Chirat cites nineteen occurrences of the word, and there are more.

⁸⁰ Lucian, *De dea Syria* 43 and 50, mentions flute players among the regular ministers of the goddess.

⁸¹ Apuleius, *Met.* 8.28, speaks of *vaticinatio clamosa* by the ministers of the Syrian goddess; and prophecy was common among the sacred slaves (*hierodouloi*) of Asia Minor: Festugière, REG 52 (1939) 615.

⁸² *Monstrum prodigiumve:* a Ciceronian pair of synonyms, *Cat.* 2.1.1, *Verr.* 3.73.171, *Div.* 1.93.

⁸³ Eunuchism was condemned by the Mosaic law (Deut. 23.1), by Hermetic doctrine (*Corp. Hermet.* 2.17, interpreted by Festugière, *Harv. Theol. Rev.* 31 [1938] 13–20), and by Roman thought. A Roman legal decision held that *Genucius quidam, Matris Magnae gallus,* could not inherit property because he was neither man nor woman: Val. Max. 7.7.6.

⁸⁴ The MS. reads *summitatem*, retained by Ziegler (Teubner ed.), Heuten, and Pastorino, but variously emended by others in violation of the canons of paleographical probability. The word, though rare, appears in late pagan writers (refs. in Souter) and five times in a source of Firmicus, Arnobius (1.25, 2.19, 3.28, 3.31, 7.36). Tage Wikström, *Eranos* 53 (1955) 183 n. 1, defends *summitatem* (despite Ziegler's adoption of *insanitatem* in his 1953 ed.), saying that just as Firmicus employs *divinitas* for *deus* in 20.7, so here he is using *summitas* for his frequent expression *summus deus;* and in general Firmicus is prone to employ abstract substantives in a concrete sense: F. Groehl, *De syntaxi Firmici-*

ana (diss. Breslau 1918) 32f. and Wikström, *Studia in Firmicum Maternum critica* (diss. Uppsala 1935) 58ff.

[85] The word *paganus*, though known even before the fourth century, was never used by Firmicus. His phrase here, *profana mens*, reappears in 24.9. Souter warrants the translation "heathen" for *profanus*.

[86] Matt. 18.12, Luke 15.4.

[87] Luke 15.11–32.

[88] A parallel to this sentence, and perhaps its source, is Clem. Al., *Protr.* 5.65.1: Περσῶν δὲ οἱ Μάγοι τὸ πῦρ τετιμήκασι καὶ τῶν τὴν Ἀσίαν κατοικούντων πολλοί. Clement said that he was quoting from a book on Persia by Diogenes, thought by Jacoby (*F. Gr. Hist.* 692 F1) to be an otherwise unknown Diogenes of about the third century B.C.

[89] Firmicus does not mean that there was a feminine Mithra as well as a masculine one, but rather that fire is represented by two divine images, one of each sex. The feminine one is clearly the triform Hecate, who was often associated with Mithra and worshiped in the Mithraea: Festugière, REG 52 (1939) 646; M. J. Vermaseren, *Corpus inscr. et mon. rel. Mith.* (The Hague 1956) no. 992. But the connection of Hecate with fire is nil and that of Mithra tenuous. A scholium to Lucian (p. 60, ed. Rabe) identifies Mithra with Hephaestus, the fire god. A feminine Persian deity, Anahita or in Greek spelling Anaitis, was closely connected with the cult of fire and there was a fire temple wherever she was worshiped: Nilsson 1.647, citing the Iranist Wikander. Very likely Firmicus has transferred the fire worship of Anahita, who was little known in the West, to Mithra.

[90] Snakes in the Mithraea and on Mithraic monuments are attributes of the lion-headed god Zervan (Aion, Cronos): Vermaseren, *op. cit.* nos. 312, 326, 777 and other examples. Festugière, REG 52 (1939) 646, thinks Firmicus confused the triform Hecate and Zervan, or else Hecate symbolized Zervan. Cumont, *Textes et monuments figurés relatifs aux mystères de Mithra* 2 (Paris 1896) 14 n. 1, declared erroneous Firmicus' statement that there were snake-entwined representations of a female deity associated with Mithra. There were, however, as Cumont observed, such statues in other Oriental cults: Macrob., *Sat.* 1.17.67 (on the statue of the Sun at Hierapolis): *ante pedes imago feminea est, cuius dextra laevaque sunt signa feminarum, ea cingit flexuoso*

volumine draco. Cumont's attribution of error to Firmicus was partially combated by Ziegler, ARW 13 (1910) 263–69, followed by P. Alfaric, RHLR 7 (1921) 161f.

[91] Cumont, *Textes* 1.169–72. Commodian, *Instr.* 1.13 (cited in Cumont, *Textes* 2.9): *Vertebatque boves alienos semper in antris sicut et Cacus Vulcani filius ille.* The tradition "goes back to an age when to steal the live-stock of a neighboring tribe was a recognized feature of warfare, and when cattle-lifting was regarded not as a crime but as an honorable achievement not unbecoming even to a god" (Cumont, "St. George and Mithra, 'the Cattle-Thief,'" *Journ. Rom. Stud.* 27 [1937] 63–71, at 67).

[92] The passage was interpreted by Friedrich and Clemen (refs. in Pastorino's edition) to mean that Firmicus was an initiate. See the Introduction, pp. 6–7. But Prosper Alfaric, RHLR 7 (1921) 159f., observed that the designation *propheta* does not occur among the priests, ministers, and functionaries of Mithraism, and is more likely to have signified an inspired author rather than the servant of a cult. The "prophet" of Mithra, according to Alfaric, would undoubtedly be Zoroaster.

[93] Firmicus quotes a good Greek hexameter, an otherwise unknown liturgical formula of Mithraism. The liturgy of Mithra was considered to be Zoroastrian, and this hexameter is cited in the Greek tradition of Zoroaster by Bidez-Cumont, *Les mages hellénisés* (Paris 1938) 2.153, cf. 1.98. The initiate is saluted in the vocative. The nonsensical vocative ΣΥΝΛΕΞΙΕ in the MS. gave rise to sundry conjectures, clearly discussed by Ziegler in his 1953 edition, 25f. The reading συνδέξιε, paleographically attractive because of the easy confusion between lambda and delta in the capital forms, was suggested in the *editio princeps* by Flacius and finally confirmed to the satisfaction of all by Cumont in 1934: "Rapport sur une mission archéologique à Doura-Europos," *CR Acad. Inscr.* 1934, 90–111, at 107. In a Mithraeum excavated at Dura there appeared repeatedly, among over 250 legible graffiti, συνδεξίῳ ἀγαθῷ συνδεξίῳ. Cumont therefore concluded: "Συνδέξιος est dans la langue rituelle un synonyme de μύστης [et] désigne celui qui a été initié par la *iunctio dextrarum*, cette poignée de mains accompagnant déjà dans la Perse ancienne un engagement solennel." Cumont's solution of the old crux was immediately welcomed by F. J. Dölger, AC 5 (1936) 286f., and by all scholars subsequently. In 1949 corrobora-

tion, if needed, came from a new Mithraic inscription that mentions *syndexii*: B. Nogara and F. Magi, *Hommages à Joseph Bidez et à Franz Cumont* (Brussels 1949) 229–44, at 231. As for the "illustrious father," Cumont was able to clarify this also. Jerome, *Ep.* 107.2, names the seven degrees of initiation into Mithraism, culminating in *pater*. Of these seven degrees, six are found in the graffiti of the Mithraeum at Dura, including *pater*. The "illustrious father" acted as initiator, and by the ceremonial *iunctio dextrarum* received the novice as an "initiate of cattle-rustling."

⁹⁴ Zoroaster was said to have dedicated to Mithra in the Persian mountains a cave: Porph., *De antro nympharum* 5f. All known Mithraea are natural caves, artificial caves, or above-ground temples which are still called "caves" (*spelaea* or synonym): Cumont, *Textes* 1.55–58.

⁹⁵ The MS. reading is *vera*. Alfons Müller, *Zur Überlieferung der Apologie des Firmicus Maternus* (diss. Tübingen 1908) 81, claimed that he could read *mira*. Ziegler thereupon proceeded to re-examine the MS. and declared that *vera* is certain: BphW 29 (1909) 1196. Editors before Ziegler did not perceive the irony and were led to make unnecessary emendations. Pastorino (lxv) lists nine occurrences of irony in Firmicus, including this passage.

⁹⁶ To fill out a lacuna in the MS. Skutsch suggested [*sacra fieri*], which was adopted by Ziegler and Pastorino.

⁹⁷ Heuten *ad loc.* suggests the approximate argument of the two lost folios. "Since you are serving the Persian religion of Mithra, why don't you abandon all patriotism, stop defending your frontiers against the Persians, accept their military conquest, and become their slaves? . . . The principal ceremonies of Mithraism are as follows, to be philosophically interpreted as follows, and of course to be condemned. The male Mithra is described and interpreted as follows; now let us take up his female counterpart." The patriotic note, probably developed after the appeal to the "Roman name," is frequently sounded by Firmicus in both his books and is always sincere. Müller (*Überlieferung* 71) believes that the lost folios may have contained further discussion of fire worship and something about Plato's tripartite division of the soul.

⁹⁸ The MS. at this point (fol. 5r) is hardly legible and Ziegler did not succeed in reading it correctly. By extremely pains-

taking and lengthy study Alfons Müller (*Überlieferung* 69) was able to make out what Ziegler later, BphW 29 (1909) 1197, acknowledged to be right: *quae armata clypeo lorica tecta in arcis summae vertice consecratur.*—At this point Firmicus is explaining and attacking the *physica ratio* whereby the pagan intelligentsia, the Neoplatonists, sought to make Mithraism respectable. It was the Neoplatonists who interpreted the triform female counterpart of Mithra as symbolizing the tripartite division of the soul, a Pythagorean idea which had been embraced by Plato (*Rep.* 4.439). The three parts were νοῦς, θυμός, ἐπιθυμία = *mens, ira, libido* = reason, passion, and desire. Firmicus gives the anatomical location of each part of the soul and, astrologer-like, relates each part to a goddess who has a corresponding nature. Passion is in the head, and is equated with Athena-Minerva ("the goddess armed with a shield and protected by a cuirass"). Reason dwells in the heart, under the auspices of Artemis-Diana, goddess of the woodlands and the wild animals. Desire is in the liver, the seat of concupiscence, under the auspices of Aphrodite-Venus. The three goddesses were taken by the Neoplatonists to be a trinity corresponding to the triform goddess of Mithraism. Very likely Neoplatonism in the fourth century influenced Mithraic theology. —The whole passage of Firmicus was first correctly interpreted by Ziegler, "Zur neuplatonischer Theologie," ARW 13 (1910) 247–69 (summarized in the notes on his translation, p. 56). Cumont, ARW 9 (1906) 331 n. 1, mentions a triple division of the soul taught in the "Assyrian mysteries," and thinks Firmicus (ex-astrologer) knew of the Chaldean fondness for triads.

[99] Firmicus follows Cicero, *Tusc.* 1. 10.20, in employing *ira* to translate Plato's θυμός as one of the three parts of the soul.

[100] Ziegler, *op. cit.* 252, exclaims over Firmicus' naiveté and his strained comparison between the tangled and wild forests where Diana roams and the tangled forests of infinitely varied thoughts in the heart.

[101] One deplores the unwarranted disrepute of the liver as the dwelling place of concupiscence and wellspring of sin. Alas for Prometheus, of whom a sympathetic poet has written:

> Prometheus, bright fire-giver,
> Suffered horrors with his liver.

[102] The MS., still hardly legible, seems to read *perficit*, but possibly *perficiat* (Müller, *Überlieferung* 70). Ziegler reads

perficit and lists this (in his *Syntactica*, p. 120 of the Teubner ed.) with six other instances of indirect question employing the indicative in the *De errore*. Better is the proposal of Friedrich (20f.), independently put forward again by Wikström, *Eranos* 53 (1955) 175f., to punctuate thus: *Quid ergo perficit ista divisio?* In the following words, *Diligenter aspicite ut facile commentum ratio veritatis impugnet*, Wikström understands *ut* as interrogative (as in 12.5 *et alibi*) and *facile* as adverbial. (For *facile* Skutsch suggested *futile*, which Ziegler adopted in his 1953 ed.; but Wikström observes that Firmicus nowhere else uses the word.) The present translation adopts Wikström's suggestions.

[103] The MS., legible at this point, fails to make sense, though J. B. Bauer, *Wien. Stud.* 71 (1958) 154f., implausibly argued that *incipit esse quod fuerat* is right as it stands. Bauer later, *Eranos* 57 (1959) 73–75, retracted his view, since he had found in Tertullian (*adv. Prax.* 27.7) a passage which provides the wording that Firmicus was imitating: *Omne enim, quodcumque transfiguratur in aliud, desinit esse quod fuerat et incipit esse quod non erat*. Reversing the sequence of Tertullian's clauses, perhaps for the sake of a good clausula, Firmicus wrote: *incipit esse [quod non erat et desinit esse] quod fuerat*. This certain correction, followed in the present translation, is a striking corroboration of the emendation proposed by Skutsch, ARW 13 (1910) 305, which was praised by Ziegler (1953 ed., 26), Wikström, *loc. cit.*, and Ernout, *Rev. de philol.* 28 (1954) 308, and adopted by Pastorino. Carl Weyman had long ago (BphW 29 [1909] 778) noticed the same wording (*desinit esse quod fuerat*, etc.) in three authors who postdate Firmicus: Optat. Milev. 5.7, Maxim. Taurin., *Hom.* 14 (ML 57.251C), and Ruricius, *Ep.* 2.11.

[104] This passage, emended by Ziegler and most other editors, is considered sound by Bauer, *loc. cit.* The MS. reads *quae per tres contrarias separata dividitur*. Asserting that *contrarias* refers back to the immediately preceding *speciem formamve*, Bauer holds that no such noun as *partes* (Ziegler) or *naturas* (Kroll) needs to be inserted. Firmicus means that the soul cannot remain as an integer if it is distributed among three distinct species; the unity of the soul is lost if it is distributed among three unities which have nothing to do with each other (*contrarias*). Ziegler's emendation of *per* to *in* on the ground that *dividere per* occurs nowhere else was an error; Wikström, *loc. cit.*, pointed to

dividere per in 28.10, Suet., *Dom.* 9, and Tert., *Adv. Valent.* 29.1. Suetonius' *divisis per veteranos agris* shows that the phrase means not "to divide into" but "to distribute among."

[105] Firmicus hoped to confound the pagan philosophies by exposing their contradictions. The Neoplatonists, who were strongly entrenched in the century of Firmicus, asserted a firm belief in immortality (C. H. Moore, *Ancient Beliefs in the Immortality of the Soul* [New York 1931] 47); but Firmicus argues that if the soul is tripartite, then it is surely perishable by Plato's own doctrine that whatever is divisible is perishable. A similar refutation of the trichotomy of the soul appears in Tertullian, *De anima* 14 (erudite notes by Waszink). The Neoplatonist Porphyry in his lost treatise on the faculties of the soul tried to rescue the soul's unity by saying that its so-called parts were really only activities or faculties; such too was the argument of Tertullian.

[106] *Necesse est esse mortale;* the triple appearance of this exact phrase in Arnobius (7.3, 7.5, 7.28) lends force to the view that Firmicus read and imitated Arnobius.

[107] The deification of fire, with its ramified sequelae.

[108] *Anima [monstratur] esse mortalis:* so Ziegler in 1953, approved by Bauer, *Wien. Stud.* 71 (1958) 156. The last word on folio 5r of the MS. is faded beyond recognition, and students of the text have offered a wide variety of proposals, discussed by Ziegler (1953, p. 27), Pastorino, *ad loc.*, and Wikström, *Eranos* 53 (1955) 178f.

[109] In general the MS. of Firmicus has no scholia, but at this point (upper margin of 5v) it has *fulgentius de fabulis*. This seems a worthless bit of lore, since the only discoverable parallel in the fifth-century mythographer Fulgentius involves the erection of a statue of a dead son by his father Syrophanes, with religious worship of the statue, as by Jupiter in Section 4 below. See Fulgentius, 1.1 pp. 15–17 Helm (much better told in Mythogr. Vat. 3 prooem.) and cf. Heuten 153. Ziegler (Teubner ed., app. crit.) dismissed the reference as a false lead.

[110] Firmicus has now concluded his discussion of the worship of the four elements, as originated and promulgated by four Oriental nations. Christian polemic against stoichiolatry usually continued with an attack on the worship of the sun and moon (also considered to be "elements," in a sense: Cumont 189): so Aristides 6. Firmicus' source did likewise, but interposed the

identification of the sun with Liber and the moon with Libera-Proserpina (see 7.7 below). Firmicus elected to dwell first on other aspects of Liber-Libera, and thus turned aside from astral symbolism: Festugière, REG 52 (1939) 646. Launching into Greek mythology (*aliae superstitiones*), he commences with a euhemeristic version of the Orphic Dionysus-Zagreus story. His numerous divagations from other known versions of that story derive from his euhemeristic source. His attack is not directed at a dead horse, for the cult of Liber was alive in the West throughout the fourth century: A. Bruhl, *Liber Pater* (Paris 1953) 169f.; Ambrosiaster, *Quaest. Vet. et Nov. Test.* 114.12.

[111] The word, whose exact meaning is relative, is always pejorative in Roman usage. Any cult of a suspicious nature or disapproved by the State was a *superstitio*. It was regularly distinguished from *religio*, as in Cic., *Nat. deor.* 2.71. Christianity, stung at being called a *superstitio* by Tacitus (*Ann.* 15.44) and many others, now hastened to fling the epithet back at paganism (also in 12.1, 18.1, 20.1): de Labriolle in the Fliche-Martin *Histoire de l'église* 3 (Paris 1945) 178.

[112] The following account pertains to Dionysus, whose Greek name seldom appears in the Latin writers (passages in Pastorino). "The old Roman Liber antedates the period of divine filiation; the attempt to equate him with Dionysus . . . multiplies complexities" (so Pease on Cic., *Nat. deor.* 3.53). Libera is the Greek Core-Persephone.

[113] Ziegler in his 1953 edition, 27f., argues persuasively for a lacuna just before these words, wherein Firmicus would have given a longer list of divinized mortals.

[114] Cicero (*Nat. deor.* 3.53) declares that Liber was the son of the Arcadian, not the Cretan, Jupiter. Firmicus here does not follow Cicero; it may be conjectured that he follows his euhemeristic source. Cook (*Zeus* 1.662) thinks that Euhemerus founded his theory on Cretan tradition.

[115] Cic., *Nat. deor.* 3.58: *Dionysos multos habemus, primum Jove et Proserpina natum;* parallel passages cited by Pease. Firmicus loses no opportunity to level the charge of adultery against the false gods of the pagans.

[116] The wicked stepmother is well known in classical drama, literature, and folklore.

[117] The Curetes: Clem. Al., *Protr.* 2.17.2.

[118] The traditions concerning the kingship of Dionysus are not uniform: that he was a deputy king, or temporary king, or permanent king as successor to Zeus: H. Jeanmaire, *Dionysus* (Paris 1951) 411. That he was personally and permanently enthroned by Zeus is the statement of the Neoplatonist Proclus on Plat., *Crat.* 396B.

[119] The Titans as slayers of the child Dionysus appear already in Clem. Al., *Protr.* 2.17.2, from an Orphic source. To the myth of Dionysus "the Orphics added the Titans": W. K. C. Guthrie, *Orpheus and Greek Religion* (London 1935) 120.

[120] Clem. Al., *Protr.* 2.17.2–18.1, says that Dionysus was deceived by children's playthings, and mentions a mirror among the symbols of Orphic initiation. The mirror appears also in the parallel list given by Arnobius (5.19), but not the rattle. The Neoplatonists gave deep, wise, and allegorical interpretations of the mirror in this myth: Guthrie, *op. cit.* 122f.

[121] Clement and Arnobius in the passages just noted record the killing, dismembering, and cooking of Dionysus by the Titans; but Clement says and Arnobius implies that the cannibalistic act was forestalled by the early intervention of Zeus. Firmicus was drawing from a euhemeristic source, not from Clement.

[122] Other sources (Clement and Proclus, *Hymn to Athena* 11–13) do not state or hint that Athena was implicated in the crime, but praise her for rescuing the sacred heart of Dionysus.

[123] Only the euhemeristic version of the Dionysus myth, therefore Firmicus' version, knows of this statue; the Orphic accounts naturally speak of the resurrection of Dionysus. Euhemerus and his Christian adherents held that statues of dear ones, set up by their bereaved relatives to comfort themselves, became objects of worship and thus started cults. Cf. Min. Fel. 20.5: *Dum defunctos eos desiderant in imaginibus videre, dum gestiunt eorum memorias in statuis detinere, sacra facta sunt quae fuerant adsumpta solacia.* Heuten 155 and Prindle (unpub. diss., Ch. 2, pp. 5f.) call attention to the parallel story of the divinization of a grieving father's dead son in Sapientia, 14.15–20.

[124] Ordinarily a slave-tutor and protector. Horace (*A.P.* 239) has the line *custos famulusque dei Silenus alumni*. The bestial Silenus is replaced by the wise Silenus in the Villa Item and elsewhere at Pompeii: M. Rostovtzeff, *Mystic Italy* (N.Y. 1927) 75f. Only in the euhemeristic tradition does Silenus appear as a priest of Dionysus.

[125] The phrase *annuum sacrum trieterica consecratione* has given rise, partly by its verbal contradictoriness, to some puzzlement and to definite mistranslations. The Greek *trieterica* signifies "biennial" according to our method of reckoning, never "triennial" (Alfons Müller and Faggin mistranslate). But how could Firmicus call a festival both "annual" and "biennial"? I have followed Ziegler's loose translation of *annuum* as "recurrent." Cook (*Zeus* 1.662) thought there was an annual rite and a biennial celebration; somewhat similarly Heuten. Just below we have *annuis commemorationibus*. Full discussion in Pastorino. The festival of the Theban Dionysus was biennial: Macr., *Sat.* 1.18.15: *In hoc monte Parnasso Bacchanalia alternis annis aguntur.* Macrobius in this passage was drawing from about the same sources as Firmicus.

[126] Firmicus is our chief source on the Cretan mysteries of Dionysus, and his account is authentic: W. K. C. Guthrie, *Orpheus and Greek Religion* (London 1935) 111. Cumont (307 n. 26) notes the similarity to the Bacchanalia at Rome, if they are correctly described by Livy (39.8): at night, in secrecy, with howlings of sacred frenzy, with the disappearance of human bodies (due to omophagy, not suspected by Livy). Firmicus' phrase *vivum laniant dentibus taurum* is a mildly overstated reference to omophagy, corroborated by the "raw feasts" of Euripides' *Cretans* (frag. 472 Nauck). Earlier doubts as to whether the Dionysiac mysteries included omophagy were dispelled when an inscriptional record thereof was published by Th. Wiegand, "Sechster Bericht über die Ausgrabungen in Milet," *Abh. Akad. Berlin*, Anhang, 1908, 22f.; cf. Nilsson 1.572f. The identification of Dionysus with a bull, even outside of Crete, is frequent: H. Jeanmaire, *Dionysos* (Paris 1951) 386.

[127] The *cista mystica* (pictured e.g., in Cumont Pl. 16.1) was a cylindrical woven basket with a cover, concealing sacred objects. Familiar in several mystery religions, but most of all in that of Dionysus, it was carried in processions and festivals by *cistophori*. See F. Lenormant, "Cista mystica," DA 1.1205–8, esp. 1206b.

[128] The *tibia Bacchica* was highly important for helping to awaken the Dionysiac frenzy: Th. Reinach, "Tibia," DA 5.300–332 at 321b. The cymbal served the same purpose, and appears in art among other attributes of Dionysiac worship: E. Pottier, "Cymbalum," DA 1.1697f. with fig. 2267.

[129] The Theban Dionysus postdates the Theban cycle of the Seven and Oedipus: Jeanmaire, *Dionysos* 339. He was reputed to be the grandson of Cadmus, king of Thebes, and son of Semele by Zeus.

[130] The best commentary would be a re-reading of Euripides' *Bacchae;* it is just possible that Firmicus knew the play, more likely that he simply knew the myth embodied in the play. The Thracian Lycurgus does not belong to the myth of the Theban Dionysus; deliberately or mistakenly Firmicus has substituted Lycurgus for Pentheus. The story of Pentheus he surely knew from Ovid, if not from Euripides; Heuten has shown the verbal parallels, individually slight but collectively persuasive, between our passage and *Met.* 3.522–63. Since Firmicus mentions stage presentations of the myth, Heuten was led to think of the *Lycurgeia* of Aeschylus. Ziegler's comment on this (notes to his translation, p. 56): "That Firmicus should have seen a presentation of the *Lycurgeia* of Aeschylus on the stage (as Heuten 157 seems to think) is quite improbable. At most it could be a case of a pantomime, or else Firmicus borrows the sentence from a much earlier source, of the time when Aeschylean dramas were still being staged."

[131] *Tragici carminis auctoribus:* so the MS. and all editors until Ziegler in 1953, followed by Pastorino, decided that he had been wrong in 1907 (Teubner ed.) and argued for *actoribus* (pantomimic actors), as Livy, 7.2.8, called Livius Andronicus *suorum carminum actor.* But Wikström, *Eranos* 53 (1955) 179f., observed that Firmicus might have remembered the phrase *carminis auctor* from Horace, *A.P.* 45; and in any case his word for a stage actor is *histrio* in 12.9, *scaenicus* in the *Math.*, never *actor.* From all Christian Latin Blaise-Chirat cites no occurrence of *actor* to mean "stage actor."

[132] All the mythological sources known to us declare that Dionysus triumphed and Lycurgus was the loser; in the Homeric passage partly cited below by Firmicus, the child Dionysus was temporarily discomfited, but Lycurgus was stricken blind as a penalty. As Section 9 shows, Firmicus reversed the identity of victor and vanquished because he desired to give a Greek parallel to the Roman Senate's enactment against the Bacchanalia: King Lycurgus triumphed over Dionysus, and in a later day the glorious

Roman consul Postumius did the same. Implied moral of the tale: Constans and Constantius, go ye and do likewise.

[133] This kind of reproach had always been effective with Roman readers, and Firmicus is leading up to a patriotic appeal; note the emphatic repetition of *virorum* in two successive sentences. The effeminate appearance of Dionysus was mentioned by Euripides (*Bacch.* 353), Arnobius (6.12), and others, and often is manifest in art: e.g. Michelangelo's *Bacchus* in the Bargello, Florence.

[134] Text and translation of this sentence are disputed. Kroll took *effeminatum cenatum* to be corrupt by dittography, emended *cenatum* to *cinaedum* (a word of frequent use in the *Math.*), and dropped *effeminatum* as a gloss. Ziegler (1953) and Pastorino have adopted Kroll's reading; so the present translation. Faggin, followed by Pastorino, took *Graecorum gymnasiis* with *amatorum servisse libidinibus;* Alfons Müller, Heuten, and Ziegler took it with *decantatur.* Faggin's version is defensible, since the Greek gymnasia were in truth not blameless in regard to pederasty: see W. Kroll, "Knabenliebe," RE 11 (1921) 897–906, at 901. But the word order favors the other interpretation, equally possible since the gymnasia were in effect clubhouses where conversation and gossip flowed freely: see Forbes, "Expanded Uses of the Greek Gymnasium," *Class. Phil.* 40 (1945) 32–42, at 42. The meaning of *decantatur* was misapprehended by Heuten ("on chante"), but its pejorative sense, known to Firmicus from Cicero, recurs in 12.9 and *Math.* 3.5.3; Blaise-Chirat correctly defines the word here as "répandre le bruit que."

[135] Vine leaves are entwined on Dionysus' wand in Ov., *Met.* 3.666.

[136] Borrowed unchanged from Verg., *Aen.* 4.215: *cum semiviro comitatu.*

[137] Maenads and Sileni were the customary retinue of Dionysus. Bacchic inebriety created intimations of an immortality of sensual bliss: Cumont, *Lux perpetua* (Paris 1949) 255f.

[138] The Bacchic procession, called *thiasos* in Greek. Representations of the *thiasos* on sarcophagi are reproduced in A. Bruhl, *Liber pater* (Paris 1953) pl. 25–26, after p. 254.

[139] Bacchants wreathed with snakes are mentioned by Clem. Al., *Protr.* 2.12.2, and Arnob. 5.19. The snakes symbolized the earth and fertility.

¹⁴⁰ Arnob. 5.19 describes the Dionysiac Omophagia, wherein the worshipers *cruentatis oribus* (*cruentus ore*, Firmicus) tore the flesh of bleating goats. Cf. Jeanmaire, *Dionysos* 254–57.

¹⁴¹ The adjective *lacer* is mostly though not wholly a poetical word, and is not found elsewhere in the writings of Firmicus. Heuten seems right in holding that Firmicus adopted the word from Ovid's account of the mangling of Pentheus, *Met.* 3.522.

¹⁴² *Iliad* 6.135–7, quoted in Greek by Firmicus.

¹⁴³ Spurius Postumius Albinus, consul of Rome in 186 B.C.

¹⁴⁴ For the MS. reading *in libris annalibus* Gronovius suggested already in the seventeenth century *in Livii annalibus*. Editors (Ziegler, Pastorino) commend but do not adopt this reading; they note that passages of the *Mathesis* show knowledge of Livy (Moore 40ff.) and that the present passage is straight from Livy, 39.8–19 (the well-known account of the suppression of the Bacchanalia in Rome in 186 B.C.). Pastorino lists verbal reminiscences of Livy, such as *mente captas* (Sect. 6) from *mente capta* (Liv. 39.13), *stuprorum et flagitiorum* (Sect. 7; each word appearing nowhere else in the *De errore* except once in Ch. 12) from *stuprum flagitiumve* (39.14), and *quaestio* (Sect. 9, nowhere else in Firmicus) from *quaestio* (bis in 39.14). Heuten, as usual, says that the source is Cornelius Labeo rather than Livy; this is to fly in the face of the obvious.

¹⁴⁵ Firmicus' words are probably, as Skutsch thought, an echo of an oft-quoted passage of Cicero (*Cat.* 1.3): *Non deest rei publicae consilium neque auctoritas huius ordinis: nos, nos, dico aperte, consules desumus.*

¹⁴⁶ Firmicus' patriotism and his pride in Roman history were sincere. His approval of severe measures actually taken against a pagan cult by the Roman Republic foreshadows his appeal to Constans and Constantius for the ruthless repression by the State of all pagan cults. Cf. L. M. Prindle (unpub. diss.) 3 and Pastorino's note.

¹⁴⁷ Livy (39.18) says that initiates who had abstained from criminal activities were simply imprisoned, but these were the minority: *plures necati quam in vincula coniecti sunt.* Firmicus for his purposes wished to give a drastic statement of what was done. By good fortune the *Senatus consultum de Bacchanalibus* is preserved, on a bronze tablet now housed in the Kunsthistorisches Museum of Vienna; its text is widely known and often

published, e.g. in Riccobono, *Fontes iuris Romani antejustiniani: Leges* (2nd ed. Florence 1941) 240f. no. 30.

[148] The corrupt *Romani nomini* of the MS. was emended by Flacius to *Romano nomine*, by Bursian (followed by Halm and Ziegler) to *Romani nominis*. Firmicus always, even in the *Mathesis*, uses *dignus* with the ablative, and in 5.2 has a duplicate of the phrase used here, *Romano nomine dignum*. The ablative should be read, as it is by Pastorino.

[149] The euhemeristic interpretation again; Arnobius (1.36) also says, following Cicero, that Ceres was a native of Sicily. Ceres is equated with the Greek Demeter. The luxuriant fertility of Sicily caused the islanders to make the goddess of grain and her daughter their chief divinities, and later they claimed that the Demeter cult originated in Sicily. The cult flourished in all the major Greek cities of the island (Leo Bloch, "Kora," LM 2.1309–11) and especially in Henna (Enna). Worth quoting is Wilamowitz, *Der Glaube der Hellenen* (reprinted Basel 1956) 2.381 n. 2: "Ever since Callimachus had introduced into poetry the originally barbarian Demeter of Henna, the rape of Persephone was localized in Sicily and Demeter began her wanderings there. To the Romans Henna was closer than Eleusis." Firmicus here states that Ceres initiated the cult of her daughter; but he contradicts himself in 7.4, saying that the people of Henna of their own accord established the cult of Proserpina. Cf. Prindle (unpub. diss.) Ch. 2, p. 8.

[150] This etymology should be commended as one of the few correct ones in the *De errore*.

[151] A small lake, with no outlet, near Henna; now called Pergusa.

[152] *Amoenitas*, just preceded by the adjective *amoenus*. The *locus amoenus* was a rhetorical *topos*, which "from the Empire to the sixteenth century forms the principal motif of all nature description": E. R. Curtius, *European Literature and the Latin Middle Ages* (New York 1953) 195. While Firmicus, as a Sicilian, may have been personally acquainted with the beauties of Henna and Percus, there is no doubt that the following description is based less on a sightseer's recollections than on the embroidered accounts in Ovid (*Fasti* 4.437–51, *Met.* 5.390–413) and Cicero (*Verr.* 4.48.107). See the detailed table of parallels in Heuten, Appendix 2, p. 194.

[153] The poetical and rhetorical flavor of the passage is heightened by the triple anaphora of *illic*.

[154] *Albae hederae*, from Verg., *Ecl.* 7.38: *hedera alba*.

[155] *Suaviter rubens amaracus*, from Verg., *Ecl.* 3.63: *suave rubens hyacinthus*.

[156] *Puellares animos*, the *ipsissima verba* of Ovid in telling the story of Proserpina (*Fasti* 4.433).

[157] For the MS. reading *reservati* M. Haupt, *Hermes* 2 (1867) 8f., suggested the slight alteration to *resecati*, as a reminiscence of Horace, *Od.* 1.6.18: *proelia virginum sectis in iuvenes unguibus acrium*. Haupt's reading is adopted by Pastorino, who lists or discusses other proposals.

[158] *Retorsit ad civitatem oculos*, imitating Cic., *Cat.* 2.1.2: *retorquet oculos ad hanc urbem:* Italo Lana, *Riv. fil.* 36 (1958) 208.

[159] This commonplace modern expression does not derive from Firmicus, but seems the inevitable translation for *ex disperatione consilium*.

[160] The corrupt reading of the MS., *qua vehiculum trahebat*, was altered by Flacius to *quae . . . trahebat* (adopted by Pastorino). But Halm proposed *qua . . . trahebatur*, and Ziegler, listening for the habitual rhythms of Firmicus, was sure this was right. Italo Lana, *Riv. fil.* 36 (1958) 204, noted that *trahebatur* is corroborated here by the necessary emendation of *sustentat* to *sustentatur* in 21.4. Though I have used the active voice in my translation, I consider *trahebatur* right.

[161] Gronovius' proposal instead of *immersus* in the MS. While *immensus* occurs four times in the *Mathesis* and is a commonplace word in all periods of Latin, *immergere* (*immersus*) is a rarer word, elsewhere unattested in Firmicus, and not often used by the Christian authors. Besides, the meaning would be strained if the literal statement is that "the lake is immersed." The scribe's eye wandered to *submersus* in the following sentence. Ziegler in 1953 adopted *immensus*. As for the realities, Firmicus is less concerned with them than with rhetorical ecphrasis; neither *profundis* nor *immensus* is warranted for a lake with a maximum depth of fifteen feet and a total area of three fourths of a square mile (*Enciclopedia Italiana*).

[162] MS.: *per alium locum . . . mersisse;* Ziegler (1953 edition, 28) argues lengthily and convincingly for *lacum* (Widmann)

and *emersisse* (Flacius); so Pastorino. Unlike Ovid and Cicero, who say that Pluto's chariot disappeared near Syracuse, the euhemeristic version followed by Firmicus says that, according to a white lie of the people, it reappeared there.

[163] The temple of Ceres at Henna was the center of the cult of Ceres in Sicily; but Cicero (*Verr.* 4.49.109) assures us that Henna also had a temple of Proserpina.

[164] In the tradition of mainland Greece Triptolemus was the first priest of Demeter-Ceres and the founder of her cult. Regarding Henna Cicero says (*Verr.* 4.49.110): *Ante aedem Cereris in aperto ac propatulo loco signa duo sunt, Cereris unum, alterum Triptolemi.* The euhemeristic version reduces Triptolemus to a *vilicus* of the rich lady of Henna.

[165] Marie C. van der Kolf, "Pandaros," no. 4, RE 18, 3 (1949) 507, thinks this Pandarus a Syracusan, not identifiable with any other Pandarus or Pandareus.

[166] The southern cape of Sicily, below Syracuse, now Capo Passaro.

[167] Two temples honoring Demeter-Ceres and her daughter were built in Syracuse by Gelon after the battle of Himera in the fifth century: Leo Bloch, LM 2.1309.

[168] The quest for Proserpina by Ceres appears in all versions of the myth; likewise the coming to Eleusis.

[169] At least in Sicilian tradition Ceres bestowed the gift of wheat first on the Sicilians: Diod. 5.2.4. All scholars acknowledge that the Eleusinian cult was basically agricultural: Nilsson 1.470.

[170] The etymology from ἔλευσις, "a coming, advent," is of course wrong. Nilsson 1.313: "Eleusis ist eine vorgriechische Siedelung, und ihr Name ist sicher auch vorgriechisch." Firmicus wrote *Eleusin*, and apparently meant that the final syllable *-in* was derived from *Henna* (rarely spelled Hinna): Ziegler, 1907 ed., *ad loc.*

[171] That notable benefactors of mankind, such as inventors of the arts and discoverers of basic foods like wheat, were deified out of gratitude was the doctrine of the Sophist Prodicus of Ceos and the early Stoic Persaeus. This view could have been known to Firmicus from his reading of Cicero, *Nat. deor.* 1.38: *At Persaeus . . . eos [dicit] esse habitos deos a quibus aliqua magna utilitas ad vitae cultum esset inventa.* Other apologists knew of the doctrine, e.g. Min. Fel. 21.2: *Prodicus adsumptos in deos*

loquitur qui errando inventis novis frugibus utilitati hominum profuerunt. Demeter and Dionysus were obvious examples, pointed out by Prodicus (Frag. 5 Diels).

[172] The mother and daughter were inseparably associated in legend and cult. Thus the article on Kora in Roscher's *Lexikon* is subtitled "Demeter und Kora."

[173] The same phrase, *Graecorum levitas,* had been used by Firmicus in the *Mathesis,* 1.10.12 (cf. *ibid.* 1.2.3: *leves Graeci*). The fact is that "Greek frivolity" had been a rhetorical *topos* ever since Cicero had repeatedly brought the indictment. *Pro Flacco* 11.24: *hominibus levitate Graecis, crudelitate barbaris; ibid.* 25.61: *Liceat mihi . . . de levitate Graecorum queri; Rep.* 1.3.5: *levitas Atheniensium; Fin.* 2.25.80: *Graecorum levitas,* fragment of *Pro Flacco* cited by Jerome, *Ep.* 10.3 and *ad Gal.* 3.1: *Graecorum ingenita levitas;* Servius *ad Aen.* 6.724: *Graecos leves videmus.* The Christian Cicero, Lactantius, had picked up the *topos, Div. Inst.* 1.15.14 (on deification): *Quod malum a Graecis ortum est, quorum levitas* etc. The implied contrast with the famed Roman *gravitas* enhanced the self-esteem of the rulers of the world. For Firmicus the well-worn phrase of obloquy was a useful weapon against a nation which had originated countless pagan cults. (Note indebted to Prindle [unpub. diss.] Ch. 1, p. 3.)

[174] In mythological geography Nysa was either a mountain or more often a city which Dionysus founded or where he was born. It was variously located in Greece, Thrace, Caria, Palestine, and India. Cf. Pease on Cic., *Nat. deor.* 3.58.

[175] The constellation of Gemini, which resulted from the translation to heaven of the athletic Spartan twins Castor and Pollux.

[176] The cremation of Hercules on a pyre atop Mt. Oeta in Thessaly, followed by his ascension to heaven, is a familiar story of Greek mythology. Hercules was worshiped at the putative site of the pyre, as excavations by Pappadakis revealed in 1920. Cf. Nilsson, "Der Flammentod des Herakles auf dem Oite," ARW 21 (1922) 310–6; Fr. Stoessl, *Der Tod des Herakles* (Zurich 1945).

[177] Cic., *Nat. deor.* 3.53 (on the three Jupiters): *tertium Cretensem, Saturni filium, cuius in illa insula sepulcrum ostenditur.* Euhemerus (cited from Ennius' translation, Lact., *Div. inst.* 1.11.46) was the first to declare that the tomb of Zeus was to be seen in Crete, at Cnossos.

¹⁷⁸ The MS. gives *hos hihomines;* Ziegler and most recent editors simply *hos homines.* Wikström, *Eranos* 53 (1955) 180f., thinks we need the word "two" (for Liber and Proserpina), recalls that in capital script B and H are often confused by scribes, e.g. *Math.* 3.5.3 *horoscopo* for *horoscopo,* and conjectures *hos bi[nos] homines.* Firmicus uses the word *bini* in the *Mathesis.* I have adopted Wikström's conjecture.

¹⁷⁹ Late Neoplatonism tried to save paganism by asserting that all the pagan divinities were merely manifestations or aspects of the sun. As a Neoplatonist astrologer Firmicus had glorified the sun as *Sol optimus maximus . . ., mens mundi atque temperies, dux omnium atque princeps,* etc. (*Math.* 1.10.14). Deeply versed in the lore of the heavens, he knew of the Neoplatonic syncretism from a now-lost treatise by Porphyry, perhaps Περὶ θείων ὀνομάτων: so P. Courcelle, *Les lettres grecques en Occident* (Paris 1948) 20, objecting to a different identification of the treatise by Heuten, "Le soleil de Porphyre," *Mélanges Franz Cumont* (Brussels 1936) 253–59. As for the equation Liber = Sol, we read in Servius, *ad Ecl.* 5.66: *Sed constat secundum Porphyrii librum quem Solem appellavit triplicem esse Apollinis potestatem, et eundem esse Solem apud superos, Liberum patrem in terris, Apollinem apud inferos.* Macrobius, *Sat.* 1.18.7f., has the same information from Porphyry. According to a possible but disputed interpretation, Vergil (*Georg.* 1.7) had already identified the Sun with Liber. Cf. also Julian, *Or.* 4.144A, and the discussion in Bruhl, *Liber pater* 264–66. The Christian apologists who attacked the worship of the four elements customarily added an attack on the deified Sol and Luna, also considered to be "elements": J. Geffcken, *Zwei griech. Apologeten* 56ff. Firmicus, after digressing on another path, is now taking a quick glance at this topic.

¹⁸⁰ That Proserpina and Luna are identical is an idea first known from Epicharmus, cited by Ennius, *Varia,* Fr. 59 (Vahlen, 2nd ed.). The source of the Ennian fragment is Varro, *L.L.* 5.68. The Neoplatonists naturally welcomed this syncretism: Porph., *De cultu simulacrorum* ap. Euseb., *Praep. ev.* 3.11.35: καὶ ἔστι συνεκτικὴ τῆς Κόρης ἡ Σελήνη.

¹⁸¹ The reading of the MS. is here retained, as in all editions save Ziegler's of 1953, but with the insertion of a transitional *enim* after *indivisam:* so Wikström, *Eranos* 53 (1955) 181f. On

this passage the remarks of Heuten are malapropos, and the only satisfactory commentary (albeit highly compressed) is that furnished by Festugière in his review of Heuten, REG 52 (1939) 646f. Firmicus, having struck out at Neoplatonism once already (5.3), is here again assailing the *physica ratio* of Neoplatonism and Hermetism. Plato in the *Timaeus* (35A) had stated that the world soul is composed of three elements: the indivisible, the divisible, and a third essence compounded from the first two. This doctrine exercised the Neoplatonists considerably, since it seemed to contradict Plato's insistence in the *Phaedo* on the indivisibility of the soul: comment or exegesis in Macrob., *Somn. Scip.* 1.12.6, Plotinus 1.1.8, and several Plotinian passages cited by Festugière. The apologist Aristides (6.1–2) declared that the sun is one in its nature but is associated with many parts; therefore we see that it could be accounted comparable with "the undivided and divided intelligence." Hermetism in fact frequently compared the sun with the intelligent universe (*Corp. Herm.* 16.12: "Just as the intelligent universe . . ., so also the sun . . .") and held that the sun is the intermediary between the divine intelligence and the individual soul. Firmicus with cryptic brevity means to argue that sun worship cannot be justified by the Neoplatonic doctrine that such worship is really directed towards the Divine Intelligence. The Greek phrase cited by Firmicus was, Festugière maintains, one in current use among the intelligentsia, and we need not suppose, with Heuten, that Firmicus derived it from Porphyry.

[182] The MS. reads *O dii miseri mortales* and repeats the phrase unchanged in 18.8. Ziegler discards *dii* in both passages and does not even mention it in the critical apparatus at 18.8. For all the manifold excellences of his work on Firmicus, Ziegler seems never to have seen the critical notes of Robinson Ellis, "On the *Octavius* of Minucius Felix and Firmicus *de errore profanarum religionum*," *Journ. of Philol.* 26 (1899) 197–202. Ellis reasonably argued that the scribe would hardly have made the same error at two widely separated spots, and *dii* (genitive) is intelligible since Firmicus elsewhere spoke of man as belonging to God (16.4 and 27.4 *hominem dei*). Wikström, *Eranos* 53 (1955) 182f., though likewise unaware of what Ellis had written, essentially repeated his argument, only adding that Firmicus probably used the spelling *dei* here as well as elsewhere.

[183] The address of the Sun to humanity is recognized as a high point in the literary efforts of Firmicus; the power of the words, thought Coman (85), is worthy of Tertullian. The imaginative idea of convoking all humankind to hear an important *contio* (not necessarily given by the Sun) occurs in Arnob. 1.29 and 6.14, and McCracken, ACW 7.281 n. 123, is able to cite no parallel except Firmicus. C. Brakman, *Miscella tertia* (Leyden 1917) 25, affirmed that Firmicus was imitating Arnobius. Aware that solar monotheism, once proclaimed as the official religion of the Roman world by Aurelian in 274 and favored by Neoplatonism, was a serious threat to Christianity, Firmicus hit upon the dramatic idea of having the Sun itself deprecate such worship. Among the 156 heresies cataloged by Filastrius (*Heres.* 10) later in Firmicus' century was a Hermetic sect in Gaul which combined heliolatry and Christianity. See J. Carcopino, *Aspects mystiques de la Rome païenne* (Paris 1942) 314; L. Homo, *De la Rome païenne à la Rome chrétienne* (Paris 1950) 151–57.

[184] Here we are to think of the identification Sol = Liber, and to recall that in 6.1–5 Firmicus recounted the death and immortal (divine) life of the Cretan Dionysus-Liber.

[185] In this sentence the Sun protests against being identified with Osiris, Attis, and the Cretan Dionysus-Liber (in that order).

[186] Osiris as the sun: Cumont (83).

[187] "When astrology and the Semitic religions caused the establishment of a solar henotheism as the leading religion at Rome, Attis was considered as the sun": Cumont (65f., E.T. 69).

[188] Adding detail to what was narrated in 6.3 about the killing and cooking of Dionysus-Liber by the Titans. Clem. Al., *Protr.* 2.18.1, gives the same details of the pot and the spits.

[189] The mystical properties of the number seven are well known. According to some accounts the slayers of the Cretan Dionysus were seven Titans, who cut up the body into seven pieces and cooked them on seven spits: W. H. Roscher, "Die Sieben- und Neunzahl im Kultus and Mythus der Griechen," *Abh. sachs. Ges. Wiss., phil.-hist. Kl.* 24,1 (1906) 24.

[190] Retaining *paululum* of the MS., as recommended by Wikström, *Eranos* 53 (1955) 183f.; so all editions except Ziegler in 1953 (*paululo ante*).

[191] The professional *auriga* in the fourth century belonged to

the lower classes; therefore to rank the Sun as an *auriga* would be insulting.

[192] Occasionally in Late Latin (Firmicus, Jerome, Victor Vitensis, *et al.*) *convenire* means "to admonish": Christine Mohrmann, *Études sur le latin des chrétiens* (Rome 1958) 423. For the verb in this meaning see 8.4, 28.2, 28.4, 28.12.

[193] Firmicus blames Porphyry for the syncretism which merged other deities with the sun, thus helping to set up heliolatry as a strong rival of Christianity. The unnamed *inimicus dei* of this passage is reintroduced in 13.4 as *Porphyrius . . . hostis dei, veritatis inimicus*, etc. See Heuten in *Mélanges Franz Cumont* 255.

[194] Several editors have felt the need of an attributive adjective with *secreta*, and Kroll suggested *caelestia* (adopted by Ziegler in 1953). Wikström, *Eranos* 53 (1955) 184f., points to the contrast *sanctum . . . secretum . . . profanus actus* in 20.1, and proposes *sancta*. This is favored by Firmicus' passion for alliteration: *secreta [sancta] profanis persuasionibus polluit*.

[195] Again with reference to the identification Sol = Liber and the mutilation by the Titans of the Cretan Dionysus-Liber.

[196] The word *ethopoeiacus* is a coinage of Firmicus, who here wishes to signify that he has been a mouthpiece for the Sun, adopting for the nonce the Sun's character and moral views. An emphatic *at ego* follows, as Firmicus begins once more to speak for himself.

[197] *Sacrarum lectionum institutione formatus.* Firmicus had numerous speech patterns and pet phrases, of which this is one. See four passages in the *Mathesis*: 2.3.4: *hac institutione formati;* 2.30.10: *tua institutione formati;* 5.7.4: *divina institutione formatum;* 6.26.1: *docta institutione sermo formatus.* Unless Firmicus had a surprising acquaintance with Christianity already when he wrote the *Mathesis*, it is idle for Heuten and others to suppose that he was, in this passage of the *De errore*, echoing the words that introduce the Lord's Prayer in the Canon of the Mass: *divina institutione formati.* Commentators are in general agreement that Firmicus is here making his only overt statement about his conversion. Pastorino shrewdly discerns a covert allusion to earnest words that Firmicus had written in the preface to Book 5 of the *Mathesis;* in a prayer to the Sun and Moon he disclaimed any ignoble motives for writing on astrology and continued (Sect. 6): *sed animus divina inspiratione formatus totum*

conatus est quod didicerat explicare. "Firmicus remembers well that former prayer of his to the Sun; here he speaks anew of the Sun but with very different language and very different doctrine" (Pastorino).

[198] Xenophanes (A 13 Diels) was often quoted to the effect that people should not mourn for beings whom they deem gods nor deem gods those for whom they mourn. This argument was welcomed by the Christian apologists (Geffcken, *Zwei griech. Apologeten* 202) and Firmicus may have found it in Clem. Al., *Protr.* 2.24.3: εἰ θεοὺς νομίζετε, μὴ θρηνεῖτε αὐτοὺς μηδὲ κόπτεσθε· εἰ δὲ πενθεῖτε αὐτούς, μηκέτι τούτους ἡγεῖσθε εἶναι θεούς. Compare also Min. Fel. 22.2: *Nonne ridiculum est vel lugere quod colas vel colere quod lugeas?*

[199] Alfons Müller (footnote in his translation) observes that the following prayer for benisons has the form and rhythm (in Latin) of the prayers of the early Church.

[200] Adonis (Phoenician *Adon*, "Lord," cf. Hebrew *Adonai*) was much worshiped in Phoenicia, Syria, and Cyprus. Cicero (*Nat. deor.* 3.59) wrote that there were four Venuses, the fourth being *Syria Cyproque concepta, quae Astarte vocatur, quam Adonidi nupsisse proditum est.* Copious material on Adonis in Frazer's *Golden Bough*, Vol. 5. The cult of Adonis, being weak in Rome, drew little attention from the Christian apologists.

[201] W. H. Roscher, "Adonis," LM 1.69–77 at 71, lists the accounts of the myth that report that Ares either sent a boar against Adonis or transformed himself for the purpose into a boar.

[202] Mars (Ares), who conquered Adonis but was entrapped *in flagrante delicto* by Vulcan (Hephaestus) according to the Homeric story: *Od.* 8.266–366.

[203] The idea is that Mars, having complete freedom of choice, should have elected to metamorphose himself into the king of beasts rather than into a *porcus* (a word used by Firmicus as a contemptuous substitute for *aper*).

[204] Steier, "Löwe," RE 13 (1926) 968–90 at 977f., shows that the lion in antiquity enjoyed good repute for its noble and magnanimous character, but its propensity for a chaste life is not mentioned elsewhere. Pastorino points to a statement of Clem. Al., *Protr.* 1.4.1, that lions are irascible and pigs are hedonists.

[205] Matt. 8.28–32, Mark 5.1–13, Luke 8.26–33.

[206] Cinyras was a legendary king of Cyprus, father of Adonis

and wooer of Venus. Unmentioned in the euhemeristic tradition, he may have come to Firmicus' attention in Clement of Alexandria (*Protr.* 2.13.4, 3.45.4) or Arnobius (4.24, 5.19, 6.6).

²⁰⁷ Both Clement and Arnobius so designated the Cyprian Venus and said that Cinyras deified her. Euhemerus, in Lact., *Div. inst.* 1.17.10, attributed to her the invention of harlotry, which therefore supposedly originated in Cyprus.

²⁰⁸ Clem. Al., *Protr.* 2.14.2: "The new initiates bring her a piece of money, as lovers do for a courtesan"; Arnob. 5.19: *Cypriae Veneris abstrusa illa initia . . . quorum conditor indicatur Cinyras rex fuisse, in quibus sumentes ea certas stipes inferunt ut meretrici et referunt phallos propitii numinis signa donatos.* Sacred prostitution (discussed by Cumont 258f., n. 58) was certainly a regular feature of the cult of the Cyprian Aphrodite, but Dölger, AC 3 (1932) 11, deplores any Christian statement or hint that the "fee" for initiation was actually payment for a prostitute. Dölger points to an initiatory fee in the Eleusinian mysteries and perhaps in Mithra worship.

²⁰⁹ Both Clement and Arnobius, in the passages just cited, say that the new initiate received a phallus. So Carl Clemen, RMP 73 (1920–24) 352. The high-minded Firmicus as a matter of policy avoided all obscene words and allusions, whereas in this respect both Clement and Arnobius delighted in writing Juvenalia.

²¹⁰ *Manifestius explicare*, a pet phrase of Firmicus: 23.1, *Math.* 2.30.11, 3.9.12.

²¹¹ The customary spelling in Greek and Latin sources is Sabazius. Sabazius was a Phrygian god of nature and vegetation, sometimes identified with Dionysus or with Zeus-Jupiter. See Cook's *Zeus* 1.390–403.

²¹² Clem. Al., *Protr.* 2.16.2, Arnob. 5.21. A snake made of gold was drawn down through the bosom of initiates, to symbolize a sacred marriage with the deity. The snake in this ceremony was a phallic emblem; the ceremony effected the sacred marriage equally well for a male as for a female initiate. Erich Küster, *Die Schlange in der griech. Kunst und Religion* (RVV 13, 2, Giessen 1913) 148–50; A. Dieterich, *Eine Mithrasliturgie* (3rd ed. Leipzig 1923) 123f.; Carl Clemen, RMP 73 (1920–24) 352f. A comprehension of what the snake meant in the mysteries of Sabazius shows what led Firmicus to append this topic to his account of the Cyprian Venus.

[213] The honor given the snake in the mysteries of Sabazius reminded Firmicus of the serpent in Eden and man's original sin.

[214] In close connection with the cults of Cyprian Venus and Sabazius, both Clement (*Protr.* 2.19.1) and Arnobius (5.19) introduce the Corybantes, the frenzied Phrygian divinities who formed part of the train of Cybele. Clement reports that two of the Corybantes killed their brother, carried the corpse's head ceremonially on a bronze shield to the base of Mt. Olympus, and there buried it.

[215] Clement (*Protr.* 2.19.4) and Eusebius (*Praep. ev.* 1.10.14) identify the Corybantes with the Cabiri, as does Firmicus. The Cabirus of Thessalonica was, as we learn from numismatics, one of the chief deities of that city in the time of the Roman Empire: Charles Edson, "Cults of Thessalonica," *Harv. Theol. Rev.* 41 (1948) 153–204 at 200; Bengt Hemberg, *Die Kabiren* (Uppsala 1950) 206.

[216] Hemberg, *op. cit.* 207, states that the Cabiric cult was bloody nowhere else except in Macedonia.

[217] This chapter deals with the immoral, criminal, and otherwise human behavior of the anthropomorphic gods of Greek mythology. Protests against the *chronique scandaleuse* of the gods had been lodged by Xenophanes, Plato, and Cicero (*Nat. deor.* 1.42, 2.70, where see the copious notes of Pease), not to mention most of the Christian apologists. The attempt of Heuten to postulate for Firmicus a single source, something similar to Lucian's *Dialogues of the Gods* or *Sacrifices*, has not met with approval. Pastorino *ad loc.*, after a lengthy discussion, says: "It is not necessary to suppose that Firmicus had before him one text rather than another. . . . It is to be believed that he drew from various sources, adapting and transposing according to his particular criteria or amplifying according to his stylistic needs." Certainly among his sources were Clement of Alexandria (*Protrepticus*) and Arnobius, as will be evident from the following notes.

[218] *Devota mente*, again in 12.9; the only instances in the *De errore* of the Late Latin substitute for an adverb (French *dévotement*).

[219] The MS. reads *eorum*. Ziegler in both editions observed that the meaning is *deorum*, but did not adopt this in his text. Pas-

torino gives [d]eorum. For once the true reading is a matter of indifference to the translator.

²²⁰ The closest parallel to this partial and condensed catalog of the amours of Jupiter is Arnob. 4.26: *modo . . . in aurum versus, modo in satyrum ludicrum, in draconem, in alitem, [in] taurum.* The four adventures alluded to by Firmicus are, in order: Leda and the swan, Europa and the bull, Antiope and the satyr, Danae and the golden rain. All four stories were well known and accessible in Ovid (e.g. *Met.* 6. 103–13 briefly alludes to each of the four).

²²¹ *Inclusam regiam virginem:* did Firmicus remember *Inclusam Danaen,* the opening words of Horace's ode (3.16)? So H. J. Rose, *Class. Rev.* 71 (1957) 234.

²²² In this sentence Firmicus has collected five of the most notorious examples of pederasty in Greek mythology. Clement (*Protr.* 2.33.5) lists exactly these five, and Arnobius (4.26) adds no others except one Roman example. Jupiter (Zeus) loved the Trojan boy Ganymede and had him wafted to heaven; Hercules took the young Hylas as companion on the Argonautic expedition and searched frantically for him after he was nympholept; Apollo loved the Spartan lad Hyacinthus; Laius of Thebes kidnaped Chrysippus, son of Pelops, in what the Greeks often called the original case of pederasty; and Poseidon loved the young Pelops (references on the last named are assembled by Bloch, "Pelops," LM 3.1871). Clement, Arnobius, and Firmicus unthinkingly parrot one another on Chrysippus, in whose case no god was involved.

²²³ Mommsen, *Römisches Strafrecht* 703f., "Päderastie." The Lex Scantinia, of uncertain date but first known from the correspondence of Cicero, established a fine of 10,000 sesterces for the violation of a freeborn boy. A sixth-century apologetic essay (Ps.-Tertullian, *De execrandis gentium diis* 5) blames Jupiter as the inventor of pederasty, and refers in vague terms to a Lex Cornelia which fixed a penalty (unstated) for this crime. Paulus, of about the year 200, states that the aggressor was liable to the death penalty: *Digest* 47.11.1.2. In December of 342 Constantius posted in Rome a law that the consenting male victim of pederasty incurs the death penalty: *Cod. Theod.* 9.7.3 = *Cod. Iust.* 9.9.30. Praising the severe Roman legislation against pederasty, Firmicus uses the word *hodie,* a word which solicits attention because it

appears nowhere else in the *De errore.* (*Hodieque* appears three times in the post-Augustan sense of *adhuc, hodie etiam:* Leumann-Hofmann 657.) Writing between 343 and 350, he appears to be alluding with approval to Constantius' new law of 342. It is true that the law of Constantius would be inapplicable to Jupiter, as an aggressor; but Firmicus, speaking here in vague terms, might have sacrificed strict accuracy for the sake of flattering the emperor and voicing patriotic pride in the Roman law.

[224] The polemicists thought such lists of the victims of divine misdemeanors were effective. Once more Firmicus drew from Clement or Arnobius or both. Clement (*Protr.* 2.32.3) lists as the recipients of Poseidon's affections Amphitrite, Amymone, Alope, Melanippe, Alcyone, Hippothoe, Chione, "and myriads more"; Arnobius (4.26) shortens the list to five: Amphitrite, Hippothoe, Amymone, Menalippe (*sic*), and Alcyone; Firmicus also names five: Amymone, Alope, Menalippe (*sic*), Chione, and Hippothoe. The close resemblance of these three lists is striking when we realize how many other names could have been chosen; A. S. Pease, "The Son of Neptune," HSCP 54 (1943) 69–82 at 70, tallied over 155 sons and about eleven daughters of Neptune. It should be noted that the misspelling Menalippe, contradicting etymology, occurs occasionally by an easy metathesis; but clearly there is a strong probability that Firmicus got it from Arnobius.

[225] Clement (*Protr.* 2.32.3) sarcastically commented that the reputation of Apollo as a chaste prophet and good counselor was sullied by his affairs with Sterope, Aethusa, Arsinoe, Zeuxippe, Prothoe, Marpessa, and Hypsipyle—though Daphne alone won laurels by escaping. The same remark, the same tone, and the same list in Arnobius 4.26. Firmicus repeats the list with the omission only of Marpessa and Hypsipyle. The reader of these three apologists might easily conclude that they were parroting a canonical list, but such is not the case. Although Arsinoe and Aethusa (as all writers except Firmicus spell her name) were known to Apollodorus (3.10.1, 3.10.3) as beloved by Apollo, the mythographers give no warrant for including Sterope, Zeuxippe, and Prothoe among the objects of the god's affections. On the count of promiscuity Apollo for the most part deserved his good reputation, so that Firmicus and his predecessors would have been well advised to dwell exclusively on the flagrant cases

of Jupiter and Neptune.—On this passage the notes of Pastorino are riddled with misprints and misinformation.

226 In this passage of carefully considered stylistic subtleties there is attractive alliteration: *et vitavit et vicit: Dafnen divinans deus.* Remarkably similar in thought is a sentence of Tatian, *Or. adv. Graecos* 8, praising Daphne for conquering the incontinence of Apollo and simultaneously discrediting his mantic power.

227 Prosymnus, called Polymnus in Paus. 2.37.5. See O. Höfer, "Polymnos," LM 3.2657–61. Firmicus adheres to his regular policy of reticence on subjects of an indelicate nature. But Clement (*Protr.* 2.34.3f.) and Arnobius (5.28), one or both of whom served as Firmicus' sources, told with brutal coarseness the story of how Prosymnus, upon request, showed Dionysus the road to Hades and was promised an indecent reward.

228 Jupiter did not kill Saturn, but according to the euhemeristic account sent an armed band to seize or kill him; eluding his pursuers, however, Saturn hid in Italy: Ennius (Euhemerus), *Hist. sacra* Fr. 5 Vahlen.

229 See Ch. 11 and n. 214 for fratricide among the Corybantes.

230 4.1: *Iunonem sane ne et hinc deesset incestum, Iovis volunt ex sorore coniugem factam.* The incest of Jupiter with his daughter Proserpina was a familiar story from countless pagan sources, and was reprehended by a host of the Church Fathers, e.g. Arnob. 5.22. Ziegler (note in his translation, 58) errs in accusing Firmicus of making an unauthorized and unparalleled charge that Jupiter committed incest with his mother. Athenagoras, *Legatio* 20 (trans. Crehan, ACW 23): "that daughter of Zeus, the one he had by his mother Rhea, or by Demeter her daughter." See Nilsson 2.660.

231 The Christian writers seldom mention the familiar tale of how Marsyas was flayed alive by Apollo as the forfeit for losing in a flute-playing contest with the god. Firmicus would have read at least the account in Ovid, *Met.* 6.382–400.

232 Firmicus may have had in mind the Tenth Commandment, though his Latin words do not resemble those of the Itala.

233 This portion of the Hercules saga was well known to the Romans; it was often located in the remotest part of Spain or islands beyond. See G. Heuten, "Les mythes du taureau et l'Espagne," *Latomus* 7 (1948) 3–7 at 7.

234 Protests against Mars's fondness for indiscriminate slaughter

are common; see e.g. Arnobius, 3.26 (trans. McCracken, ACW 7): "Mars brings together from different places so many thousands of mortals and, before you can say a single word, piles the fields with corpses."

235 Another allusion (cf. Section 2) to the myth of Danae.

236 A mythological error; there is no known story that Jupiter was assisted by traitors in his overthrow of his father Saturn. H. J. Rose, *Class. Rev.* 71 (1957) 234, thinks Firmicus may have had in mind the Hekatonchires and other primeval figures who sided with Zeus.

237 The story, not a favorite in the apologists, is sufficiently told in every handbook of mythology. Tantalus rashly tested divine omniscience by serving the gods at a banquet with the cooked flesh of his son Pelops.

238 The translation endeavors to reproduce the intentional parechesis of *O infelicis imitationis cruenta meditatio!* Other examples of parechesis in Firmicus are collected by Pastorino (lx).

239 After voicing some sweeping generalities about the dramatic aspects, comic and tragic, of the life of the gods as portrayed by Homer and the Greek mythological writers, Clement of Alexandria exclaimed (*Protr.* 4.58.4): σκηνὴν πεποιήκατε τὸν οὐρανόν. Firmicus' words, *scaenam de caelo fecistis*, reproduce Clement's striking remark and give the most notable example of his verbal imitation of Clement.

240 Presumably Firmicus' gratitude is directed chiefly at Euhemerus, who taught the mortality of the so-called immortal gods. Cic., *Nat deor.* 1.119: *Ab Euhemero autem et mortes et sepulturae demonstrantur deorum;* Min. Fel. 21.1: *Euhemerus . . . [deorum] sepulcra dinumerat.* But the Greek poets and mythological writers had furnished ammunition for Euhemerus, as the following sentences of Firmicus point out.

241 This section aims to select from Greek mythology a few familiar examples of divine mischances, failures, sins, humiliations, griefs, wounds, and even deaths. See *Iliad* 5.330–42 and 855–61 on the discomfiture of first Aphrodite and then Ares at the hands of Diomedes. The laudatory adjectives for Diomedes merely signify that a man of ordinary chastity worsted the unchaste Venus, and a man of ordinary temperance overcame the intemperate Mars.

242 These twin giants, enemies of the Olympians, imprisoned

Ares for thirteen months in a bronze jar: *Iliad* 5.385–91. The story was known equally to the Greek apologists and to their Latin confreres: Clem., *Protr.* 2.29.3; Ps.-Justin, *Coh. ad graecos* 2; Tert., *Apol.* 14.3, *Ad nat.* 1.10.39; Arnob. 4.25.

²⁴³ This rare adjective was an invention of Ennius (*Ann.* 181 Vahlen), but was picked up by Vergil and his epic imitators and by a very few Christian writers.

²⁴⁴ The mourning of Zeus for the impending death of his son on the battlefield is recorded in the *Iliad* 16.433f. and the death itself on the following pages. Numerous apologists, attacking the frailty of the pagan gods, mentioned the tears of Zeus for Sarpedon: e.g. Clem., *Protr.* 4.55.3 (quoting Homer's words); Tert., *Apol.* 14.3, *Ad nat.* 1.10.39; Min. Fel. 23.4. Arnobius omitted Sarpedon.

²⁴⁵ *Iliad* 21.441–53. The Trojan king who defrauded Poseidon of his pay was Laomedon. The incident appears in Clement (*Protr.* 2.35.1), Arnobius (4.25), and other apologists; succinctly in Min. Fel. 23.5: *Laomedonti vero muros Neptunus instituit, nec mercedem operis infelix structor accipit.*

²⁴⁶ Euripides, *Alcestis*, prologue; Min. Fel. 23.5: *Apollo Admeto pecus pascit;* Clem., *Protr.* 2.35.1; Arnob. 4.25, etc.

²⁴⁷ The all-seeing Sun (*Od.* 12.323) failed to see the killing of his sacred cows by the men of Odysseus, and the news had to be brought to him by the nymph Lampetie (*Od.* 12.374f.).

²⁴⁸ The usual Latin *Castores* for Castor and Pollux. Firmicus' thought is that the death and burial of demigods weakens the case of paganism. Cf. 7.6.

²⁴⁹ 7.6.

²⁵⁰ Pagan and Christian testimonia on the death of Aesculapius are collected by E. J. & L. Edelstein, *Asclepius* (Baltimore 1945) 1.53–56. Zeus killed him with a thunderbolt as a punishment for using his medical skill to effect anabiosis. See Clem., *Protr.* 2.30.2; Arnob. 4.24; Min. Fel. 22.7.

²⁵¹ *Iliad* 1.590f. Clem. *Protr.* 2.29.5; Arnob. 4.24: *claudum pede . . . Vulcanum.*

²⁵² 6.8.

²⁵³ The song of Demodocus about the misbehavior of Ares and Aphrodite is in the *Odyssey* 8.266–366; cf. Clem., *Protr.* 2.33.9, 4.59.1, and other apologists. For Aphrodite's alliance with Anchises, cf. *Iliad* 2.820f.

²⁵⁴ Seeking to insure the early demise of any potential heirs to his throne, Cronus systematically ate each of his children immediately after childbirth: Hes., *Theog.* 459–62. From this relentless pedophagy Rhea saved Zeus by trickery, and in good time Zeus dethroned his father, who thereupon took refuge in Italy. Firmicus was following a euhemeristic account, echoed also by the proof in Min. Fel. 21.5–7 that Saturn was a mere *homo*.

²⁵⁵ Heuten *ad loc.* thinks that Firmicus, using partly Greek and partly Latin sources, was unaware that *Catamitus* is simply the archaic Latin equivalent of *Ganymedes*—whose case Firmicus had already adduced in Section 2 of this chapter. Arnobius used indifferently *Catamitus* or *Ganymedes*.

²⁵⁶ The story of the Moon's love for Endymion appears in the mythographers and elsewhere, e.g. Lucian, *Dial. deorum* 11; brief allusions in Clem., *Protr.* 2.33.8, and Arnob. 4.27.

²⁵⁷ This concluding example of divine frailty is from the *Iliad* 14.153–351. As both Heuten and Pastorino observed, Alfons Müller did not reread the Homeric passage and erroneously translated *contra voluntatem* with *dormit* instead of with *auxilium ferens*.

²⁵⁸ A general reference to the persecutions of the Christians by various emperors.

²⁵⁹ An ironic reprise of the scornful *Scaenam de caelo fecistis* of Sect. 7.

²⁶⁰ The Latin *histriones facite sacerdotes* is ambiguous; which accusative is predicate? Alfons Müller and Faggin take *histriones* as the predicate; Heuten and Ziegler, *sacerdotes*.

²⁶¹ For the lacuna . . . *ntur* Halm conjectured *saltentur*, adopted by Ziegler and Pastorino. Better is Wikström's *monstrentur*: *Eranos* 53 (1955) 185, comparing the earlier sentence (Sect. 7) about the theatricality of the pagan heaven: *facinorum via de deorum monstratur exemplis*. That Firmicus had in mind this earlier sentence is seen from his reuse of *deorum exemplis* in the sentence which immediately follows the lacuna.

²⁶² *Mens perdita* also in 8.5; *perditas mentes* in *Math.* 2.30.14. Firmicus so labels the unregenerate pagan soul or mentality, which is an easy victim of temptation and sin. The *mens perdita* is a remediable misfortune; *adulterium* and *facinus* are irremediable misdeeds. Alfons Müller and Ziegler are entirely wrong in

taking *mens perdita et adulterium et facinus* as a triple subject of *docetur*. They were understandably troubled by the thought of accusatives after a passive verb; but Löfstedt, PKPer 291–93, found in vulgar and medieval Latin several examples of the accusative with an impersonal passive. Here the passive is not impersonal, but the construction parallels the "retained accusative" of such an English sentence as "He was taught arithmetic." Heuten, Faggin, and Pastorino regard *adulterium* and *facinus* as accusatives.

²⁶³ Serapis, "the divinity whose worship was started at Alexandria by Ptolemy" (Cumont 70, E.T. 74), identified with the Egyptian Osiris. His cult was such throughout the Roman Empire that Minucius Felix (22.2) could exclaim: *Haec Aegyptia quondam nunc et sacra Romana sunt.*

²⁶⁴ The following passages of Genesis are pertinent: 30.23f. (birth of Joseph to the patriarch Jacob), 41.54–56 (the seven-year famine in Egypt), 41.25–32 (Joseph's interpretation of Pharaoh's dream), 39.7–20 (Joseph's resistance to the blandishments of Putiphar's wife and his consequent imprisonment), 41.39–57 (Joseph's share in the rule of Egypt during the seven fat and seven lean years).

²⁶⁵ Isidore Lévy, *Rev. de l'hist. des relig.* 40 (1899) 372, has traced to a rabbinical source (Rabbi Juda ben Ilai, *ca.* A.D. 150 in Tiberias) the notion, founded on a fanciful Semitic etymology, that Serapis was a divinized Joseph. From this or some other source the Christian writers adopted the idea, using a Greek etymology as unacceptable as the Semitic: Melito of Sardis, *Apol.* 5; Tert., *Ad nat.* 2.8.10; Rufinus, *Hist. eccl.* 2.23; Paulinus Nol., *Carm.* 19.100; the Suda *s.v.* Σάραπις. The true etymology of "Serapis" is still disputed: Roeder, RE 1 A (1920) 2397f.

²⁶⁶ Roeder, *ibid.* 2425: "Das wesentliche Attribut des S., das nie fehlt, ist der Kalathos (Modius) auf dem Kopf."

²⁶⁷ Gen. 21.1–5, but the passage does not record her exact age.

²⁶⁸ The statue of Serapis at Alexandria is discussed by Clem., *Protr.* 4.48.

²⁶⁹ Several early Christian writers, beginning with Minucius Felix, held that demons lurked under the statues of pagan deities. Min. Fel. 27.1: *Isti igitur impuri spiritus, daemones . . . sub statuis et imaginibus consecratis delitescunt et adflatu suo auctoritatem quasi praesentis numinis consequuntur*, etc.

²⁷⁰ Here Firmicus delivers his third specific assault on Neoplatonic doctrine; cf. 5.3 and 7.8. While still a Neoplatonist astrologer he had spoken respectfully of *noster Porphyrius: Math.* 7.1.1. Porphyry (233–*ca.* 304) was the most important follower of the Neoplatonist Plotinus and the author of many books besides the youthful treatise about to be cited by Firmicus. To the neophyte Firmicus, Porphyry was anathema because of his smashing attack on Christianity (*Against the Christians*, 15 books).

²⁷¹ This book, cited under its Greek title by Firmicus, survives only in fragments, edited by G. Wolff, *Porphyrii de philosophia ex oraculis haurienda librorum reliquiae* (Berlin 1856, reprinted 1962). In preparation is a new edition of the fragments of Porphyry's writings, based on the collections made by J. Bidez.

²⁷² Wolff, *Porph. rel.* 111 (after citing this fragment of Porphyry's book): "Responsum ipsum Firmicus omittit." The adherents of pagan demonology held a belief, evidently shared by Porphyry, that oracles issued from human beings who were temporarily possessed by a demon or a god, such as Serapis. These agents through whom demon or deity spoke were mediums, not identical with the priests who performed the invocations. Firmicus refers here to two persons: the oracle priest who invokes and commands and encloses the demon or deity in the body of the medium, and the medium who is used to transmit the oracular response. So Dölger, AC 3 (1932) 170 n. 70.

²⁷³ Clement, *Protr.* 4.48.1, equating pagan gods with demons, called Serapis ὁ μεγαλοδαίμων. Min. Fel. 27.6: *Ipse Saturnus et Serapis et Juppiter et quicquid daemonum colitis.* . . . The oracular responses of Serapis at Alexandria are discussed by A. Bouché-Leclercq, *Hist. de la divination dans l'ant.* (Paris 1879–82) 3.380–83.

²⁷⁴ The reference is to the formulas of exorcism. On early Christian exorcism see pages 163–71 of Dölger's essay, "Teufels Grossmutter," AC 3 (1932); and the same pages give abundant parallels for Firmicus' equation in this passage of pagan gods with demons. Also H. Leclercq, "Exorcisme," DACL 5.1 (1922) 964–78.

²⁷⁵ The claim that Christian believers had the power to torment, flagellate, and scorch the demons who took lodgment in human beings was asserted by Minucius Felix (27.5: *a nobis tormentis verborum et orationis incendiis de corporibus exiguntur*), Ter-

tullian, and Cyprian (passages listed and quoted by Pastorino in his commentary).

²⁷⁶ Of Prodicus of Ceos Cicero says (*Nat. deor.* 1.118): *ea quae prodessent hominum vitae deorum in numero habita esse dixit.* To explain the Penates and Vesta Firmicus adopted Prodicus' method, which he knew via Cicero: so Prindle (unpub. diss.) Ch. 2,·p. 10. In Section 2 Firmicus shows that he accepts the usual etymology of *Penates* from *penus* and therefore understands the Penates to be gods of the larder. But Stefan Weinstock, "Penates," RE 19 (1937) 417–57 at 423, and A. S. Pease, on Cic., *Nat. deor.* 2.68, trace the word to *penes* and regard the Penates as gods of the hearth, house, and home.

²⁷⁷ *Divini oraculi.* Pastorino draws attention to the invariable meaning of *oraculum* in Firmicus (except 12.3): the word of God or of Holy Writ, or a prophecy of the Old Testament prophets.

²⁷⁸ Ziegler, 1953 ed., 30f., observed that in all the other five passages where Firmicus used this expression he wrote *dominus noster I.C.;* therefore [*noster*] should be restored in the text here. But J. B. Bauer, *Wien. Stud.* 71 (1958) 157, rightly holds that the stylist Firmicus deliberately omitted *noster* in view of *pro nostra salute* a few words later.

²⁷⁹ Quoted by memory from Matt. 4.3f. and Luke 4.3f., with slight variations from the pre-Vulgate and Vulgate versions.

²⁸⁰ In these words (*Nam omne quod vescuntur homines penus vocatur*) Firmicus borrowed what Cicero said (*Nat. deor.* 2.68): *Est enim omne quo vescuntur homines penus.* Skutsch suggested emending Firmicus' *quod* to *quo,* in order simultaneously to improve the grammar and strengthen the resemblance to Cicero. Wholly gratuitous is Heuten's assumption of Cornelius Labeo as an intermediary between Cicero and Firmicus; the idea is rebuked by Pastorino.

²⁸¹ Firmicus continues the explanation of the domestic deities as personifications. He does not offer an etymology of "Vesta," but presumably accepts Cicero's statement (*Nat. deor.* 2.67) that the etymon is Ἑστία, "hearth." This etymology is doubted by Boisacq, Ernout, and others: see references in Pease, on Cic. *loc cit.* Ovid's view was in harmony with Cicero's, *Fasti* 6.291: *nec tu aliud Vestam quam vivam intellege flammam.*

²⁸² The passage is not unintelligible, *pace* Heuten (8 and 171);

see also Pastorino's discussion. The allusion is to the glory of Christian virginity. Firmicus implies that virginity is noble and worth while in the cause of Christ, but wasted in honor of a deified hearth-fire. The praises of voluntary Christian virginity were regularly sung by the early Fathers, often in special essays: E. Dublanchy, "Chasteté," DTC 2.2319–2331 at 2323. Prudentius (c. Symm. 2.1055–1113) drew a comparison between Christian virgins and the Vestal virgins, greatly to the disadvantage of the latter. The most recent treatment of the Vestals is by Carl Koch, "Vestales," RE 8 A (1958) 1732–53.

[283] L. Ziehen, "Palladion," RE 18, 3 (1949) 171–89, discusses the varied and conflicting legends about the protective image called the Palladium. Firmicus makes a natural transition from Vesta to the Palladium, because a Roman legend held that either the original Trojan Palladium or at least a Palladium was kept in Rome's temple of Vesta under the care of the Vestal virgins: Dion. Hal., Ant. Rom. 1.69. In art the Palladium appears as an archaic figure of Athena with shield and poised spear. In the warlike Mycenaean period the armored Palladium was kept in the interior of a palace as a guarantee of the city's survival. See Nilsson 1.433ff.

[284] That the Palladium was an image made of bone, and specifically from the bones of Pelops, is not genuine legend but pedantic rationalism which Firmicus could have learned from Clem. Al., Protr. 4.47.6. Clement cited as his source Dionysius of Samos, F. griech. Hist. 15 F 3. A brief statement to the same effect is in Arnobius 4.25.

[285] A fabled thaumaturge, dated variously from the 8th to the 5th century: E. Bethe, "Abaris," RE 1 (1894) 16f. No writer except Firmicus associates Abaris with the bones of Pelops.

[286] Firmicus had already voiced a severely unfavorable opinion of the Scythians: Scythae soli immanis feritatis crudelitate grassantur (Math. 1.2.3). The Greek and Roman writers in general gave the Scythians a bad reputation: K. Kretschmer, "Scythae," RE 2 A (1921) 923–46 at 935f. Moore (49) pointed out that Firmicus liked poetical and rhythmic turns of phrase, and here employed or quoted (but from no known poet) two thirds of a hexameter in describing the Scythians: effera gens hominum et crudeli.

[287] See n. 222. Vase paintings provide much of the proof that

Pelops had Poseidon as a lover: Karl Scherling, "Pelops," RE
Suppl. 7 (1940) 849–66 at 858f. The principal literary passage is
Pind., *Ol.* 1.25. The Christian apologists say little of this, but
Tatian (*adv. Graecos* 25) comments on the paradox that Pelops
was cooked and served as a banquet for the gods in spite of his
being the beloved of Poseidon. Clem. Al., *Protr.* 2.33.4, and
Arnob. 4.26 say that Pelops had a divine lover; they seem to be
confident that popular knowledge will identify him.

[288] The expression *damna pudoris* is found in *Math.* 1.7.25 and
could be, but need not be, from Ovid, *Ars amat.* 1.100. Moore
(18) lists the six occurrences of *prostitutus pudor* in the *Mathesis.*

[289] Myrtilus, the charioteer of King Oenomaus of Pisa, accepted a bribe or the promise of a reward from Pelops and betrayed his master to death in a chariot race. To avoid paying the
reward, Pelops hurled Myrtilus over the cliffs into the sea. The
whole story, much as it is synopsized by Firmicus, appears in
Apollodorus, *Epit.* 2.4ff., and Hyginus, *Fab.* 84; the gradual growth
of the myth is traced by Weizsäcker, "Oinomaos," LM 3.764–83.

[290] The sequence of tenses here (*quid se maneat . . . vidit*) is
defended against Ziegler by Ernout, *Rev. de philol.* 64 N.S. 12
(1938) 241 n., and I have adopted his suggested translation. "He"
refers to the Palladium, not to Pelops himself. By using the
present tense (*maneat*) Firmicus implies that doom had not yet
been visited on the Palladium.

[291] Ancient writers do not agree on what befell the Palladium
in the sack of Troy, but one tradition held that Aeneas rescued
it and brought it to Italy with the Penates: L. Ziehen, "Palladion,"
RE 18, 3 (1949) 171–89 at 182–84. Since the Vestals reputedly had
the care of the Palladium in Rome, presumably they enjoy the
credit for preserving it when Rome was burned by the Gauls in
390 or 387 B.C.

[292] Firmicus consciously strove for assonance here to heighten
the effect of the antithesis: *dilatum . . . non liberatum.* Anticipating the destruction of paganism and its idols, he denies that
the Palladium is not for burning.

[293] Clement (*Protr.* 4.53.2f.) declared that fire can cure superstition and had already done signal service by burning the Argive
Heraeum, the Ephesian Artemisium, and several other pagan
temples—a prelude to its future conquests. Arnobius (6.23) parallels or copies the passage of Clement.

[294] *Absconsa,* "colloquial and unliterary participle of *abscondo*" (Souter). The form occurs in a known source of Firmicus, Ps.-Quint., *Decl. mai.* 17.15, and is a favorite word in the *Mathesis.* Ph. Thielmann, *Archiv f. lat. Lex.* 6 (1889) 165: "*Absconsus* ist durch alle Zeiten Vulgärform geblieben. . . . Firmicus Maternus der Astronom hat 55 *absconsus,* 2 *absconditus,* die vielleicht zu corrigieren sind."

[295] Mal. 4.1: *Ecce enim dies veniet succensa quasi caminus.* Cyprian (*Test.* 2.28) gives the wording *Ecce dies Domini venit ardens velut clibanus.* Firmicus used Cyprian as a source of scriptural quotations, but here introduced minor variants: *Venit enim dies Domini ut ardens clibanus.*

[296] The MS. has *Audisti quid veniat, audisti quid veniat.* Alfons Müller (*Überlieferung* 86) pointed to similar iterations in 24.2: *Disce, disce quod nescis, disce quod non vides;* 24.4: *Aperite, aperite;* 26.2: *Fugite, o miseri homines, fugite;* and 28.6: *Tollite, tollite,* and observed: "Es entsprechen diese Wiederholungen dem oft übertriebenen Pathos des Firmicus." Ziegler was convinced by Müller's argument and adopted the iteration in his 1953 edition; Pastorino gives only *Audisti quid veniat, audisti.*

[297] In this and the previous sentence Firmicus may be vaguely recalling Matt. 13.30 (Vulg.): *Colligite primum zizania et alligate ea in fasciculos ad comburendum: triticum autem congregate in horreum meum.*

[298] Retain *servatur* from the MS., although Ziegler in his 1953 ed. emends to *convertitur.* The MS. reading is defended by all other editors, by T. Wikström, *Eranos* 53 (1955) 185–87, and by J. B. Bauer, *Wien. Stud.* 71 (1958) 157. The latter cites several biblical texts where *servare in* shows purpose: e.g. Job 21.30: *in diem perditionis servatur malus.*

[299] The verbiage of Firmicus in this whole clause is elevated and poetical; he may have remembered *rapax ignis* from Ovid, *Met.* 8.837, or some other poet.

[300] Pleonasm, of which Pastorino (li–liv) cites dozens of examples in Firmicus, may take the form of synonyms—either in parallel, as here, or with one of the pair subordinated in the genitive. For the concept of "death and doom" in Firmicus, Moore (22) cites six passages: (the present one) *exitus finisque;* 2.3: *necis exitium;* 3.1: *funeris exitium;* 28.13: *exitium mortemque; Math.* 3.4.37: *necis morte; id.* 6.15.7: *mortis exitium.*

[301] A. Michel, "Feu de l'enfer," DTC 5.2 (1939) 2196–2239.

[302] A. J. Festugière, "Arnobiana," VC 6 (1952) 216: "Dès l'âge hellénistique et sous l'Empire, on s'est plu à collectionner les noms divers grecs et barbares, que porte une même divinité en vertu de l'*interpretatio* usuelle depuis Hérodote." A lengthy discussion of homonymous deities is presented by Cicero, *Nat. deor.* 3.53–60, and Pease in his commentary points to lists of such deities in Ampelius 9, Clem., *Protr.* 2.28.1–29.1, Arnob. 4.13–15, Lact. in Stat. *Theb.* 4.482, Lydus, *De mens.* 4. See the thorough study of the topic by Rudolf Hirzel, "Die Homonymie der griechischen Götter nach der Lehre antiker Theologen," *Ber. d. sächs. Ges. d. Wiss.* 48 (1896) 277–337. On the subject of the five Minervas Pastorino shows in tabular form the verbal parallelism in the accounts by Cic., *Nat. deor.* 3.59, Ampel. 9, Clem., *Protr.* 2.28.2, and Arnob. 4.14, and argues convincingly for Clement as the closest parallel to Firmicus and therefore his probable source (with Firmicus contributing rhetorical amplification).

[303] This genealogy for the Athenian Minerva is found in Ampelius and Arnobius, *loc. cit.* The tradition may have arisen from a misunderstanding of Plato, *Tim.* 23D-E, where it is said that Athena received the seed of the Athenian race from Earth and Hephaestus.

[304] This "Minerva" is obviously Athena Polias, the patroness and defender of the polis.

[305] The parallel passages (above, n. 302) in Cicero, Ampelius, Clement, and Arnobius all describe the Egyptian Athena as daughter of Nilus (the river god), but Egyptology knows no such paternity for Neith. Plato, *Tim.* 21E, says that the Egyptians in Sais identified their goddess Neith with the Greek Athena. Each was a goddess of war and had an owl as emblem. In the district of Sais, where weaving was an important industry, the weavers looked to their city goddess Neith as patroness or even inventor of weaving. See A. Rusch, "Neith," RE 16 (1935) 2189–2218, esp. 2191–92 (syncretism with Athena) and 2206–7 (goddess of weaving).

[306] So the parallel passages in Clement and Arnobius; but Cicero and Ampelius assert that the third Minerva was daughter of Jupiter. Since Saturn was a peaceable deity of agriculture, Firmicus expresses surprise that his daughter should be a sort

of warrior amazon. That the third Minerva actually invented war is the assertion of Clement and Arnobius.

[307] The grammarian Aristocles of Rhodes, cited in Schol. Pind., *Ol.* 7.66b, declared that Athena was born in Crete, from a cloud which was struck by Zeus. In Ch. 6 Firmicus has already discussed the Cretan king Jupiter, the murder of Liber, and the report thereon by Minerva.

[308] Pallas was a giant and according to some sources husband of the Oceanid Titanis: Otto Seel, "Pallas (nr. 2b)," RE 18,3 (1949) 235.

[309] A rather close parallel, using the verb *nuncupare*, is Arnob. 4.16: *Minervam me esse genitore ex Pallante procreatam testis omnis est poetarum chorus, qui Palladem me nuncupat derivato a patre cognomine.*

[310] The MS. offers no sense with the plural *ornatae sunt;* the singular, which is needed, offers a good clausula, is supported by κεκόσμηται in the parallel passage of Clement (*Protr.* 2.28.2), and is adopted by Ziegler in his 1953 edition. Less good is the emendation by T. Wikström, *Eranos* 53 (1955) 187f.: *exuviis corporis eius ornat et suum.*

[311] *Pontificalis lex* here; *ius pontificium* in Cic., *Legg.* 2.23.58. See Georg Rohde, *Die Kultsatzungen der römischen Pontifices* (RVV 25, Berlin 1936). The *pontifex maximus* of course was deeply concerned with the vestal virgins and the Palladium which they guarded.

[312] *Flammis ultricibus* (also in *Math.* 8.17.8) from Vergil's *ultricis flammae* (*Aen.* 2.587). In this passage *continuatione,* adopted by Dieterich, Ziegler, and Pastorino in lieu of the MS. reading *imitatione,* is strongly supported by several parallels in Firmicus, e.g. 27.2. Reject the un-Firmician *incitatione* proposed by T. Wikström, *Eranos* 53 (1955) 188f. Firmicus is alluding to the perpetual fire maintained at Rome by the vestals, the keepers of the Palladium.

[313] The idea of temples being downgraded to tombs originated with Tiberius, who said of temples erected in his honor: *quae saxo struuntur si iudicium posterorum in odium vertit, pro sepulcris spernuntur* (Tac., *Ann.* 4.38). The Christian writers probably hit on the idea independently and found it useful in apologetics. Athenagoras (*Suppl.* 14) criticized the Egyptians for burying sacred animals in temples. Clement (*Protr.* 3.44.4) said

"temples" was a euphemism for tombs: νεὼς μὲν εὐφήμως ὀνο-μαζομένους, τάφους δὲ γενομένους. Min. Fel. 8.4: *templa ut busta despiciunt.* Arnob. 6.6: *templa (numinum) mortuorum superlata sunt bustis.* The word *bustum*, hapax in the *De errore*, was obviously borrowed by Firmicus from his Latin source.

[314] What Firmicus literally calls for is "amputation," a drastic term which was a favorite with him (6.9, 20.5; literally 8.2).

[315] Skutsch and later commentators draw attention to this phrase in 1 Tim. 6.11 and 2 Tim. 3.17; again in *De errore* 27.4. But I. Lana, *Riv. fil.* 36 (1958) 209, observes that by "man of God" Firmicus merely meant man as the creature of God, whereas Paul meant a man who was in close contact with God.

[316] The remainder of this chapter is packed with medical vocabulary, as Firmicus develops the easy analogy between an infidel and a sick man needing to be cured; similarly Ambrose, *Exp. Luc.* 6.57, on Christ as a *medicus e caelo* for nonbelievers. Firmicus' penchant for employing medical terms, here and elsewhere, may have survived from his career as an astrologer; under the Empire medical science was friendly toward astrology, and iatromathematics was a recognized branch of applied astrology: F. H. Cramer, *Astrology in Roman Law and Politics* (Philadelphia 1954) 188–90. Firmicus voiced his respect for physicians in *Math.* 3.7.19, 3.8.3, 8.25.7, and 8.26.12.

[317] *Et ignis et ferrum.* Again, as often, Firmicus had been reading Clement of Alexandria's *Protrepticus*, where (1.8.2) Christ appears as the Good Physician, resorting sometimes to the knife, cautery, and even amputation.

[318] In this chapter Firmicus tilts at the gods in an effort to demolish them by an onslaught of Ciceronian etymology. Once more he has resorted to the *De natura deorum* (2.68): *cum Sol dictus sit vel quia solus ex omnibus sideribus est tantus vel quia cum est exortus obscuratis omnibus solus apparet.* Cicero in turn had accepted Varro's view of the etymology: *L.L.* 5.68. The wide acceptance enjoyed by the etymology, even among the Greeks, appears in the parallel passages cited by Pease in his note on the Ciceronian passage; and other astrologers besides Firmicus lent their approval: Mart. Cap. 2.188 (p. 74 Dick).

[319] About twenty words at this point, beginning with *quaedam velut in fixa*, are borrowed *verbatim et litteratim* from one of Firmicus' recognized sources: the declamation on astrology by

the Pseudo-Quintilian (4.13). Firmicus' astrological interests rather than the demands of the present subject led him to insert this brief digression on the difference between the planets and the fixed stars.

[320] Still quoting from the same Ciceronian passage, and this time the etymology is correct, since *Luna* and *Lucina* are both traced to *lucere*. Joshua Whatmough, HSCP 48 (1937) 194, remarks on "a certain degree of syncretism of the Roman Juno (as Lucina) and Diana (as Lucifera, or Luna) before the end of the Republic" and refers to the well-known stanza of Catullus' hymn (34.13–16):

Tu Lucina dolentibus
Iuno dicta puerperis,
tu potens Trivia et notho es
dicta lumine Luna.

Lucina, goddess of childbirth, is studied by K. Latte, RE 13 (1927) 1648–51.

[321] The etymology of *Diana* from *dies* is the third in this series from Cicero (*Nat. deor.* 2.69): *Diana dicta quia noctu quasi diem efficeret.* The two words do seem to be etymologically related, according to modern views.

[322] The fourth item from Cicero (*Nat. deor.* 2.66): *Neptunus a nando paulum primis litteris immutatis;* but Cicero himself (*op. cit.* 3.62) admitted the forced nature of this etymology, depending on a single letter. Of course it is unacceptable.

[323] The fifth consecutive etymology from Cicero (*op. cit.* 2.66), this time a correct one. In this sentence Firmicus retained much of the Ciceronian vocabulary and phrasing. In the story of the rape of Proserpina (7.1) Firmicus had already correctly explained the name of Dis (Pluto): *dives rusticus cui propter divitias Pluton fuit nomen.*

[324] Cicero, *loc. cit.*, mentions Proserpina immediately after Dis, but does not etymologize. No source has been found for Firmicus' unfortunate etymology. The idea that the pagan deities were allegorical representations of aspects of nature (e.g. Proserpina = grain) was copiously criticized by Arnobius 5.32–45.

[325] *Cum seri coeperint.* Pastorino drew attention to the pleonastic *coepi*, familiar in vulgar Latin (Petron. 29.9; *Itinerarium Egeriae* 3.7) and ably discussed by Löfstedt, PKPer 209f.

326 In this seventh item Cicero's etymology and phrasing were again available: *op. cit.* 2.67: *Mater autem est a gerendis frugibus Ceres tamquam geres.* Cicero had it from Varro 5.64, but Varro was again wide of the mark. Where Firmicus wrote *Terram ipsam Cererem nominant*, Arnobius (5.32) had written *pro tellure Cererem nominat.*

327 The eighth item from Cicero, *loc. cit.*: *Iam qui magna verteret Mavors.* Wrong, but not by the fault of Varro. Ziegler (1953 edition, but not in the earlier edition) wished for the sake of etymology to alter the orthography to *vort-* in both Cicero and Firmicus. This is not necessary, and there is no MS. support for the change.

328 *Quasi aut minuat aut minetur*, from Cic. *loc. cit.*: *quae vel minueret vel minaretur.* Erroneous and non-Varronian.

329 This item is the tenth and last in the sequence drawn from Cicero. But Cicero, *op. cit.* 2.69, avers that *Venus* is derived from *venire* and that the abstract *venustas* was formed from *Venus* and not vice versa. In the latter remark he is right. Firmicus' inversion of the facts may be due to a negligent reading of his source on an unimportant detail. Arnobius 3.33 followed the Ciceronian etymology, leaving *venustas* unmentioned.

330 The attempt to derive "Apollo" from the verb ἀπόλλυμι, "lose," is misguided; all ancient etymologies of the name are summarily dismissed by Boisacq, *Dict. étym. de la langue grecque* (4th ed. 1950) *s.v.* The Greekless reader may be helped at this point by recalling Apollyon, "the Destroyer," in *Pilgrim's Progress.* Apollyon's name is from the verb just cited, but Apollo's is not. Firmicus' false etymology of "Apollo" appears also in Macrob., *Sat.* 1.17.7, and Serv., *ad Ecl.* 5.66; Servius says he got it from a book of Porphyry.

331 After the short non-Ciceronian discussion of Apollo, Firmicus here reverts to the thought and phraseology of Cicero (*Nat. deor.* 2.70): *Videtisne igitur ut a physicis rebus bene atque utiliter inventis tracta ratio sit ad commenticios et fictos deos? Quae res genuit falsas opioniones erroresque turbulentos et superstitiones paene aniles. Et formae enim nobis deorum et aetates et vestitus ornatusque noti sunt.* Pease *ad loc.* notes that this Ciceronian summation was condensed or quoted for polemic purposes not only by Firmicus but also by Lact., *Inst.* 1.17.2, *Epit.* 17.4, Aug., *De civ. Dei* 4.30.

³³² The flight of eloquence in this and the next two sentences soars on wings borrowed from the declamation on astrology by Pseudo-Quintilian (*Decl.* 4.14): *Haec credo, pater, terrori primis fuisse mortalibus, mox admirationem consumpta novitate meruisse. Paulatim deinde hoc quod stupemus, animus ausus diligenter adtendere, in arcana naturae sacrum misit ingenium, et ex adsiduis observationibus notisque redeuntibus latentium ratione collecta pervenit ad causas.* Here Firmicus has somewhat expanded and retouched Pseudo-Quintilian, whereas in 17.1 he reproduced his statement almost verbatim. For example, unwillingness to concede "sacred talent" to paganism caused Firmicus to alter *sacrum ingenium* to *sagax ingenium;* cf. Albert Becker, "Julius Firmicus Maternus und Pseudo-Quintilian," *Philologus* 61 N.S. 15 (1902) 476–78. The idea embodied in the poetic phrase *Primus in orbe deos fecit timor,* found in Petronius, *Fr.* 27.1, and Statius, *Theb.* 3.661, is traced by G. Heuten, *Latomus* 1 (1937) 3–8, not to Lucretius but to Stoic and Neoplatonic sources, whence it became known to astrological writers such as Pseudo-Quintilian and Firmicus. Pastorino's note, in part: "The declamation of Quintilian is on astrology and the defender of that science attributes popular beliefs to the weakness of the primitive intellect. Once strengthened, the human intellect can get at the true causes, i.e. can be initiated into astrology. For Firmicus, turned Christian, the focal point will no longer be astrology, but Christianity."

³³³ Firmicus here concludes the second major section of his argument. By partly euhemeristic and partly naturalistic explanations he has sought to discredit the old-time pagan worships of the Greco-Roman world. The elevated language of 17.4 is designed to emphasize the conclusion that mankind's religious progress has been from fear (*terror*) to wonderment (*admiratio*) to truth (*veritas*).

³³⁴ The symbols of the mystery religions are the topic of the third and final section of Firmicus' treatise (Chs. 18–27); Chs. 28 and 29 are a concluding exhortation to the ruling emperors. Firmicus' general interpretation is that the symbolism of the mysteries is a diabolically inspired imitation of biblical words, usages, and symbols. Quoting Ziegler (1953 edition, p. 17): "This section is particularly valuable because it contains much information not otherwise known to us about the mystery religions." Coman (111) observes that Firmicus was contemporary with the matters under

discussion and besides could read the Greek sources of information; thus by direct and indirect means he was able to amass good information. The bitterer tone adopted in the following chapters Boll, RE 6 (1909) 2377, ascribes to the fact that the mystery cults were alive, flourishing, and dangerous, whereas the traditional relation of the emperors to the Roman state religion could have prompted Firmicus, in a treatise addressed to the emperors, to be milder in his attack on the official but moribund religion.

335 The different meanings of σύμβολον are historically discussed by Friedrich (28–36), who successfully impugned the arguments of G. Wobbermin, *Religionsgeschichtliche Studien zur Frage der Beeinflussung des Urchristentums durch das antike Mysterienwesen* (Berlin 1896) 177, and earlier writers that the word never signified "password" or "token of recognition." The first formula recorded by Firmicus (18.1) was in the nature of a password, but the others were not; therefore the general assertion of the opening sentence of this chapter that the formulas were passwords is substantiated only by a single instance. The rest of the *symbola* quoted by Firmicus were formulaic responses to questions put by priests of the mysteries: Arnob. 5.26: *verba quae rogati sacrorum in acceptionibus respondetis;* cf. P. Foucart, *Les mystères d'Eleusis* (Paris 1914) 377, and Heuten's note on the present passage of Firmicus. All the *symbola* cited in the ensuing chapters "refer to the peripetia, either that in the life of the god or to the parallel one in the life of his adept": G. van der Leeuw, "The σύμβολα in Firmicus Maternus," *Egyptian Religion* 1 (1933) 61–72 at 69. It has been noticed that Firmicus reserves the words *symbolum* and *sacramentum* (occurring only in 20.1) for pagan affairs, using *secretum* and *arcanum* for either pagan or Christian affairs.

336 Firmicus' theology "gave the devil his due," as appears particularly from this and the ensuing chapters.

337 The urge, felt by many, to interpret *moriturus* as an allusion to a mystical "death" of the initiate is rebuked by Heuten, Pastorino, and Ziegler and regarded doubtfully by Nilsson 2.658. Heuten follows Père Lagrange in thinking *moriturus* means that the devotee of Cybele courts damnation by performing the pagan rites. Cf. *perituros homines* in 27.1 and *morituri draconis* in 26.3.

[338] The Latin formula here cited (*De tympano manducavi, de cymbalo bibi, et religionis secreta perdidici*) does not correspond in its third and final clause with the authentic Greek words which immediately follow. For an unknown reason Firmicus substituted in the Latin a vague interpretation of the Greek instead of a translation. Discarding the words of the *symbolum*, he has used his own favorite phraseology, for we read in *Math.* 1.4.11 *divinae dispositionis secreta perdidicit*, and in 5.1.26 *absconsarum religionum secreta perdiscens*, and *religionis* (*-num*) *secreta* in three other passages.

Three Greek sources (Clem. Al., *Protr.* 2.15.3; Euseb., *Praep. ev.* 2.3.18; and Schol. Plat., *Gorg.* 497C) cite a formula of Attis worship in the following words (the Platonic scholium erroneously referring it to the Eleusinian mysteries): ἐκ τυμπάνου ἔφαγον· ἐκ κυμβάλου ἔπιον· ἐκερνοφόρησα· ὑπὸ τὸν παστὸν ὑπέδυν. In Pastorino's notes one may find a review of scholarly opinion regarding the divergence between this wording and that given by Firmicus. I adhere to the view of Ziegler (in his note to his translation, p. 60): "Offenbar ist nicht etwa die eine Form richtig, die andere falsch, sondern es handelt sich um zwei sakramentale Formeln des Attis, das eine nur auf ein Speisesakrament, das andere ausserdem auf ein Sakrament der geschlechtlichen Vereinigung mit dem Gott bezüglich. Dass Firmicus nur das Speisesakrament im Auge hat, zeigt die ganze folgende Darlegung, die dem todbringenden heidnischen Symbol die heilsamen alttestamentlich-christlichen Speisungen entgegenstellt." Communion for the votaries of Attis was under both species, but no record reports on the exact contents of the tambourine and cymbal. See Cumont (65, E.T. 69): "Towards the end of the empire, moral ideas were particularly connected with the assimilation of sacred liquor and meats taken from the tambourine and cymbal of Attis. They became the staff of the spiritual life and were to sustain the votary in his trials."

[339] The odd expression *vitalem venam stringit in mortem* is from Ps.-Quint., *Decl.* 10.4: *omnes in mortem strinxerat venas*, and had already been used by Firmicus, *Math.* 1.9.1: *venas stringit in mortem*.

[340] F. J. Dölger, AC 3 (1932) 225f., noted the heightened tendency in the fourth century to label pagan usages and cult

formulas as spurious or imitated, while Christianity possessed the authentic and the original. He cited the present passage of Firmicus and others to come: 19.1, 20.1, 20.6, 21.4, 27.8.

341 The Introduction has already discussed the fact that Firmicus was more familiar with Cyprian's two collections of biblical passages than with the Bible itself. Up to this point in the treatise Firmicus has quoted Scripture only a couple of times, but henceforward he does so frequently. As a matter of policy the present notes will point to Firmicus' source both in the Bible and (where possible) in Cyprian. Here the quotation is from Prov. 9.5, cf. Cypr., *Test.* 2.2; the Vulgate has *comedite,* Cyprian *edite,* and Firmicus *manducate.*

342 The incident is related in Gen. 14.18–20.

343 Gen. 27 gives the whole story of the blessings imparted by Isaac. Verse 37 is the one quoted by Firmicus, a verse not found in Cyprian. "There appears to be no other early citation of this verse": E. J. Martin, "The Biblical Text of Firmicus Maternus," *Journ. of Theol. Stud.* 24 (1923) 318–25 at 323. The correspondence with the Vulgate is feeble. Firmicus: *Dominum illum feci tuum et omnes fratres eius feci servos, tritico et vino confirmavi illum.* Vulgate: *Dominum tuum illum constitui, et omnes fratres eius servituti illius subiugavi: frumento et vino stabilivi eum.*

344 Isa. 65.13–15 (in part); Cypr., *Test.* 1.22.

345 Ps. 33(34).9; Cypr., *loc. cit.*

346 Ps. 33(34).10–11; Cypr., *loc. cit.*

347 Pastorino has invited attention to partial parallels, in thought and diction, between this sentence and Min. Fel. 37.10, Cypr., *ad Don.* 3 and 11. The parallels are insufficient to indicate borrowing. Firmicus has here displayed literary artistry, notably with *aut auro . . . aut lauro* and *paupertatis . . . pondus.* He may have purposely taken *turpis egestas* from Vergil, *Aen.* 6.276.

348 The following passage is of course an abbreviated paraphrase of Luke 16.19–26.

349 John 6.35; Cypr., *loc. cit.*

350 *In sequentibus;* the second quotation immediately follows the first in Cypr., *loc. cit.,* but not in John, where the first is 6.35 and the second 7.37–38. Firmicus has betrayed himself into referring to the sequence that is visible in Cyprian more than in John.

351 John 6.54; Cypr., *loc. cit.*

[352] *O dii miseri mortales* is the exact wording of the MS. both here and at 7.9 (n. 182 above). Pastorino follows the MS.; not so Ziegler.

[353] *Vivificat*, apparently from John 6.64 (so Ziegler). The word in the sense "to give spiritual life" is common in the Vulgate and the Latin Christian writers: Blaise-Chirat *s.v.* and H. Rönsch, *Itala und Vulgata* (Marburg 1875) 178.

[354] Spiritual death comes from partaking of the sacramental feast of Attis, a counterfeit and mockery of the Eucharist.

[355] All the editors agree that there is a lacuna at this point, affecting Ch. 19 rather than the end of 18. The scribe of P showed no awareness of a lacuna, which Ziegler suggests may have amounted to one or more folios.

[356] The beginning of this religious formula or *symbolum* is lost because of the lacuna, but the MS. reports correctly the surviving portion. Because νύμφος was an unknown word, and because Firmicus glossed it with *sponsus*, Flacius and nearly all succeeding editors prior to 1934 emended νύμφε to νύμφιε. But Cumont in that year, examining the 250 graffiti deciphered by Rostovtzeff on the Mithraeum of Dura-Europus, noticed repeatedly νύμφῳ or ἀγαθῷ νύμφῳ. He recalled the passage in Jerome (*Ep.* 107.2) where the seven degrees of initiation into Mithraic worship include *nymphus* as the second. Hilberg in his edition of Jerome's letters emended *nymphus* to *cryphius*, but the data from Dura show that any emendation is wrong. (It is regrettable that Labourt in his recent edition of the letters of Jerome is not *au courant* in this passage.) What would be the meaning and interpretation of the newly discovered word? In his original observations, Cumont, "Rapport sur une mission archéologique à Doura-Europos," *CR Acad. Inscr.* 1934, 90–111 at 108, interpreted it simply as "adolescent," but he eventually believed it to mean "fiancé" or "bridegroom." In notes published posthumously, *Hommages à Joseph Bidez et à Franz Cumont* (Brussels 1949) 237, he supported his final opinion by saying that the degree of *nymphus* was under the patronage of the planet Venus, and an initiate of this degree was portrayed in the Mithraeum of Santa Prisca as nuptially dressed in long veils and holding a lamp. LSJ, 9th ed., Addenda, confines itself to defining νύμφος as "a grade in Mithraic initiation," and Blaise-Chirat defines *nymphus* as "le marié(?)." It appears that Firmicus was justified in equating

the Greek word with *sponsus*. F. J. Dölger, AC 5 (1936) 286–88, warmly greeted Cumont's discovery regarding Firmicus, and added the view that the latter was quoting from a Mithraic hymn.—Since we belatedly know, thanks to Cumont, that the religious salutation of this *symbolum* is addressed to Mithra (and not, as was formerly thought, to Bacchus), we are in a better position to understand why the god is saluted as "new light." Mithra was a god of light, often equated with Helios. F. J. Dölger, "Lumen Christi," AC 5 (1936) 1–4, has shown that χαῖρε, φίλον φῶς in late classical Greece was a greeting familiarly used by lovers of either sex, and therefore applicable to a bridegroom. Since Firmicus is about to advance the argument that Christ is the true bridegroom and the true light, he first cites the salutation to a pagan deity as the bridegroom and the light. "Zu beachten ist freilich, dass der Gruss χαῖρε φῶς, χαῖρε φίλον φῶς, χαῖρε νέον φῶς richtige Sonnenbegrüssungen waren" (Dölger, citing H. Usener, *Götternamen* [Bonn 1896] 185 n. 24).

[357] *Audire* has the meaning "to be called" in Horace, *Epp.* 1.1.17, and elsewhere in classical Latin. Alfons Müller is the only recent scholar who failed to recognize that this is the meaning in the present passage of Firmicus.

[358] *Perpetuus* is a favorite word with Firmicus, occurring thirteen times in the *De errore* and often in *Math.* Firmicus could have found *perpetua nox* in one of his known sources, Ps.-Quint., *Decl.* 1.6, and it appears earlier in Sen., *Ep.* 82.16.

[359] *Erige vultus*, a known but not common locution, is from Ps.-Quint., *Decl.* 5.6: noted by A. Becker, *Philol.* 61 N.F. 15 (1902) 478. Other occurrences in Curt. 5.5.23, Petron. 60.2, *et alibi*.

[360] *Desertis his.* Skutsch believed that some noun such as *tenebris* has dropped out of the text. The pronoun *his* could allude to the whole collection of dismal-sounding nouns in the previous sentence.

[361] John 8.12; Cypr., *Test.* 2.7.

[362] The *variatio temporum* in this sentence (*orietur, insinuat, possumus*) is paralleled by several instances in *Math.*, listed by C. Brakman, *Mnem.* 52 (1924) 444f. Generalizing from this passage and others, Ernout says of Firmicus (*Rev. de philol.* 64 N.S. 12 [1938] 244): "Sa langue présente bien des tours décon-

certants: les modes et les temps y sont souvent confondus, sans
qu'il soit toujours possible de discerner si la faute en revient à
l'auteur lui-même, ou au copiste." The prevalence of such incon-
sistencies leads to the belief, supported by Pastorino, that we
should attribute them to Firmicus himself, not to the scribe.

[363] A historical treatment of the Church as bride and as mother
can be found in, respectively: C. Chavasse, *The Bride of Christ:
An Enquiry into the Nuptial Element in Early Christianity*
(London 1940), and J. C. Plumpe, *Mater Ecclesia* (Washington
1943). Firmicus was a reader of Cyprian, who alludes to the
Church as *sponsa Christi* in *De eccl. unit.* 6. The concept of
mater ecclesia was particularly frequent in Tertullian and Cyprian.

[364] The heading of Cyprian, *Test.*, 2.19, is: *Quod Ipse sit sponsus
ecclesiam habens sponsam, de qua filii spiritales nascerentur.* Immediately following, as in Firmicus, is the relevant passage of Joel.

[365] Joel 2.15f.; Cypr., *Test.* 2.19. The MSS. of Cyprian exhibit
textual variants, but the text by Hartel (CSEL) gives for the
words of Joel exactly the same as we find in Firmicus, with note-
worthy divergences from the Vulgate. Thus Cyprian and Firmicus have *indicite curationem* where the Vulgate has *vocate
coetum;* the Septuagint with κηρύξατε θεραπείαν supports the
tradition represented by Cyprian and Firmicus. Cyprian's *excipite
maiores natu* again resembles LXX ἐκλέξασθε πρεσβυτέρους, not
the Vulgate *coadunate senes.*

[366] Jer. 7.34; Cypr., *Test.* 2.19. Except for orthography and
the omission of one phrase Firmicus has again copied the wording of Cyprian, which varies from the Vulgate.

[367] Ps. 18(19).6f.; Cypr., *loc. cit.* Here the text of Cyprian is
essentially that of the Vulgate, but Firmicus gives a notably
different text.

[368] Apoc. 21.9f.; Cypr., *loc. cit.* In this passage Firmicus and
Cyprian are in full textual agreement, with slight variation from
the Vulgate. In this and the four other passages (24.7, 27.7, 28.8,
28.13) where Firmicus quotes from the Apocalypse his introductory words show monotonous regularity and never allude to
authorship. *Sancta revelatio,* says Firmicus repeatedly; but he did
not believe in Johannine authorship: A. Vecchi, *Convivium* 25
(1957) 651.

[369] John 3.28f.; Cypr., *loc. cit.* Firmicus reproduces Cyprian's
text; *aliter* Vulg.

370 Immediately after the citation from John both Cyprian and Firmicus have the phrase *Huius rei mysterium ostensum est.*

371 The parable of the wise and foolish virgins is in Matt. 25.1–13.

372 *Pervigili cura* (repeated later in this chapter) is quoted not from Matthew but from *Math.* 8.33.4.

373 Luke 12.35–37; Cypr., *loc. cit.* Firmicus followed Cyprian except on two words, where he employed synonyms; *aliter* Vulg.

374 *In acerbis casibus constitutus*, a phrase repeated verbatim from *Math.* 1.2.6.

375 The word *sacramentum* occurs in the *De errore* only here.

376 Mithra. M. J. Vermaseren, *Corpus monumentorum et inscriptionum religionis Mithriacae* (The Hague, 1956–60), refers to dozens of monuments depicting the rock birth of Mithra: see e.g. figs. 100, 165,166. The rock was called *petra genetrix.* Cumont, *The Mysteries of Mithra* (Chicago 1903) 130f.: "The light bursting from the heavens, which were conceived as a solid vault, became, in the mythology of the Magi, Mithra born from the rock. The tradition ran that the Generative Rock, of which a standing image was worshipped in the temples, had given birth to Mithra on the banks of a river."

377 Firmicus now proceeds to quote a hodgepodge of scriptural passages which exhibit the key word "stone." The relationship of these passages to the Generative Rock of Mithra is nil. But Justin Martyr, *Dial. c. Tryph.* 70, had preceded Firmicus on this false path, saying that the devil had borrowed from Dan. 2.34 and Isa. 33.13–19 the idea of the birth of Mithra from a rock.

378 Christ the Rock is a Pauline concept, 1 Cor. 10.4: *Omnes eumdem potum spiritalem biberunt: bibebant autem de spiritali, consequente eos, petra: petra autem erat Christus.* Also one recalls 1 Peter 2.4–6: *Lapidem vivum . . . lapidem summum angularem, electum, pretiosum: et qui crediderit in eum, non confundetur.* The Church Fathers naturally made frequent use of this concept, e.g. Tert., *ad Marc.* 3.16.5: *Petra enim Christus.*

379 *Ruina sequitur et cadentium culminum funesta conlapsio.* Firmicus was picking up an alliterative phrase that he had already used, *Math.* 6.29.10: *cadentium culminum ruinis.* Very likely he had noticed Ps.-Quint., *Decl.* 2.24: *conlabentium culminum fragor.*

380 Isa. 28.16, but Firmicus took the wording unchanged from

Cypr., *Test.* 2.16, and Cyprian in turn took the wording mostly from the loose quotation of Isaias in 1 Peter 2.6 (just quoted in n. 378).

[381] Ps. 117(118).22f., quoted in Matt. 21.42; Cypr., *Test.* 2.16 (all texts in agreement except in the choice of the pronoun to mean "this"). The MS. of Firmicus reads *in centesimo et septimo psalmo*, perhaps through an error of the author rather than the scribe (Ziegler).

[382] Zach. 3.8f.; Cypr., *loc. cit.* The MS. of Firmicus yields incomprehensible words at this point, in an apparent corruption of Cyprian's text; *aliter* Vulg.

[383] Deut. 27.8; Cypr., *loc. cit.* Again Firmicus followed Cyprian faithfully, not the Vulgate.

[384] The MS. gives merely *Hiesus Nave*, as in Cyprian, *loc. cit.* The names appear in the Vulgate as *Iosue filius Nun*.

[385] Jos. 24.26f.; Cypr., *loc. cit.* The texts of Firmicus and Cyprian, closely resembling each other, are remote from the Vulgate.

[386] Dan. 2.31–35; Cypr., *Test.* 2.17. Firmicus gives Cyprian's text with minuscule differences; *omnino aliter* Vulg.

[387] *Septemtrion*, not literally the North Star; but the translator has here been carried away by the sweep of Firmicus' rhetoric.

[388] Firmicus is of course indulging in a rhetorical exaggeration, contradicted both by the facts and by his own assertions; for example, in 13.3 he asserted of Serapis: *Hic in Aegypto colitur, hic adoratur, huius simulacrum neocororum turba custodit.* Speaking of the period one generation after the death of Firmicus, J. R. Palanque (*The Church in the Christian Roman Empire*, tr. by E. C. Messenger [London 1949–52] 685) writes: "There were still many pagans within the Empire. They were found especially in two classes of society, the ruling and cultivated aristocracy, and the poor and ignorant rural masses." Cf. Introd. 10–13 and Pastorino's note on the present passage.

[389] A metaphor which Firmicus liked, and which he seemingly did not borrow from his known sources. The phrase here, *ut . . . hoc malum funditus amputetur*, echoes his words about the SC de Bacchanalibus (6.9): *quamdiu hoc malum fuisset radicitus amputatum.*

[390] In the MS. only the prefix *con-* can be read. Flacius, followed by most editors, gave *coniungit;* but Ziegler prefers *con-*

ponit, a verb commoner in Firmicus and used (22.3) in the locution *membra conponis*. The difference in meaning will be imponderable.

391 *In cinerem favillasque converso*, borrowed from *Math.* 1.9.1: *in cinerem favillasque convertitur*.

392 A short lacuna leaves us without a subjunctive, presumably transitive, verb at the end of this sentence. T. Wikström, *Eranos* 53 (1955) 189, proposed (and I adopt) *sortiatur*. The locution *imperium sortiri* is in 5.3 and *Math.* 4.1.6; and *Math.* exhibits *sortiri* commonly with such objects as *dominium, potestatis licentiam, regimen potestatemque hominum*.

393 *Terrena fragilitas*, a phrase and concept of which Firmicus was enamored: 18.2, *Math.* 1.4.4, 1.7.11, 8.1.5. Once in Arnobius: 4.28.

394 The brother-emperors did not heed this clear invitation to sainthood.

395 Pertinent are two items, *Cod. Theod.* 16.10.2 and 3, discussed in the Introduction 11. The reader is reminded that these laws did little to eradicate or even to discourage paganism.

396 *Veneni virus*, also in 18.2, 18.5, *Math.* 1.9.1, 5.2.16, 6.15.7. Firmicus rejoiced in the phrase because it combined two of his favorite usages: alliteration and *genetivus inhaerentiae*.

397 Emending *eminentis* to *enim* [*vinc*]*entis*, with T. Wikström, *Eranos* 53 (1955) 189f. Ziegler (1953 ed.) emended to [*omnipot*]-*entis*. Other suggestions by J. B. Bauer, *Wien. Stud.* 71 (1958) 157f.

398 The MS. has: *inter acervos cesarum hostium prostravistis exercitum*. Editors since Flacius have contrived various emendations. Italo Lana, reviewing Pastorino's edition in *Riv. fil.* 36 (1958) 204f., observes that the MS. occasionally has *a* where it should have *o*, so that Flacius and later editors were warranted in reading *caesorum*. Wikström, *Eranos* 53 (1955) 190f., agrees with Ziegler that the sentence requires an attribute for *exercitum* that will allude to its paganism or cult. Observing *profani homines* in 28.12 and *Math.* 4.22.1, he offers and I adopt [*profanorum hominum*]. I agree with Heuten and Pastorino that Firmicus refers to a military victory which in a sense was a double victory, for the beaten foes of the Roman state were also foes of Rome's newly espoused Christianity.

399 At the beginning of this sentence the MS. is hardly legible.

For the first two words Ziegler (1953 ed.) and Pastorino give
Felices [quos] instead of the traditional reading *Felices vos.* All
that can be read of the third word is *p–p–s;* Ziegler (1907)
printed *principatus,* but admitted this word was too long for the
available space. *Imperii* (Ziegler [1953] and Pastorino) yields a
good meaning but has nothing else to commend it. Wikström,
Eranos 53 (1955) 191, suggests (and I adopt) *propositi,* as somewhat shorter than *principatus* and yet containing the three legible
letters. *Propositi* is well balanced with *voluntatis* as a near
synonym.

⁴⁰⁰ I translate here a portion of G. Faggin's note (p. 168 of his
Italian version): "The whole Christology of Firmicus is based on
the destruction of the rule of the devil, who triumphed from the
time of Adam's sin until the coming of Christ. The Christian
interpretation of Genesis 3.15 developed in the Christian writers
the idea of the struggle between the principle of good and that
of evil, which in Manicheism took on a gloomy outlook. The
triumph of Christ over the principle of evil is expressed, among
the first, by Justin, Ignatius of Antioch, Origen, *et al.*"

⁴⁰¹ Firmicus was convinced that the devil had warped and mis-
quoted Scripture for his own purposes. Justin Martyr, *1 Apol.*
54.4, claimed that the demons did not fully understand the O.T.
Prophets, but imitated them with errors. Tertullian, *De praescr.
haer.* 40.6, arguing that the rites and cults introduced in Rome
by Numa resembled Judaism, said: *Nonne manifeste diabolus
morositatem illam Iudaicae legis imitatus est?*

⁴⁰² This formula or *symbolum* is rightly ascribed to the Dionysiac cult by A. Dieterich, *Eine Mithrasliturgie* (Leipzig 1923)
Anhang, no. 7. Dieterich pointed to the Orphic Hymn to Dionysus (30, vs. 3, ed. W. Quandt), where we find the two adjectives διϰέρωτα, δίμορφον side by side amidst a great cluster of
epithets for Dionysus. "Der Vers wird als Klage um den Gott
gesprochen sein," says Dieterich. Zagreus, identical or identified
with Dionysus, was, according to a feeble tradition, born tauriform: Arnob. 5.21. Another version had it that Hera set the
Titans to kill the child Zagreus, and he tried vainly to escape by
metamorphosis into animal forms, including that of a bull:
Johannes Schmidt, "Zagreus," LM 6.534. Plutarch, *De Is. et Os.*
35, shows knowledge of a tauriform Dionysus and reports,
Quaest. Gr. 36, p.299B, that the women of Elis at a festival sang

to Dionysus a hymn with the refrain ἄξιε ταῦρε. Roman poetry knew of a Bacchus who was bicorn if not fully tauriform: Tib. 2.1.3f.: *Bacche, veni, dulcisque tuis e cornibus uva pendeat.*

[403] Firmicus, probably not personally familiar with the basilisk, read of it in Ps. 90(91).13: *Super aspidem et basiliscum ambulabis.* If the scorpion does not appear in this text of the Psalms, it does in Luke 10.19: *Ecce dedi vobis potestatem calcandi supra serpentes et scorpiones.*

[404] The anguiform devil in Gen. 3.13 was blamed by Eve for deceiving her (*Serpens decepit me*); the quest for his head is an allusion to God's plan of enmity between woman and serpent (3.15: *Ipsa conteret caput tuum*); and the doom of mortality was the penalty for original sin (3.19).

[405] Job 40.20: *An extrahere poteris leviathan hamo?* But Firmicus would have known the wording antedating the Vulgate and more closely resembling his own: *Adduces autem dracones in hamo?*

[406] Killing the water snake that infested the marshes of Lerna in Argolis was the second labor of Heracles.

[407] Firmicus is inexact, since the myth represented the hydra as a single serpent with nine heads; and the amputation of heads by Heracles caused new heads, not new serpents, to sprout in succession.

[408] The reading *vitiata*, "tainted," is a conjecture by Halm, adopted by all recent editors. *Plebs Dei* or simply *plebs* recurs in 27.3 and 5 to mean "the community of Christians." In this sense *plebs* is amply attested, e.g. in Lactantius and Ambrose (Blaise-Chirat *s.v.*); and *plebs Dei* is found in Commod., *Instr.* 2.18.17: *in plebe Dei facultatis dona demonstres*, and Prud., *c. Symm.* 2.901f.: *ite procul, gentes! consortia nulla viarum sunt vobis cum plebe Dei.* The familiar Christian meaning of *plebs* as "laity" (λαός) as distinguished from the clergy is not found in Firmicus.

[409] An allusion to αἰαί, the first word of the quoted *symbolum*.

[410] Justin, *Dial. c. Tryph.* 91, trying to interpret the "rhinoceros horns" of Deut. 33.17, was the first to speak of the arms of the cross as "horns" and on this basis to give a fantastic interpretation of an allusion to horns in the Old Testament. Wm. A. Irwin, "The Psalm of Habakkuk," *Journ. Near East. Stud.* 1 (1942) 10–40 at 13, reaffirms a widely held view that by "horns" Habacuc (3.4) meant shafts of lightning.

⁴¹¹ Irwin (*op. cit.* 10) rates the third chapter of Habacuc "among the very difficult and obscure passages of the Old Testament." The interpretative sentence of Firmicus, explaining *obscurum per obscurius*, entitles him to an exceedingly low mark as an exegete of Habacuc. To make matters worse, the text of the sentence is corrupt, causing Ziegler (1907 ed.) in his critical apparatus to say: "Structuram misere turbatam certo restitui posse desperamus." I have endeavored to translate the conjectural reading hesitantly offered by T. Wikström, *Eranos* 53 (1955) 191f.: *ut si[t] totus orbis tripertita stabilitate firmatus, c[um] fixi operis immortal[i] radic[e] fundamenta teneantur.* The grammatical confusion of the text at this point may reflect the scribe's inability, shared by me, to fathom the mystical and grandiose language. Pastorino points to sundry other mystical interpretations of the Cross in the Fathers; but his false reference to Jerome should be corrected to Ps.-Hier., *Exp. in Marc.* 15 (ML 30.661C), a passage dependent on Sedulius, *Pasch. carm.* 5.188–95. Ziegler (trans., p. 61), referring to Robert Eisler, *Weltenmantel und Himmelszelt* (Munich 1910), reminds us that the idea of the Cross of Christ holding up the cosmos is rooted in the ancient Oriental concept of the sky as a canopy stretched over the world.

⁴¹² Hab. 3.3–5, slightly shortened and altered from the wording given in Cypr., *Test.* 2.21. Cyprian's text resembles the LXX more than it does the Vulgate.

⁴¹³ This and the preceding clause are transparent allusions to the Carrying of the Cross.

⁴¹⁴ Isa. 9.6, cf. Cypr., *loc. cit.;* again closer to the LXX than to the Vulgate.

⁴¹⁵ Exod. 17.9–12. Firmicus refrains from quoting the passage, which appears at full length in Cypr., *loc. cit.;* but he follows Cyprian's interpretation: *Hoc signo crucis et Amalech victus est ab Iesu per Moysen.* This symbolical interpretation of Moses with outstretched arms as prefiguring the Cross is encountered first in *Epist. Barn.* 12. The latter part of Firmicus' sentence (*ut facilius impetraret quod magnopere postulabat, crucem sibi fecit ex virga*) does not refer to Num. 21.8f., *pace* Alfons Müller, but still to Moses versus Amalec. What Moses greatly wanted was a victory over Amalec; what he did was to stretch out his arms high and sidewise, holding the rod horizontally, and making a

T-shaped cross out of his vertical body and the horizontal rod. Also in 21.4 Firmicus had in mind a T-shaped cross, whose three (not four) *cornua* gave the cosmos a *tripertita stabilitas*. Such is the exegesis by J. B. Bauer, *Wien. Stud.* 71 (1958) 159.

⁴¹⁶ *Festina celeritate*, a good phrase borrowed by Firmicus from himself, *Math.* 4.1.6 (cf. *celeri festinatione* in 4.1.7).

⁴¹⁷ The thought, much bandied about in the present century, that Christianity has remarkable analogies with the mystery religions or is even indebted to them, has been rebuked by M. J. Lagrange, "Les mystères d'Eleusis et le christianisme," *Rev. bibl.* 28 (1919) 157–217, and A. D. Nock, "Hellenistic Mysteries and Christian Sacraments," *Mnem.* ser. 4, 5 (1952) 177–213. Nock (212) says: "To argue as I have done is not to suggest that pagan mysteries had no influence on the development and acceptance of Catholic Christianity; the surprise is that on the evidence they had so little."

⁴¹⁸ *Per numeros digestis fletibus plangitur*. Alfons Müller understood *numeros* to refer to groups of mourners; but Faggin, Heuten, Ziegler, Pastorino, and others prefer to take *numeros* in the musical sense, "rhythms."

⁴¹⁹ According to R. Reitzenstein, *Die hellenistischen Mysterienreligionen* (3rd ed. Leipzig 1927) 400, the anointing by the priest gave the initiates a promise of immortality, since the same ointment was used that was used to effect the resurrection of the deity. A reference to anointing the goddess, i.e. her statue, appeared in 1914 in a newly discovered segment of the *Acta fratrum Arvalium*: O. Marucchi, *Not. Scav.* 1914, 466: *deam unguentavit* (1.29f.), *deam unguentaverunt* (1.32). The goddess was Dea Dia, equivalent to Ceres, and the act of anointing was presumably intended to effect the annual resurrection of the grain (Ceres).

⁴²⁰ *Lento murmure*. Carl Weyman, *Archiv f. lat. Lex.* 14 (1906) 496f., was the first to observe that *lentus* in this passage means "low" or "soft." E. Löfstedt, *Coniectanea* (Uppsala 1950) 81f., offered several parallels for this meaning in late and medieval Latin.

⁴²¹ The Greek formula consists of two iambic trimeters, imitated in the translation. The genitive of the first trimeter is correctly understood as a genitive absolute by Heuten, Ziegler, and others; as a possessive genitive by Alfons Müller. Clinching the

case is the ablative absolute, *liberato deo suo*, in Firmicus' own paraphrase of the Greek formula (24.1). Since the formula is found only here and Firmicus does not identify the god in question, controversy has arisen: Adonis, Attis, or Osiris? See the history of the discussion in Pastorino's note. Though Heuten and several others have argued for Attis, the authority of Loisy, Lagrange, Cumont, Nilsson, and Ziegler favors Osiris. Lagrange, "Attis et le christianisme," *Rev. bibl.* 28 (1919) 419–80 at 448, wrote as follows: "Le dieu sauvé n'est pas Attis mais sûrement Osiris. En effet, à partir du chap. xviii, l'apologiste expose tous les *symbola* des mystères. Les mystes d'Attis paraissent dès le debut du ch. xviii; d'autres suivent, et le ch. xxii se rapporte au dieu égyptien comme le prouve le detail de la lumière, qui rappelle l'exhortation *quaere exordium lucis* (2.9), à propos d'Osiris. Cette statue qu'on apporte dans une litière et dont on rassemble les membres gisants et sans doute épars (22.3) représente beaucoup mieux Osiris qu'Attis, comme M. Loisy l'a très bien vu." Cf. Cumont 226 n. 46; Nilsson 2.612f.; Ziegler's trans. p.61. Nilsson observed that to have a god's stone image dismembered and then put together again (22.3) was a cult action appropriate to Osiris and not to Attis. Cumont, *Lux perpetua* (Paris 1949) 404, traced the thought and some of the wording of the liturgical formula to the Pythagorean *Golden Verses*, 63 and 66:

'Αλλὰ σὺ θάρσει ἐπεὶ θεῖον γένος ἐστὶ βροτοῖσιν . . .
ψυχὴν δὲ πόνων ἀπὸ τῶνδε σαώσεις.

[422] Firmicus means that for Osiris there was no inspired prophetic literature foretelling his resurrection, as there was for Christ; and he goes on to say that in the case of Osiris there was no epiphany to verify the supposed resurrection.

[423] *Praecedentibus exemplis;* the translation, to suit the context, was suggested by an anonymous reviewer of Heuten, *Suppl. crit. Bull. Budé* 10 (1938) 110. The allusion is to the resurrection of Lazarus, the daughter of Jairus, and the young man of Nain.

[424] Though Firmicus speaks contemptuously, he actually condenses in this short sentence the essential doctrine of the mystery religions: that the mystae by initiation and ritual acts gained a share in the divine life and a guarantee of immortality.

[425] *Quo dolore* of the MS. was easily emended by Bursian to *quod olore*. Bursian suggested and Halm adopted *quod odore*.

A. Ernout, *Rev. de philol.* 12 (1938) 244 n. 2, pointed out that *olor* is a vulgar spelling of *odor*, under the influence of *olere*.

426 The verb *dispicere* occurs only twice elsewhere in the *De errore* (2.5 and 18.6), in both passages transparently in the meaning of *despicere*. In his critical note on the first passage Ziegler calls attention to the orthography and the correct meaning. It is therefore regrettable that Alfons Müller and Ziegler have both gone astray on this third occurrence of the verb, rendering it by "durchschauen."

427 Firmicus, knowing Greek, was aware that *christus* means "anointed." Blaise-Chirat cites no parallel for the pejorative sense of the word here.

428 The word "Antichrist" is familiar in Tertullian and Cyprian. Firmicus had read 1 John 2.18–27, with its discussion of Christ, Antichrist, unction, and immortality. Cf. R. Reitzenstein, *Die hell. Mysterienreligionen* (3rd ed. Leipzig 1927) 401.

429 In the dialogue of Minucius Felix (12.6) the pagan Caecilius criticizes the Christians because they do not perfume themselves while living but save the ointment for the dead: *Non corpus odoribus honestatis: reservatis unguenta funeribus.*

430 The reference is to the anointment of confirmation. Canons 38 and 77 of the Synod of Elvira in Spain (*ca.* A.D. 306: Denzinger, *Ench. symb.* nos. 52 d-e) define confirmation as the perfection and complement of baptism. Baptism was a sacrament for adults, and in the time of Firmicus it was usually followed at once by confirmation; in such cases there was only one anointing, viz. in connection with the latter sacrament. This view, not shared by Pastorino, is maintained with detailed arguments by A. Vecchi, "Giulio Firmico Materno e la 'Lettera agli Ebrei,'" *Convivium* 25 (1957) 641–51 at 645–47.

431 *Ut sepulto primo homine ex eodem statim homine homo alius felicius nascatur.* Vecchi argues that the phrase *sepulto primo homine* alludes to baptism (cf. Rom. 6.4: *Consepulti enim sumus cum illo per baptismum in mortem*), whereas the remaining words allude to confirmation, which involved unction and followed immediately (*statim*) after baptism.

432 Ps. 44(45).3–9; cf. Cypr., *Test.* 2.29 (vss. 3–5) and 2.6 (vss. 7–8). In this instance Firmicus has not derived his citation from Cyprian, and in general he was not dependent on Cyprian for his knowledge of the Psalter. E. J. Martin, "The Biblical Text of

Firmicus Maternus," *Journ. of Theol. Stud.* 24 (1922–23) 318–25, thinks Firmicus may have used a Spanish Psalter that showed residual African influences.

[433] *Virtutem.* Martin, *op. cit.* 322, regards this word (unattested here in the Septuagint, Vulgate, and Cyprian) as surely a copying error for *veritatem.* Wower, Bursian, and Pastorino have thought best to replace *veritatem* in the text of Firmicus.

[434] Ps. 2.1f.; cf. Cypr., *Test.* 1.13.

[435] Several passages in the Synoptic Gospels, e.g. Matt. 5.22 and 18.9, allude to Gehenna or "the Gehenna of fire," and the patristic writers made free use of the Hebrew word. For a learned treatment cf. J. Chaine, "Géhenne," DB Suppl. 3.563–79.

[436] The sentence is obviously a Latin paraphrase of the Greek formula whispered by the priest, 22.1.

[437] Cumont, *Lux perpetua* (Paris 1949) 401–5, has a complementary note entitled ἀγαθὴ ἐλπίς, showing that ἀγαθὴν ἐλπίδα ἔχειν was a religious formula pronounced in the Eleusinian mysteries, to assure the mystai of a happy existence beyond the grave. Hence Socrates averred that his trip to the next world was "with good hope" (*Phaedo* 67B). The formula, signifying salvation, was later borrowed by some of the other mystery religions and became widely current. Cumont holds that Firmicus was quoting faithfully the sacerdotal formula.

[438] See a full discussion of the topic by H. Quilliet, "Descente de Jésus aux Enfers," DTC 4.565–619. The rhetorical exaltation of Firmicus on the subject justified Pastorino in quoting the words with which Cumont concluded his chapter "Transformations des Enfers," *Lux perpetua* (Paris 1949) 234; "Obscurcie dans l'eschatologie de la Grèce antique, l'idée d'une défaite de la Mort hideuse a été développée dans la littérature de l'Empire, et lorsque les écrivains chrétiens voulurent dépeindre la Descente du Christ aux Enfers, ils en empruntèrent le coloris violent à leurs prédécesseurs païens. Elle devient un drame grandiose qui s'associe à la perturbation de tout l'univers produite par la mort du Sauveur, et l'émotion que faisaient éprouver aux âmes pieuses les péripéties du combat triomphal livré par le Libérateur aux puissances infernales, assura la transmission jusqu'aux mystères du moyen-âge d'un thème scénique éminemment propre à impressioner l'imagination des foules."

[439] The O.T., influenced by ancient Babylonian traditions, re-

peatedly speaks of the gates of death, of Sheol, or of Hades: Job 38.17, Wisd. 16.13, Isa. 38.10.

[440] Luke 23.44f.: *And there was darkness over all the earth until the ninth hour. And the sun was darkened.* The good phrase *mundi rotata vertigo*, only with the substitution of *caeli*, had already been used twice by Firmicus (*Math.* 1 prooem. 5 and 1.3.2) and much earlier, as *tantae molis rotata vertigo*, by Pliny (*N.H.* 2.6). Similarly Arnob. 1.2: *vertigo haec mundi.*

[441] Matt. 27.51: *And behold the veil of the temple was rent in two from the top even to the bottom.*

[442] *Omnia elementa turbata sunt*, perhaps from Arnobius' dramatic retelling of the phenomena attending Christ's death, 1.53: *universa mundi sunt elementa turbata.*

[443] Ps. 43(44).22–26. This passage of the Psalms appears nowhere in Cyprian, except that the first sentence is quoted (*Test.* 3.18) from Romans 8.36. Again Firmicus shows that he knew more of the Psalter than he could get from Cyprian.

[444] *Triumphales currus eius iustorum ac sanctorum turba comitatur.* Firmicus had an easy familiarity with Ovid, and this passage echoes an Ovidian line (*Am.* 1.7.37) about a triumph: *Quaeque tuos currus comitatus turba sequetur.*

[445] 1 Cor. 15.55; Cypr., *Test.* 3.58. *Aculeus* in Cyprian and Firmicus; *stimulus* Vulg.

[446] *Licentia* to mean "power" in Christian Latin is recognized by Moore (12f.) and Blaise-Chirat.

[447] Ps. 23(24).7; Cypr., *Test.* 2.29 (varying from the Vulgate). Since this text from the Psalter reappears a few lines below, Italo Lana, *Riv. fil.* 36 (1958) 205, is justified in commending Bursian for emending the first citation to make it conform with the second. Thus Bursian's [*vos*] after *extollite* has been readily adopted by Halm, Ziegler, and Pastorino. But, as Lana said, Bursian should have taken the further step of emending the genitive *principis vestri*, which does not match the sense of *qui praeestis illis* in the second version. Hartel's text of Cyprian (*loc. cit.*) shows the vocative *principes*, which we need, but not the expected alteration of *vestri* to *vestras.* One MS. of Cyprian, followed by most editors, gives *vestras;* so we should read in Firmicus. Cf. M. Bévenot, S.J., in ACW 25.123 n. 190: "It has often been regretted that in *Testimonia* Hartel followed the Sessorianus

MS A, which presents only a 'subsequent version'; the alterations 'are most evident in the Psalms, where half the quotations are entirely reworded.'"

[448] Ps. 23(24).8; Cypr., *Test.* 2.29.

[449] Ps., *loc. cit.*, and Cypr., *loc. cit.*

[450] This interpretative variant is not in the Vulgate nor in Cyprian.

[451] Dan. 7.13f.; Cypr., *Test.* 2.26. Firmicus reproduces Cyprian's text with minuscule differences; *aliter* Vulg.

[452] Apoc. 1.12–18; Cypr., *loc. cit.* Firmicus gives just the seven verses that Cyprian quoted, and with few verbal changes; *aliter* Vulg.

[453] Matt. 28.18–20; Cypr., *loc. cit.* Firmicus follows Cyprian *litteratim* (with one change of word order, according to Hartel's text of Cyprian); *aliter* Vulg.

[454] Ps. 109(110).1–4, only the first two verses of which are quoted by Cypr., *loc. cit.* In the Psalter, here as elsewhere, Firmicus' wording differs considerably from that of both Cyprian and the Vulgate.

[455] Firmicus is explaining what the Psalmist, in the passage just quoted, meant by "the enemies of God."

[456] There is a small lacuna at this point. Ziegler, followed by Pastorino, suggests [*qualia*] *commenti sunt.* The present translation adopts this reading.

[457] *Sanctarum aurium vestrarum mihi commodate patientiam.* This rare expression is partly paralleled in a writer whom Firmicus read, Arnob. 5.33: *si modo commodare patientiam vultis,* and in Arnobius' pupil Lactantius, *Div. inst.* 1.1.22: *audiendi patientiam commodare.*

[458] Pastorino *ad loc.*: "In questo capitolo v'è un tentativo di conciliare il Vecchio col Nuovo Testamento, affermandone il valore universale della dottrina. . . . Si afferma, in Firmico, la dottrina paolina per cui Cristo, perduto il suo valore messianico, limitato alla nazione ebraica, si inserisce nella storia dell'umanità, in tutto il suo valore universale. Non v'è in Firmico, naturalmente, nessuna dottrina originale."

[459] *Cum hominem primum . . . ad imaginem suam deus faceret,* rather closely following Gen. 1.27: *Et creavit Deus hominem ad imaginem suam* (Vulg).

⁴⁶⁰ *Lignum in paradiso.* *Lignum* is the word regularly used in the Vulgate for the tree of paradise, e.g. Gen. 2.16: *Ex omni ligno paradisi comede.*

⁴⁶¹ Gen. 2.7: *Formavit igitur Dominus Deus hominem de limo terrae* (Firmicus: *de virginis terrae limo*).

⁴⁶² *Nondum enim . . . supra terram pluerat*, from Gen. 2.5: *Non enim pluerat Dominus Deus super terram.*

⁴⁶³ Rom. 5.12: *Propterea sicut per unum hominem peccatum in hunc mundum intravit, et per peccatum mors, et ita in omnes homines mors pertransiit, in quo omnes peccaverunt.*

⁴⁶⁴ *Praevaricatio* in Christian Latin from Tertullian onwards often means "transgression." The choice of the word here may have been to fit an alliterative pattern: *praevaricatione propria promissam perdidit vitam.*

⁴⁶⁵ The Pauline comparison of Christ with Adam is in three passages: 1 Cor. 15.21f., *ibid.* 35–49, Rom. 5.12–21. It reappears often in the patristic writers. Cf. X. Le Bachelet, "Adam figure de Jésus-Christ," DTC 1.384–6; A. Vitti, "Christus–Adam," *Biblica* 7 (1926) 121–45, 270–85, 384–401. Alberto Vecchi "Giulio Firmico Materno e la 'Lettera agli Ebrei,'" *Convivium* 25 (1957) 641–51 at 647, has noted the dramatic nature of Firmicus' 24th and 25th chapters: "Il mondo appare come il teatro di un dramma smisurato. . . . I protagonisti del drama sono Adamo disobbediente ed il Cristo obbediente. Adamo è l'umanità colpevole e sofferente, il Cristo è l'eroe di un'opera enorme di salvezza. I testi scritturali sono prodotti secondo questa necessità scenica."

⁴⁶⁶ Folio 25ᵛ of the MS. ends with the word *virginem.* In the lower right-hand corner the following comment is written in majuscules: *Et hic non ante definitum arborem cuius poma edentes primi homines peccaverunt venenatam fuisse atque pestiferam.*

⁴⁶⁷ The MS. has *accepit* but shows the early scribal correction *recepit* (adopted by Ziegler in his 1953 ed.).

⁴⁶⁸ A similar parallelism in Irenaeus, *Adv. haer.* 5.17.4: *Firmum verbum Dei, quod per lignum negligenter amiseramus nec inveniebamus, recepturi essemus iterum per ligni dispositionem.* Faggin (170 n. 55) says such intellectual parallelisms blossomed into the Italian popular legends of the Middle Ages, to the effect that the tree of Adam's fall was the very one that produced the

wood of Christ's Cross: F. Kampers, *Mittelalterliche Sagen von Paradiese und vom Holze des Kreuzes Christi* (Cologne 1897).

[469] Irenaeus, *Adv. haer.* 5.16.3, draws the same contrast between the disobedience of Adam and the obedience of Christ in connection with the "tree" (*lignum*): (*Dominus*) *eam quae in ligno facta fuerat inobedientiam, per eam quae in ligno fuerat obedientiam sanans.*

[470] Irenaeus was the first of the Fathers to aver specifically that the purpose of the Incarnation was that Christ might make up for the transgression of Adam: *Adv. haer.* 3.18.1: *ut quod perdideramus in Adam . . . hoc in Christo Jesu reciperemus.* This view, found in Irenaeus and Firmicus, became dogma in 529 at the Second Council of Orange; that council's 21st canon (Denzinger, *Ench. symb.* no. 194) declared the purpose of the Crucifixion: *ut natura per Adam perdita per illum repararetur qui dixit venisse se quaerere et salvare quod perierat.* The passages cited in this and the preceding notes argue for the probability that Firmicus knew the writings or at least the views of Irenaeus.

[471] *Novissima paene saeculorum ebdomade.* Some Christians, perhaps indirectly influenced by Pythagorean mysticism of numbers, held that the duration of this world is a *hebdomas*, while eternity, or the time subsequent to the Last Judgment, is an *ogdoas.* On this matter cf. the learned note of Waszink on Tertullian, *De anima* 37.4 (pp. 429f.). For Firmicus' stress on the lateness of the hour when the Incarnation took place, cf. Heb. 9.26: *nunc . . . in consummatione saeculorum . . . apparuit.*

[472] No editor or translator of Firmicus has seen the indebtedness of the following passage to the Epistle to the Hebrews. Pastorino in the course of a dense note says: "La concezione di Firmico sulla liberazione dei giusti e dei Patriarchi dell'Antico Testamento risale anch'essa a Ippolito ed a Ireneo." Only recently Alberto Vecchi, "Giulio Firmico Materno e la 'Lettera agli Ebrei,'" *Convivium* 25 (1957) 641–51, has shown that Firmicus reached behind Irenaeus to Hebrews. From the magnificent eleventh chapter of Hebrews come Firmicus' dramatic power, his doctrinal assertions, and his catalog of patriarchs. Firmicus dwells on *spes* and *fides*; cf. Heb. 11.1: *Now, faith is the substance of things to be hoped for.* "The justice of the saints who have lived and died in the expectation of Christ propounds again the pairing of faith and hope, as viewed in the Epistle to the Hebrews" (Vecchi

648). As examples of just patriarchs who earned merit by faith Firmicus lists seven, in this order: Abel, Henoch, Noe, Sem, Abraham, Isaac, Jacob. Hebrews gives a longer list, but begins with six, in this order: Abel, Henoch, Noe, Abraham, Isaac, Jacob. In Heb. 12.23 Firmicus understood *the church of the first born who are written in the heavens* to mean Abraham and the patriarchs, whose merits won them immortality and admission to the City of God—but only after and through the Incarnation. Consult Vecchi's article for further arguments.—Biblical scholars are well aware that Hebrews was little known in the West from 150 to 350, and never appears at all in the copious scriptural citations of Firmicus' favorite source of biblical knowledge, Cyprian: W. Leonard, in *A Catholic Commentary on Holy Scripture* (London 1953) 1154. Vecchi (650 f.) advances the hypothesis that Firmicus made direct use of Hebrews, but in his polemic against paganism thought it unnecessary or unwise to enter the debate over its canonicity and Pauline authorship; therefore he gave no verbatim citation and did not use the name of Paul.

473 The Vergilian *ineluctabilis* is a rarity in late Latin and used only here by Firmicus, who considered it appropriate in this exalted passage. Though he is likely to have found it in Vergil, he could have seen it also in Arnob. 7.49.

474 Gen. 22.17: *I will multiply thy seed as the stars of heaven* (partly quoted in Heb. 11.12). Heuten mistranslates, being unaware of the late Latin ablative of comparison introduced by *a, ab*: *Thes. ling. lat. s.v.* "a," "ab," p. 39, line 71 (citing this passage of Firmicus). Ernout, *Rev. de philol.* 64 N.S. 12 (1938) 248, rebuking Heuten, himself mistranslates through heedlessness of the scriptural source: "Dieu avait promis la royauté à Abraham plus clairement que les astres du ciel." C. Brakman, "Firmiciana," *Mnem.* 52 (1924) 443, noted the ablative of comparison with *a* in 24.4 (*lucidior a solito dies*) and in the *Math.*

475 *Ne* in vulgar and late Latin may be equivalent to *si forte*: W. Heraeus, *Arch. f. lat. Lex.* 14 (1906) 123; H. Rönsch, *Itala u. Vulgata* (Marburg 1875) 401; A. Blaise, *Man. du lat. chrét.* (Strasbourg 1955) 154. Rönsch refers to another clear case in Firmicus 24.12. Both instances are noted in the *Syntactica* compiled by Ziegler (1907 ed.) 120.

476 Among examples of Firmician alliteration Pastorino (lx) lists the fivefold initial p in this passage.

[477] Cf. Ch. 10 and notes. The formula, last in the series cited by Firmicus, belongs to the Sabazian mysteries and is known from Clem., *Protr.* 2.16 (copied verbatim by Eus., *Praep. ev.* 2.3.21) and Arnob. 5.21. Clement records the myth as follows: Zeus in the guise of a bull united with his own mother Demeter and begat Proserpina. When Proserpina came to womanhood, Zeus in the guise of a serpent united with her and begat the tauriform Dionysus-Zagreus. As for the Greek iambic trimeter quoted by Clement and Firmicus, and in Latin by Arnobius, the latter says it was a familiar one by a Tarentine poet; but the attempt of O. Crusius, RMP 45 (1890) 265–72, to assign the authorship to Rhinthon of Tarentum has not found favor.

[478] Firmicus' Christian interpretation is that the serpent of the Greek formula or "symbol" is a demon, identifiable with the Satanic serpent of Genesis.

[479] Gen. 3.5, a passage not found in Cyprian. Firmicus has *Eritis quasi dii*, the Vulgate *Eritis sicut dii*. E. J. Martin, *Journ. of Theol. Stud.* 24 (1923) 323, calls *quasi* in this passage a feature of the African text of the O.T.

[480] Heuten (186) comments on the rarity of the idea that the Satanic serpent taught false religion in Eden, but he cites Ps.-Justin, *Cohort. ad graec.* 21, to the effect that the devil beguiled Adam and Eve to believe in nonexistent gods and as a next step to believe that they themselves could become gods.

[481] *Venenati oris*, an expression already used, always with reference to the devil, in 21.2.

[482] Firmicus of course alludes to the devil in serpentine disguise. The sacred snakes of Asclepius in Epidaurus probably had free run of the temple: Paus. 2.28.1. Juno had sacred snakes in her precinct in Lanuvium: E. Küster, *Die Schlange in der griech. Kunst und Religion* (RVV 13.2, Giessen 1913) 126.

[483] Clement, *Protr.* 3.42, accused the demonic pagan gods of enjoying human sacrifices, and cited a few cases such as the Taurian Artemis. He did not mention Jupiter Latiaris or Carthaginian Moloch.

[484] Human sacrifice on the Alban Mount for Jupiter Latiaris is asserted by only one pagan writer, Porph., *De abst.* 2.56; I agree with Pastorino in seeing here Firmicus' source. The accusation is frequent in Christian apologists and Fathers, but may be based on a misunderstanding of Tert., *Apol.* 9, a passage which is

not necessarily alluding to human sacrifice. Modern scholars decline to believe that Rome had human sacrifices for Jupiter Latiaris: so Geffcken, Heinze, Wissowa, and Wünsch, cited with approval by F. Schwenn, *Die Menschenopfer bei den Griechen und Römern* (RVV 15.3, Giessen 1915) 180f.

[485] The allusion is to the well-attested offering of children as a sacrifice by fire in Semitic worships: at Carthage, Diod. 20.14. "Moloch" appears to be a name for this type of sacrifice, and not the name of a god: H. Cazelles, "Molok," DB Suppl. 5 (1957) 1337-46.

[486] Isa. 27.1, a verse never cited by Cyprian. The text given by Firmicus is unparalleled in the Vulgate or elsewhere.

[487] *Voluntas dei perfecti operis substantia est;* cf. *Math.* 5 praef. 3: *(deus) cuius voluntas perfecti operis substantia est.* Although F. Skutsch, "Ein neuer Zeuge der altchristlichen Liturgie," ARW 13 (1910) 291-305 at 303, believes the occurrence of this doctrine in the *Mathesis* a proof that Firmicus was practically a Christian or at least intimately acquainted with Christianity when he wrote the *Mathesis*, we need not accede to this view. The thought that with God to will is to accomplish was familiar to the pagan Hermetic thinkers as well as to the Christian Catechetical School of Alexandria in the second century. The Hermetic writers: *Herm.* 10.2 (p. 113 Nock-Festugière): ἡ γὰρ τούτου ἐνέργεια ἡ θέλησίς ἐστι; *Asclep.* 8: *Voluntas etenim dei ipsa est summa perfectio, utpote cum voluisse et perfecisse uno eodemque temporis puncto compleat.* In Alexandria Pantaenus declared that God made everything by His will (R. E. Witt, *Albinus and the History of Middle Platonism.* [Cambridge 1937] 130), and his successor Clement wrote of God that τὸ θέλημα αὐτοῦ ἔργον ἐστί (*Paed.* 1.6.27). Firmicus did not need to be a Christian or near-Christian in order to encounter a thought which enjoyed pagan as well as Christian circulation. See further Introduction, pp. 7-8.

[488] Firmicus has now lost sight of the euhemerism which he espoused in earlier chapters. Several of the Fathers, especially the apologists, held a noneuhemeristic view that the pagan gods really existed as demons and would suffer in hell along with their worshipers. Min. Fel. 35.2: *Juppiter . . . destinatam sibi cum suis cultoribus poenam praescius perhorrescit.* Also Tatian 14.2; Athenag., *Suppl.* 12.2; Tert., *Spect.* 30.3; Cyril, *c. Iul.* 6.211.

⁴⁸⁹ In Ch. 21 Firmicus discussed pagan counterfeits of the "horns" (arms) of the Cross; here he takes up diabolically inspired counterfeits of the wood of the Cross. "Die von Firmicus vorgenommene Parallelisierung heidnischer, auf Baumkultus beruhender Begehungen mit alttestamentlich-christlichen Geschichten, in denen Baum oder Holz irgendwie eine Rolle spielen, vorgetragen in dem Sinne, dass auf der heidnischen Seite eine vom Teufel eingegebene Nachäffung vorliege, haftet wiederum ganz am Äusseren" (Ziegler, trans. 62).

⁴⁹⁰ Arnob. 5.16f. tells of the sacred pine in the Attis cult and says it symbolized the tree under which Attis emasculated himself. But only Firmicus informs us that an image of a youth (Attis) was attached to the tree trunk. From the time of the Emperor Claudius Rome had a prolonged festival each March in honor of Attis, and on the 22nd the brotherhood of *dendrophori*, "tree bearers," cut a pine and carried it into the temple of Magna Mater on the Palatine: Cumont (52). Excavations on the Palatine by Romanelli have dated Attis worship in Rome almost as early as 191 B.C.; cf. C. Picard, *Numen* 4 (1957) 1 n.1.

⁴⁹¹ The MS. correctly reads *seminibus;* Wower's ingenious emendation *segminibus* was proved invalid by W. Spiegelberg, "Das Isis-Mysterium bei Firmicus Maternus," ARW 19 (1916–19) 194f. Referring to discussions by Egyptologists and by Frazer, *Adonis, Attis, Osiris* (323f.), Spiegelberg showed that Egyptian literature and tombs furnish copious evidence that priests in the month of Choiak, at the festival of sowing, buried small effigies of Osiris made of mud and seed grain. The seed soon sprouted, and grain then appeared to be growing out of the dead body of Osiris. Frazer (324): "The corn-god produced the corn from himself: he gave his own body to feed the people: he died that they might live." The pine container of the effigy probably represented the tree which surrounded and concealed the corpse of Osiris at Byblos: Plut., *De Is.* 15. An evergreen was necessary to symbolize immortality.

⁴⁹² This rite for Kore-Proserpina is not elsewhere attested, and religionists have been unable to localize it. Is it a cult usage known to Firmicus from his own island of Sicily? Nilsson 2.656: "Der Brauch macht einen altertümlichen Eindruck; vielleicht handelt es sich um ein Jahresfeier."

⁴⁹³ Heuten thinks there is hidden reference here to Porphyry,

for the word "fablings" (*commenta*) is the word used in 7.7 to designate Porphyry's equation of Liber with the Sun. The insistent remarks of Firmicus against fire worship would be aimed against Porphyry's Sun worship. Porphyry's treatise on the Sun-god is lost.

⁴⁹⁴ Pastorino: "Ogni legno del *V.T.* diviene, nella primitiva esegesi biblica, un simbolo della croce e Firmico, in questo capitolo, non fa che accumulare confronti, assai diffusi tra i primitivi cristiani."

⁴⁹⁵ *Nulla ratione* MS. and edd.; only Ziegler (1953 ed.) reads *nulla [alia] ratione*, with a defense of this reading on pp. 33f.

⁴⁹⁶ The ensuing biblical references seriatim are: Noe, Gen. 7–8; Abraham, Gen. 22.6; Moses' rod, Exod. 14.16 and 21; waters of Mara, Exod. 15.23–25; the water-finding rod, Exod. 17.9–13 (fully quoted by Cypr., *Test.* 2.21); the ladder to heaven, Gen. 28.12; the ark of setim wood for the tabernacle, Exod. 37.1. At the time of the Flood, wrote Augustine (*De cat. rud.* 32), *per lignum iusti liberati sunt.*

⁴⁹⁷ Puzzling over *amarae myrrae fontibus* (MS.), Heuten, Pastorino, and Ziegler (1953 ed.) have naturally sought enlightenment in Exod. 15.23 (Μεϱϱά, LXX) and Num. 33.8f. (Πιϰϱίαι, LXX). The thirsty Hebrews in the wilderness of Sur came to a nameless spot, were unable to drink its brackish water, and named the spot Mara or Bitterness. At God's command Moses cast a piece of wood into the water, which thereupon became sweet and potable. Readers of the LXX, ignorant of Hebrew, tried to etymologize Merra and thought of "bitter myrrh." Similarly readers of the Latin versions thought they understood the etymology when they read *nec poterant bibere aquas de Mara, eo quod essent amarae.* J. B. Bauer, *Wien. Stud.* 71 (1958) 158f., has shown that where the Fathers allude to this passage the MSS. waver among Merra, Myrra, and Mirra: e.g. Cypr. Gall., *Hept.* 551 (CSEL 23.76); *defessi Myrram (v.l. mirram) veniunt.* Whereas Heuten emends to *amaris Marae fontibus*, Pastorino to *amarae Merrae fontibus*, and Ziegler (1957 ed.) to *amaris Merrae fontibus*, Bauer prefers to regard the MS. reading as sensible and defensible: "wood restored a sweet taste to the waters of bitter myrrh." But Bauer was unaware that Pastorino had shrewdly looked in Cyprian, Firmicus' chief biblical source, for some reference to the waters of Mara, and had found it in *De zelo et livore*

17, where we read the counsel: *Amaritudo omnis quae intus insederat Christi dulcedine leniatur. De sacramento crucis et cibum sumis et potum, lignum quod apud Merrham profecit in imagine ad saporis dulcedinem tibi in veritate proficiat ad mulcendi pectoris lenitatem.* Once again Firmicus was indebted to Cyprian for biblical lore, including the view that the *lignum* used by Moses at the waters of Mara (Merra, Merrha) prefigured the Cross. Pastorino's reading *amarae Merrae fontibus* is to be preferred for Firmicus as a follower of Cyprian.

⁴⁹⁸ The MS. has *alios ascendere, alios ascendere,* but an early corrector (designated by Ziegler as p) altered the second *ascendere* to *descendere.* Considerations of clausula caused Ziegler and Pastorino to reverse the order of the infinitives, but Firmicus need not have heeded the rules of clausula in exact or approximate scriptural quotations. J. B. Bauer, *Wien. Stud.* 71 (1958) 159, observed that the order "ascend-descend" in Gen. 28.12 is found in the Hebrew, in all the translations, and in all citations of the passage by patristic writers.

⁴⁹⁹ *Caeli machina,* cf. μηχανὴ οὐράνιος in an unknown Greek writer of Firmicus' century, Ps.-Athan., *De passione Domini* (MG 28.1056 B). The exalted claims here made for the *mysterium crucis* were frequently heard after Irenaeus, *Adv. haer.* 5.18.3, stated that Christ on the Cross was a recapitulation of cosmic history. Cf. Hugo Rahner, *Griechische Mythen in christlicher Deutung* (Zurich 1945) 80: "Von da aus geht nun durch die ganze antik christliche Literatur ein unaufhörlicher Hymnus auf das kosmische Mysterium des Kreuzes." Rahner gives numerous citations from the Fathers and the Middle Ages.

⁵⁰⁰ For the lacuna in the text before *ratione tractetur* Kroll suggested *diligenti:* cf. *Math.* 4 prooem. 4: *diligenti ratione tractabitur,* and 6.39.1: *diligenti ratione tractare.* Ziegler in the notes to his translation argues that the lacuna represents the loss of several words, with a first reference to the *tauribolium vel criobolium* mentioned at the end of the chapter.

⁵⁰¹ The tree was a pine. In the lost part of the sentence Firmicus may have told whether the usage here described was part of the cult of Attis, Osiris, or Proserpina. Ziegler in the notes to his translation associates the *criobolium* (27.8) with the Attis cult, and tentatively assigns to the Attis cult the ritual slaying at the tree roots of a ram as a sin offering to appease the tree spirit

for the felling of the tree. H. Strathmann, "Attis," RAC 1 (1950) 889–99 at 891, has no doubt that Firmicus in this passage is describing a feature of the Attis cult.

502 For this Pauline phrase cf. n. 315.

503 Gen. 22.13: *a ram amongst the briers sticking fast by the horns.*

504 Exod. 12.3–11, fully quoted by Cyprian, *Test.* 2.15. The Vulgate has *agnus masculus,* Cyprian *ovis masculus;* the latter would appear to be the text known to Firmicus and interpreted by him as "ram." The Christian interpretation of the Hebrew Pasch began with Paul 1 Cor. 5.7: *For Christ our Pasch is sacrificed,* and 1 Peter 1.19.

505 Isa. 53.7f.; Cypr., *loc. cit.* Firmicus rather closely follows the text that we see in Cyprian, widely at variance with the Vulgate. A close comparison reveals that Cyprian knew the text from the N.T. version in Acts 8.32f., not from the O.T. Ziegler (1953 ed., 34f.) desires to read *nativitate,* (abl. temp.) for *nativitatem,* but the unanimous testimony of the MSS. of Cyprian forbids such a vagary. The accusative is supported by all the biblical texts of Isaias, including the Dead Sea Scroll: cf. J. B. Bauer, *Wien. Stud.* 71 (1958) 159f.

506 Jer. 11.18f.; Cypr., *Test.* 2.15 and 20. Firmicus follows Cyprian (but *pane* for *panem*); *aliter* Vulg.

507 Apoc. 5.6–10; Cypr., *Test.* 2.15. Firmicus quotes, with trifling changes, all the verses appearing in Cyprian, in a text resembling the Vulgate.

508 When Firmicus, immediately after quoting from the Apocalypse, says *Iohannes quoque* and goes on to cite the fourth Gospel, he clearly demonstrates his belief that the Apocalypse was not written by St. John the Divine. See Heuten's note and n. 368.

509 John 1.29; Cypr., *Test.* 2.15. Firmicus' text coincides with Cyprian's except in tenses, where the MSS. of Cyprian are not unanimous.

510 Altering MS. *invenit* to *inveniat.* I am convinced that the true explanation of this passage has not been found, despite the varied suggestions of Alfons Müller, Ziegler, Heuten, Ernout, and Pastorino.

511 *Per varios casus,* a verse tag from Verg., *Aen.* 1.204.

512 *Peremit,* balancing *redemit* in the previous clause. So Ziegler

(1953 ed.) and Pastorino. In 1907 Ziegler had read *premit*. The MS. is not clear.

⁵¹³ *Tauribolium istud vel criobolium*. The origin and meaning of these religious usages, known in the worships of Magna Mater, Ma-Bellona, Anahita, Mithra, and Venus Caelestis, are discussed by Cumont (63f.). A worshiper entered a pit beneath a platform and joyfully received "a red baptism" from the blood of a bull or ram which was slaughtered above him. The blood bath gave the worshiper's soul a temporary or permanent rebirth. Striving to compete with Christianity, the Phrygian priests of Magna Mater complained that the Christians plagiarized their *dies sanguinis* (Ambrosiaster, *Quaest. Vet. et Nov. Test.* 84.3) and "attributed to the blood shed in the taurobolium the redemptive power of the blood of the divine Lamb" (Cumont ix, E.T. xviii). Naturally Christian apologists struck back at such blasphemous pretensions: references in Cumont, RHLR 8 (1903) 424. In the lifetime of Firmicus the taurobolium was a commonplace in the Western Roman Empire, and in Rome was performed on the present site of St. Peter's: Platner-Ashby, *Topog. Dict. of Anc. Rome* (Oxford 1929), *s.v.* "Magna Mater in Vaticano." Cf. Cumont (67, E.T. 71): "But all efforts to maintain a barbarian religion stricken with moral decadence were in vain. On the very spot on which the last taurobolia took place at the end of the fourth century, in the *Phrygianum*, stands today the basilica of the Vatican."

⁵¹⁴ Here begins the third and concluding section of the *De errore*. The first was an account of the Oriental and Greco-Roman cults, with naturalistic and euhemeristic explanations; the second was a discussion of the symbols, with a *rudis indigestaque moles* of mythology, magical formulas, scriptural citations, and Firmician rhetoric. The third section asserts that the triumph of Christianity must now be made complete by the disappearance of all vestiges of paganism. Cf. Coman (96).

⁵¹⁵ *Fontes ingenuos*. Since Firmicus, unlike Arnobius, was not a reader and admirer of Lucretius, we need not trace this phrase to Lucr. 1.230: *ingenui fontes*.

⁵¹⁶ *Incandidet*, a neologism of Firmicus, rare in subsequent Christian Latin.

⁵¹⁷ By "higher authority" Firmicus means the scriptural passages which he is about to quote. As Pastorino says, the closing exhortation to the emperors to stamp out paganism by forcible

means will be more effective if Firmicus can show that his advice is simply an expression of God's will.

⁵¹⁸ Arnobius (6.8–27) devotes much space to an attack on idolatry. McCracken, ACW 8.592 n. 65: "Criticism of the pagan cult of statues and images was a favorite theme of the apologists: see Justin, *Apol.* 1.9; Tatian 33f.; the writer *Ad Diogn.* 2; Theophilus, *Ad Autol.* 2.2; Minucius 23.9–13; Firmicus Maternus 28.2–6; also Tertullian, *Apol.* 12; the *Martyrium Apollonii* 14, etc."

⁵¹⁹ *Divino magisterio nobis traditum. Magisterium,* though found only here in the *De errore,* is a favorite word of Firmicus, occurring about twenty-five times in the *Math.,* e.g. 2.11.1: *nobis . . . Graecorum magisteriis traditum est.* Here Firmicus proclaims the divine magisterium revealed to us in the Bible. See E. Dublanchy's discussion of "Le dogme catholique sur le magistère de l'église," DTC 4.2 (1939) 2175–2200.

⁵²⁰ Wisd. 15.15–17; Cypr., *Test.* 3.59, *Ad Fort.* 1. Here Firmicus was borrowing from the latter treatise of Cyprian, whence come further biblical citations in the present chapter.

⁵²¹ Firmicus liked the sound and the melancholy thought of *fragilis et caduca mortalitas,* which he here repeats from *Math.* 1.7.4. F. Gabarrou, *Le latin d'Arnobe* (Paris 1921) 184, observes that both Arnobius and Cyprian use *mortalitas* to mean *mortales.*

⁵²² Firmicus' habit of self-imitation gives three parallel passages: 8.2: *in exitium vestrum mortemque properatis;* 28.2: *in exitium suum mortemque properaret;* 28.13: *in exitium tuum mortemque festinas.*

⁵²³ Ps. 134(135).15–18; Cypr., *Test.* 3.59, *Ad Fort.* 1. Firmicus follows the latter text in Cyprian, especially in using present tenses for all the verbs.

⁵²⁴ In speaking often of the divine inspiration of the Scriptures, Firmicus liked to use a formulaic ablative absolute: 20.1: *iubente spiritu sancto;* 21.3: *sancto spiritu iubente;* 27.2: *divino spiritu iubente;* 28.4: *deo iubente.* In the present passage Firmicus has in mind the words (Bar. 6.1) introducing and stating the purpose of the Epistle of Jeremias to the Jews of the Babylonian captivity: *ut annuntiaret illis secundum quod praeceptum est illi a Deo.*

⁵²⁵ Bar. 6.5–10 (Epist. Jer.), a passage not found in Cyprian except a few words of vs. 5 in *De domin. orat.* 5 (p. 269 Hartel,

CSEL). Jerome did not translate the Epistle of Jeremias. The text given by the MS. of Firmicus is widely at variance with the Septuagint, and is surely corrupt at verses 6–7, where the pre-Hieronymian Latin version gives: *Ipse autem exquiram animas vestras; nam lingua ipsorum polita a fabro*, and Firmicus: *Lege autem exquiram ab animas vestras. Lingua eorum polita fabro*. G. Heuten, "Une variante de la Bible latine pré-hiérony-mienne," *Latomus* 3 (1939) 261–63, résumé in *Rev. belge de philol. et d'hist.* 18(1939) 1102f., deserves credit for recognizing here an intruded gloss. By writing between the lines *lege: ab* (or *lege autem: ab*) the glossator meant: "Read *ab* before *fabro*," where indeed *a* or *ab* is needed and has been inserted (on the theory of haplography after *polita*) by Bursian and all subsequent editors. The copyist, not comprehending, inserted in the text *lege* instead of *ipse* and inserted *ab* in the wrong place. Variants on Heuten's theory, but in agreement that *lege* points to a gloss, were suggested by A. Ernout, *Rev. de philol.* sér. 3, 12 (1938) 246–48, and Pastorino. Perhaps we are justified in supposing that, however the copyist garbled it, Firmicus really wrote *Ipse autem exquiram animas vestras*, just as in the pre-Hieronymian Latin version, and I have translated accordingly.

[526] In the Epistle of Jeremias we find in vs. 29, but not in vs. 10, *diis argenteis et aureis et ligneis*. Firmicus uses this as if it were part of vs. 10.

[527] Bar. 6.21–25. Again Firmicus exhibits many variants from the pre-Hieronymian text.

[528] The MS. has *conflabantur sentiebunt*. The simplest change, which also has the advantage of restoring the correct biblical text, is *sentiebant*: so Bursian, Halm, Ziegler (1907), Alfons Müller, Pastorino. Ziegler in his 1957 edition has made the im-probable alteration to *conflabuntur sentient*.

[529] Bar. 6.28. Here Firmicus reproduces the biblical text as we know it, except that he substitutes *timueritis* for *timeatis*.

[530] Bar. 6.30f. Firmicus' text corresponds well enough with the LXX and the old Latin text, except in the last phrase: ἐν περιδείπνῳ νεκροῦ (LXX), *in coena mortui* (old Latin text), *in gehenna mortui* (Firmicus). A. Ernout, *Rev. de philol.* sér. 3, 12 (1938) 247f., despairs over this total divergency, saying: "La différence entre le grec et le latin me paraît irréductible." I ascribe the error to the copyist, a medieval man of the ninth

or tenth century, in whose medieval pronunciation of Latin there was hardly any difference between *coena* and *gehenna*. Not understanding *coena mortui*, he wrote *gehenna mortui*.

[531] Bar. 6.50–57, quoted here with some omissions and some alterations of tenses, cases, and forms.

[532] Constantius and Constans did not heed any of this advice. Heuten (189) thinks Firmicus derived his idea from Cic., *Nat. deor.* 3. 83f., or Clem., *Protr.* 4.53, where he could have read of historical examples of the spoliation or partial spoliation of temples by kings and potentates.

[533] This sentence clearly implies that Constantius and Constans destroyed some pagan temples, a fact otherwise unknown to historians. The latter part of the sentence, *in maius dei estis virtute provecti*, is an echo of Hor., *Carm.* 3.4.66: *Vim temperatam di quoque provehunt in maius*. Destroying pagan temples, says Firmicus by implication, is an exhibition of *vis temperata*.

[534] Firmicus is writing in the best style of panegyric, where plain truth is obscured by the bright colors of flattery. Constans whipped the Franks in Gaul in 342: O. Seeck, "Constans," RE 4 (1901) 949. In the prolonged and spasmodic war against the Persians under Sapor, the Romans lost most of the battles, but Constantius had a worth-while victory in the autumn of 343: O. Seeck, *Gesch. des Untergangs der antiken Welt* (Stuttgart 1921) 4.78. Of course no expansion of the Empire had taken place.

[535] For the good rhetorical phrase *tumentes ac saevientes undas* Ziegler found a close parallel in Min. Fel. 7.2: *(ira) tumens et saeviens*. One familiar with the English Channel will applaud Firmicus' choice of words to describe it. In midwinter of 342–43 Constans crossed the Channel with an escort of a hundred soldiers to negotiate for more peaceful conditions on the Scottish frontier: Liban., *Or.* 59 (*Basilikos*).137–39; Amm. 20.1.1, 27.8.4; F. Sagot, *La Bretagne romaine* (Paris 1911) 237f.

[536] *Unda contremuit;* Ziegler saw that the source is Verg., *Aen.* 3.673: *Contremuere undae penitusque exterrita tellus*.

[537] *Virtutibus vestris victa*, heralded by *vultis* at the end of the previous sentence, shows more extensive alliteration than is usual even in Firmicus.

[538] Exod. 20.23; Cypr., *Test.* 3.59, the latter's text being followed by Firmicus.

[539] Exod. 20.4; Cypr., *Test.* 3.59, *Ad Fort.* 1. Firmicus' text is identical with that given twice by Cyprian.

[540] Isa. 42.17, a text not found in Cyprian. The Vulgate version is far different from that of Firmicus.

[541] Deut. 6.13; Matt. 4.10; Luke 4.8; Cypr., *Test.* 3.10, *Ad Fort.* 2.

[542] Deut. 5.7; Exod. 20.3. The exact wording in Firmicus is from Cypr., *Ad Fort.* 2.

[543] Deut. 32.39; Cypr., *Ad Fort.* 2. Firmicus follows Cyprian; *aliter* Vulg.

[544] Apoc. 14.6f.; Cypr., *Ad Fort.* 2. Again the text of the Vulgate is remote from that exhibited by Cyprian, which is duplicated by Firmicus with only two minuscule alterations.

[545] A conflation of Mark 12.29–31 and Matt. 22.37–40, a conflation already made by Cypr., *Ad Fort.* 2 and *De cathol. eccl. unit.* 15.

[546] John 17.3; Cypr., *Ad Fort.* 2, *Ad Demet.* 23, *Epp.* 73.17.

[547] Exod. 22.20, a favorite quotation of Cyprian (*Ad Fort.* 3, *Ad Demetr.* 16, *De lapsis* 7, *Epp.* 59.12), who invariably cites it in the words repeated by Firmicus (*Sacrificans diis eradicabitur praeter domino soli*), far different from the Vulgate (*Qui immolat diis occidetur, praeterquam domino soli*).

[548] Deut. 32.17; Cypr., *Test.* 1.1, *Ad Fort.* 3.

[549] *Ne ab inferioribus speres auxilium.* Blaise-Chirat lends no encouragement to Alfons Müller and F. J. Dölger, AC 3 (1932) 172, in supposing that *inferioribus* is neuter, meaning "the lower world." Ziegler correctly gives "Schwächeren"; Faggin, "essere che sono a te inferiori."

[550] F. J. Dölger, AC 3 (1932) 170f., shows that Firmicus is here speaking of exorcism. A Christian exorcist adjured the trembling, stammering demon of the possessed person to tell his name and received in reply a god's name. The man to whom the demon kept clinging, despite the use of violence against him, was of course the possessed person.

[551] Ziegler, 1953 ed., 35f., argues that *comminatione* of the MS. is correct, though the word is *hapax* in Firmicus; but at the same time he sets forward the claims of his tentative emendation *commonitione*, wondering if it will win favor. It does not. In front of Firmicus' eyes was Cyprian's chapter heading for *Ad Fort.* 3: *Quae comminatio Dei sit adversus eos qui idolis sacrificant.* Hence

came the word *comminatio*, and any thought of emendation is grievously misguided. Cyprian in the above chapter cited six scriptural passages in a certain order. Firmicus in 28.10–13 cites the same six passages in the same order. Ziegler, though perfectly aware of Firmicus' indebtedness to Cyprian (cf. 1953 ed., 19), made the mistake of never looking at Cyprian.

⁵⁵² Isa. 2.8f.; Cypr., *Ad Fort.* 3. Firmicus follows Cyprian exactly except in giving *deos* instead of *eos* as the second word; *aliter* Vulg.

⁵⁵³ Isa. 57.6; Cypr., *loc. cit.* Here Firmicus and Cyprian agree in every detail; *aliter* Vulg.

⁵⁵⁴ *Salutaris deus*, repeated in 29.4; Ps. 23(24).5 has *deus salutaris suus.*

⁵⁵⁵ Jer. 25.6; Cypr., *loc. cit.* Firmicus quotes from Cyprian with the omission of two words; *aliter* Vulg.

⁵⁵⁶ *Titubantia suspende vestigia*, cf. Claud. Mamert., *De statu animae* 1.2 (CSEL 11.25.3): *suspenso vestigio.* See Blaise-Chirat *s.v. suspendo.* Firmicus saw *vestigia titubata* in Vergil, *Aen.* 5.331f.

⁵⁵⁷ Apoc. 14.9–11; Cypr., *loc. cit.* Firmicus follows Cyprian with some omissions and altered tenses; *aliter* Vulg.

⁵⁵⁸ Concluding his book, Firmicus launches his most drastic appeal to the emperors: they too, as well as God, must castigate paganism, demon worship, and idolatry. Cf. Coman (117): "Il comprenait que le paganisme ne disparaitrait que si les empereurs intervenaient et l'arrachaient de force, comme cela se produisit sous Théodose."

⁵⁵⁹ Moore (11) observes that the rather rare adverb *omnifariam*, first in Gell. 12.13.20, was a favorite with Firmicus: sixteen passages in *Math.* and *De errore* 6.1 and 29.1.

⁵⁶⁰ Deut. 13.6–10; Cypr., *Ad Fort.* 5. The heading of the chapter just cited from Cyprian is this: *Quod sic idololatriae indignetur Deus ut praeceperit etiam eos interfici qui sacrificare et servire idolis suaserint.* Cyprian then begins his chapter with the two passages from Deuteronomy which Firmicus here presents in almost exactly Cyprian's wording. As often, the wording in the Vulgate differs *toto caelo.*

⁵⁶¹ *Gladium vindicem*, cf. 6.9: *vindices gladii.*

⁵⁶² Deut. 13.12–18; Cypr., *loc. cit.*

⁵⁶³ In 346, the year or approximate year when Firmicus wrote the *De errore*, the Persian king Sapor unsuccessfully besieged for

three months the Mesopotamian city of Nisibis, which was held by the Romans. Cf. O. Seeck, "Constantius nr. 4," RE 4 (1901) 1044–94 at 1060. At the time Emperor Constantius was in Antioch, not in Nisibis. Theodoret, *Hist. eccl.* 2.30 (ed. Parmentier), relates that Bishop James of Nisibis by prayer and miracle aided in the defense of the city and the discomfiture of the Persians.

[564] See n. 534 for the victory of Constans in Gaul in 342 and of Constantius on the Persian frontier in 343.

[565] Pastorino complains that Firmicus' closing paragraph is again remote from the spirit and teaching of Christ, since it promises the emperors material rewards for the diffusion of truth by force and violence.

INDEXES

INDEXES

1. OLD AND NEW TESTAMENT

2. AUTHORS

233

3. GREEK WORDS

ἀγαθός, 154, 197, 209
αἰαῖ, 90, 204
ἀμέριστος, 61
ἄξιος, 204
ἀπόλλειν, 129
'Ασία, 153
"Αττις, 81
βιβρώσκειν, 81
βοοκλοπίη, 52
βροτός, 207
γένος, 207
δίκερως, 90, 203
δίμορφος, 90, 203
δράκων, 102
ἔλευσις, 129, 167
ἐλπίς, 209
ἐνέργεια, 216
ἐπιθυμία, 156
ἔργον, 216
εὑρίσκειν, 47
θαρρεῖν, θαρσεῖν, 93, 207
θεῖος, 169, 207
θέλημα, 216
θέλησις, 216
θεός, 87, 93, 173
θρηνεῖν, 173
θυμός, 156
κατοικεῖν, 153
κερνοφορεῖν, 195
κόπτειν, 173
κόρη, 169
κύμβαλον, 81, 195
λαός, 204
Μάγοι, 153
μεγαλοδαίμων, 183
μερίζειν, 61
μύστης, 52, 81, 93
νεκρός, 223

νέος, 84, 198
νομίζειν, 173
νοῦς, 61, 156
νύμφιος, 197
νύμφος, 84, 197
ὄνομα, 169
οὐρανός, 30
παῖς, 71, 129
παστός, 195
πατήρ, 52, 102
πενθεῖν, 173
περίδειπνον, 223
Πέρσαι, 153
πέτρα, 87
πίνειν, 81, 195
ποιεῖν, 30
πόνος, 93, 207
πῦρ, 153
Σάραπις, 182
Σάρρα, 71, 129
Σελήνη, 169
σκηνή, 30
συγχαίρειν, 47
σύμβολον, 194
συνδέξιος, 52, 154
συνεκτικός, 169
σώζειν, 93, 207
σωτηρία, 93
ταῦρος, 102, 204
τιμᾶν, 153
τύμπανον, 81, 195
ὑποδύειν, 195
φαγεῖν, 195
φίλος, 198
φῶς, 84, 198
χαίρειν, 84, 198
ψυχή, 207

4. GENERAL INDEX

Abaris, 74, 185
Abel, 101, 214
Abraham, 71, 81, 83, 101, 105 f., 214, 218
Abydos, 146
Achaia, 4
Acropolis, 52
Acta fratrum Arvalium, 206
actors, 162, 181
Adam, 31, 100 f., 203, 212 f., 215
Admetus, 180
Adonis, 21, 64 f., 148, 173, 207
adultery, 44, 46, 65, 70, 143, 181 f.; of the gods, 67, 147 f., 159
Aebutius, 57
Aeneas, 186
Aesculapius, 69, 180, 215
Aethusa, Aethyssa, 67, 177
Africa, 3 f., 129, 150
African Latin, 3, 129 f., 140
Africans (Carthaginians), 50
Aion, 153
air, divinized, 23, 150 f.; as Juno or Venus the Virgin, 50, 150; cult of, in Syria and Carthage, 50, 150
Alban Mount, 215
Alcyone, 177
Aldine edition, of *Mathesis*, 129 f.
Alexandria, 70, 182 f.; catechetical school at, 216
Alope, 67, 177
Amalec, 92, 105, 205
Amphitrite, 177
Amymone, 67, 176
Anahita, Anaitis, 153, 221
Anchises, 70, 180
angel, angels, 98, 105, 109, 111
Antichrist, 94, 208
Antioch, 227
Antiope, 176

Antoninus Pius, 133
Anubis, 44, 139, 144
Aphrodite, 156, 179 f.; Cyprian, 21, 28, 174
Apocalypse, 85, 98, 106, 111, 114, 199; Johannine authorship of, 199, 220
Apollo, herdsman, 69, 180; sun-god, 23, 80, 169; amours of, 177 f.; and Hyacinthus, 67, 176; and Marsyas, 68, 178; etymologized, 80, 129, 192
Apollyon, 192
apologetics, 10, 18 f., 24, 27–30, 34, 133, 142, 147, 167, 169, 173, 175, 177, 179 f., 186, 189, 215 f., 222
Arabic astrology, 6
Archimedes, 2; sphere of, 5
Ares, 173, 179 f.; see Mars
Argonautic expedition, 176
ark, of Noe, 105; of the tabernacle, 218
Arsinoe, 67, 177
Artemis, Taurian, 215
Artemisium, Ephesian, 186
Asclepius, 215; see Aesculapius
Asia, 4, 153; Asia Minor, 149, 152
Assyrians (Syrians), 50; "Assyrian mysteries," 156
astrology, 4–9, 24 f., 26, 131, 135, 171, 190, 193; medical science friendly toward, 190; Christian attitude toward, 7 f.; never renounced by Firmicus, 19 f.; opposed by Ambrosiaster and Augustine, 20
Athena, 160, 185, 188 f.; Polias, 188; Egyptian, 188; see Minerva
Athens, Athenians, 76, 129, 188
Attica, 60